1001
quick fixes
& kitchen tips

First published by Parragon in 2009

Parragon
Queen Street House
4 Queen Street
Bath BA1 1HE, UK

ISBN: 978-1-4075-3395-7
Printed in China

Author: Manidipa Mandal
Editor: Fiona Biggs
Illustrators: Kunal Kundu, Suresh Kumar, Rajita Kashyap, Nitin Chawla
Layout: Eleven Arts

WARNING:

This book is intended only for adults (aged 18 and over) and the kitchen tips and hints contained in this book should not be used by children under 18.

Some of the cleaning agents and other substances recommended in this book are volatile, and extreme caution must be exercised when using them. Never mix chemical cleaning agents and always follow the advice printed on the packaging of any proprietary cleaning product.

When using any kitchen equipment or other products in conjunction with this book, you should follow all instructions and warnings given by the manufacturers and only use such equipment and products for the purposes for which they were intended.

The publishers accept no liability for any loss or injury sustained as a result of using any of the tips and hints contained in this book.

The information in this book is provided for general guidance only and may not be suitable for all individuals. Please consult your health professional if in doubt.

1001

quick fixes
& kitchen tips

A must-have collection of
household tips

Bath • New York • Singapore • Hong Kong   Cologne • Delhi • Melbourne

Contents

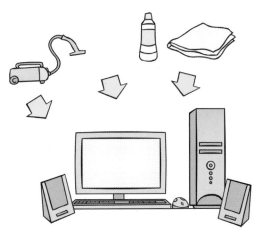

Introduction

Across seas, seasons and diverse societies, one thing bonds us all – our attachment to the comforts of home and the happiness of enjoying it with our loved ones. And that is what this book aims to do. Help you enjoy your home. And your family. And the friends who extend your family circle and expand the definition of 'home'.

This is not to say that all readers will find this book handy for the same reasons. Rather, each of you – depending on who you are – will have your own unique reason to put this book on your shelf. (And to dip in, we hope, regularly and often!)

The 1001 ideas in this book are arranged in two parts. The first section, **'In the Kitchen'**, focuses on food selection, preparation and storage. Here you will find advice on raw and larder ingredients, kitchen equipment, time-saving tips, substitutions, techniques for 'professional results', even hints on salvaging recipes gone woefully wrong! Considerable space is devoted to entertaining – from serving suggestions to table décor.

The second, **'Around the House'**, covers a larger spectrum: providing for house guests; aesthetics throughout the home; cleaning and laundry tips, including a dedicated chapter on stain removal; pest control and pet care; child safety and child-specific entertainment/décor ideas; as well as organizational aids to simplify everyday living.

Each tip is accompanied by an illustration for quicker, at-a-glance understanding. Some are even complemented by a step-by-step drawing. And throughout the book, in the selection of ideas, modern safety norms and practices have been a paramount concern – whether it's a question of how soon to give your infant peanuts or of collaring the hazardous chemicals hidden around your household.

The arrangement of these hints and tips is in logical clusters *within* chapters – situations (for entertaining), ingredients (for recipes) or offenders (for pest control and stain removal), age groups (for children), species (when it comes to pets), even rooms (when it comes to cleaning schedules). At the same time, clever cross-referencing complements the self-sufficiency of each tip. This means you can either master every trick in the area of your interest (just turn to the relevant chapter), or simply dip in daily for a mind-blowing new addition to your repertoire of survival skills! And there's yet a third way into this mine of information – that all-important index at the back!

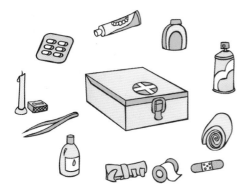

We have tried to mix up easy-peasy with advanced elegance, seriously functional with no-nonsense fun. Because we hope that this book will be your companion for a very long time – your guide out of a tight spot as well as an enjoyable read.

IN THE KITCHEN

The Right Equipment

Choosing your gadgets and tools; getting the best use from them; maximizing efficiency and ease of use; even multitasking with common tools!

■ Pottering around

1. Pottery for the pot

Unglazed pottery, such as terracotta, can be tricky to cook in – but it can do wonderful things to food if you follow the instructions carefully.

- Avoid using it in the microwave unless it is specifically made for the purpose.
- Season before you use it for the first time by soaking in water, then filling with water with a layer of oil on top and simmering (on the hob or in the oven, as indicated by the manufacturer) until dry.

2. Spotless pots

Unglazed pottery absorbs moisture and food stains and isn't easy to wash up.

- Don't use any abrasive harsher than baking soda on unglazed pottery, or you could scratch the surface badly.
- Rinse with plenty of water to flush out any bits lodged in the tiny pores.
- Allow to air dry for a couple of days after washing – just because the surface feels dry, it doesn't mean it's dry to the core. If possible, place in a sunny position by an open window to draw out moisture.

3. Use lower temperatures for glassware

Glass retains heat longer than any other material used for baking.

- Keep an eye on your glass dishes when baking – the heat retained by the glass can cause overcooking, quicker browning and uneven cooking (those parts in contact with the container will cook faster than those raised off the surface, especially when roasting meat).
- For most baked dishes, reducing the temperature by 4–5°C/10–12°F after putting the item in the oven will reduce the chances of burning.
- Be very careful to avoid moisture coming in contact with hot glass – either from your hands or from the work surface.

4. The magic of silicone

Silicone bakeware needs no greasing – cakes pop out readily, biscuits slide off at a nudge. It is cool to touch within minutes of removal from the oven. You can even freeze batter in it and transfer straight to the oven – less washing up!

It needs some care, though:

- Foods sometimes brown unevenly.
  - Because of their flexibility, larger containers or heavily filled ones need support from a baking sheet placed underneath. This can cause the base to brown faster.
    - If crumpled or crushed repeatedly, silicone bakeware can crack.
    - Greasing leaves silicone tacky!

6. A wok for all seasons

Season a traditional carbon-steel wok for years of service.

- Wash your new wok and dry on high heat.
- When smoking hot, wipe the inner surface with rapeseed oil – or another oil with a high smoking point.
- Return to heat.
- Repeat the heat-and-season cycle twice; rinse and dry.
- You now have a fairly non-stick wok that won't rust readily. It may, however, darken with use.
- After every use, wash gently – no abrasives!
- If you notice rust spots or food 'catches' more than usual, gently remove deposits with fine steel wool; re-season.

5. Keep your enamel bright

Resilient as they might seem, enamel pans can chip or scratch if roughly handled.

- Don't scrub them with bleach, steel wool or abrasive powders.
- Clean them with half a lemon dipped in borax, or buff with a paste made of bread soda and a little water.

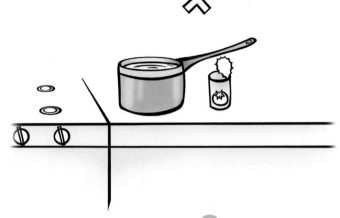

7. Smooth as steel

Stainless steel is one of the most versatile cooking materials – sturdy, with a good heat response, no rusting or tarnishing.

However, there are a couple of things you'll need to avoid for your best-quality stainless to stay that way:

- Don't wash up with steel wool! It leaves scratches.
- Rinse immediately and thoroughly after cooking acidic or salty foods. Never leave them in the pan to cool. Acids and salt pit the surface of steel!
- Dry promptly to avoid white water spots.
- Avoid overheating – it can cause rainbowing (*see Tip 8*).

8. Avoid the rainbow effect

If you notice rainbow-hued smudges on your saucepans, you're cooking on a higher heat than is good for them!

This is most obvious on stainless steel, but anodised aluminium is also susceptible. Ultimately, this will shorten the life of your utensils.

- Make sure the flame extends to only two thirds the diameter of your pans.
- Don't leave an empty pan on the stove too long – when your hand 'feels the heat' at 2 inches/ 5 cm above the surface, you should start cooking.

9. Silver and steel?

Never soak silver and stainless steel utensils together – the silver will turn black!

10. Look after the family silver!

Although versatile, silver is one of the more delicate metals.

Here's a list of things to avoid:

- Rough handling – because silver is quite soft and yields readily to pressure, you must be careful not to bend, twist or apply too much pressure.
- Abrasives – silver will scratch readily.
- Haphazard polishing – work in light strokes in only one direction, or you'll end up with a 'crazed' surface!
- Egg – this is one of the worst tarnishers.
- Rubber – rubber bands can damage silverware even through layers of tissue paper, so keep all rubber well away from those spoons!
- Moisture – place a sachet of silica gel in the silver drawer to delay tarnishing.
- Acid and bleach – wrap in acid-free paper or soft well-worn cloth.
- Steel – see Tip 9.

11. Keep your copper shining bright

Bright copper pots and pans aren't just fabulous to look at, the great conductivity means a good sturdy piece should get a lot of use. Buy pieces that are lined with stainless steel, otherwise they'll react with anything acidic: vinegar, fruit, tomatoes, even eggs!

Sadly, the gleaming surface will still tarnish on the outside, even if you keep it spotless. You can revive the mirror shine:

- Rub with half a lemon dipped in salt.
- Leave for just a minute (and no longer than two!).
- Rinse thoroughly.
- Dry with a soft cloth, wiping thoroughly.

Can you see your face in it?

12. Hard water pitfalls

Hard water and salt can leave white spots. This is not just an eyesore – on some materials it is advance notice of damage. Fine porcelain or crystal could end up with a permanent yellowish stain; metal utensils could become pitted.

- Wash by hand and dry thoroughly to avoid spots.
- Avoid adding salt to an empty pan – except to gently scour away burnt-on food (soaking with baking soda should be your first resort).
- When you season foods, allow the liquid to come to the boil first; stir until salt dissolves before removing from heat.

■ Time- and tedium-savers

13. One-handed chopping

Chefs mince herbs so beautifully with just their cook's knife and the standard chopping board. That's because they've had lots of practice.

Since you've got lots of other things to do besides slicing and dicing, it's worth investing in a hachoir and mezzaluna set, preferably a one-handed model. Much faster, and no chasing the sprigs back to the knife with every few passes.

14. No-boil sterilizing

If the thought of boiling all those jars puts you off making your own jams and preserves (*see Tip 156*), heave a sigh of relief and turn on the oven!

- Preheat to 180°C/350°F while you put the jars through a warm rinse – either in the dishwasher or by hand.
- Instead of drying them with a tea towel place them in the oven for 10 minutes, and you're ready to fill 'em up!

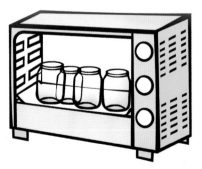

15. Flavour saver

Garlic is lovely in so many foods, from roasts to stews to dips. Peeling it can be a pain, though. Here's a time- and trouble-saver:

- Pop several heads of garlic into a sturdy freezer bag.
- Using the base of a small glass bottle or spice jar, gently crush the garlic pods to loosen the peel – no mess or sticky, smelly hands.
- Use a fork to scrape out the loose garlic skins and bung the bag in the freezer for when you need it later.

You'll never be short of flavour again. By the way, you can use a bottle or jar to lightly crush spices or soften herbs to release their aromas too, if you don't have a mortar and pestle.

16. Fine pin!

Need a clean rolling pin in the middle of a batch of furious baking?

- Remove the label from a wine bottle and use that.
- If you have only full bottles, wrap one in clingfilm and roll away!
- To clean, wash the label-free bottle – glass cleans up easily; simply unwrap the full bottle and discard the clingfilm!
- Just make sure the bottles aren't so chilled as to 'sweat', or you'll end up with soggy, sticky dough!

This is very handy when you are making different kinds of pastry or dough, both savoury and sweet, on the same day.

17. Labour-saving oven liners

If you bake a lot, you probably have to put a lot of elbow grease into cleaning the oven – sweeping out crumbs, softening spills, degreasing…

To minimize labour, start by protecting the surface – the oven 'floor' gets the worst of it.

- Reuse kitchen foil from tenting roasts or refrigerating foods to line the oven 'floor'.
- Foil bags, cut up one side and unfolded, can be used too.
- Lay foil with the food-stained or greasy side uppermost.
- When the oven has cooled, ease out carefully (to hold spills in), scrunch up and bin!

18. Slice with string

Waxed cotton thread or dental floss (unflavoured) makes light work of splitting delicate sponge cakes into layers or slicing squishy roulades.

- For cakes, use a toothpick to 'dot' a guideline along the side. Level the string along it, cross over ends and pull together.
- For roulades, use like cheese wire. Hold the thread under your thumb on one side; draw it taut by the other end and slice!
- This works for soft to medium-hard cheese too.
- It lets children slice rolls of dough until they're old enough to wield a knife.
- Good for most soft rolls or wraps – Japanese-style egg rolls, cinnamon rolls, a 'cylinder' of mousse…

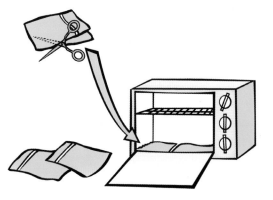

19. Versatile vegetable scrub!

No, this isn't a recipe for a body scrub – it's a new use for loofahs and exfoliating mitts. Now you can use them to scrub vegetables such as potatoes and carrots, even courgettes and aubergines. They're much gentler than those scratchy nylon bristles that rip the peel and may even score the flesh of softer veggies.

Keep a separate one for use in the bath!

20. Scissors are safer (and swifter)...

When:

- snipping tubular herbs or vegetables such as chives
- topping and tailing beans
- trimming leeks
- slicing up bacon or ham strips
- cutting fat and tendon off meats
- butterflying prawns
- spatchcocking chickens and other poultry

It will be quicker and easier than using a knife. It also leaves your chopping board clean.

■ Make the most of your appliances and gadgets

21. Faster than a speeding microwave!

A pressure cooker makes shorter work of cooking for a crowd than a microwave oven.

- Choose the right size, or you'll waste fuel and/or food.
- Check the handle – it needs to be comfortable even when hot and full. Exposed metal bits along the underside can scald!
- A quick-release feature lowers the pressure fast. Never open a cooker until the pressure has dissipated – a steam burn is worse than boiling water!
- Instead of old-fashioned vent weights that rock and hiss, opt for calibrated spring-valve rods – quieter, safer, easier to use.

22. Creamy café

For your everyday espresso, choose a smaller pot rather than a larger one.

- The trick to a smooth, full-flavoured coffee with a nice rich crema on top is to pass the minimum quantity of water through the maximum quantity of grounds.
- You'll only get the froth from that first cupful! Which means a two-cup espresso maker is best.
- Pour an inch into both cups before you top them up.

Keep the larger pots and the 6-cup worktop machines for larger gatherings when you need to make a lot of espresso quickly.

23. Frost-free freezing

If you don't have a frost-free freezer, do a fortnightly defrost.

- Transfer all food to a thermos bag.
- Switch off the fridge.
- Line shelves with towels.
- Place another towel in the bottom of the fridge or on the floor beneath to catch spills.
- Pour hot water into shallow metal containers placed on the shelves. Shut the door. (Replace hot water as it cools, until all ice melts.)
- Wipe interior with a solution of baking soda in water; dry thoroughly.
- Turn on the fridge. Wait half an hour before replacing foods.

24. Minimize mould

A periodic vinegar wipe will keep the door seal on your fridge from sprouting mould or mildew in the creases.

25. Quick fix for a smelly fridge

When your refrigerator gets that musty odour but you haven't time to clean it out thoroughly:

- Put some coffee grounds in a shallow tin with holes poked in the lid. Place it in the fridge for a few hours to kill any nasty niffs and absorb moisture.

This is just a quick fix – you will have to use the baking soda solution eventually, and better sooner than when the mould gets a grip!

26. Blend it clean

The easiest way to clean a blender is to actually run it on empty!

- Run it half filled with hot water and a few drops of concentrated dishwashing liquid.

27. Mint-fresh mixer

All those lovely Asian spice pastes we've lately adopted are storehouses of health. But they (and even the humble carrot or juicy berries, all full of antioxidants) can stain the plastic bowl of your food processor or mixer. The flavours will also linger – so that delicate vichyssoise will smell of curry! The good news is that many of these pigments are fat-soluble, rather than water-soluble.

- Try oiling the jar or bowl before you process the colourful stuff! It should keep stains from lodging too deeply.
- What won't wash away can often be coaxed out with an oil-moistened rag or kitchen towel.
- Use a pinch of enzyme-based detergent to take out all of the residue, then rinse very thoroughly.
- To get rid of the smell, try pulsing a few mint leaves or used lemon rinds – it should refresh your processor.

28. How to hollow a pumpkin

Yes, you can buy one of those 'claws' to scoop the stringy bits out of a pumpkin. But, honestly, how many times a year will you use it?

- Your trusty pasta server, which dollops out the spaghetti on a weekly basis anyway, will do the job just as well.
- If you've got good wrist action, your ice cream scoop will work too.

29. The slice is right!

Make the most of that egg slicer or tomato slicer gadget you hardly ever use.

- Make quick work of a bowlful of potatoes boiled for a salad.
- Clean mushrooms with a stiff-bristled natural brush and pop in the slicer.
- Those cute blobs of mozzarella or petit Suisse should slice up a treat too.
- Slicing up marzipan for biscuits and cake decorations? Put it right here!
- Sausages (softer ones such as frankfurters, Cumberland or black pudding) may take a few chops to do from end to end – it's still worth it when you have a party's worth of people to feed.
- That tomato slicer will have fun with bananas, unpeeled kiwi fruit and kumquats – *so* much neater, and easier to eat.

30. Hammer and hatchet

These might sound like odd tools for the kitchen, but they are handy for splitting open large, thick-skinned vegetables – such as pumpkins – and shellfish.

The 'hammer' should be a sturdy, long-handled wooden mallet. The 'hatchet' is ideally a large, heavy-bladed cleaver – the Oriental kind with a metal handle all cast in one piece is best.

Please take care with hands and fingers!

- To crack a pumpkin open, use a controlled, careful swing to embed the cleaver lightly in the flesh (make sure the pumpkin is stable and won't roll about if rocked a little). Delivering a sharp tap or two from the mallet should swing the blade all the way in and split it in half.
- The mallet is handy for cracking up crab claws and shells after cooking. Easy does it! You don't want shell shrapnel flying everywhere.

■ Mindful maintenance

31. Tangled tongs and tines

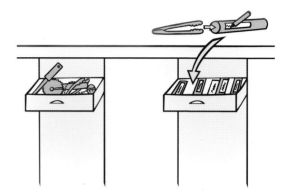

We all have at least one kitchen drawer of awkward implements, all tangled up:

- barbecue tongs
- turkey baster
- melon baller
- tea ball
- measuring spoons
- pizza wheel

… and the kitchen fairy alone knows what else.

Sort them out:

- Mount softboard inside a cabinet door; add hooks. Hang up small objects with loops – measuring spoons, tea balls.
- For the rest, use cardboard cylinders from used-up rolls of kitchen paper and foil.
- Tape one end shut with masking tape.
- Pop tools in these 'sleeves', label along the sides and stuff scrunched-up foil or paper to 'close'.
- Arrange neatly in the drawer.

32. Oil the boards

If you scour your wooden chopping boards after every use they may split.

- Once a fortnight or so, rub your chopping board with a little salad oil to season it. (You can use some kitchen paper dipped in oil to do this.)
- Make sure the chopping board is absolutely dry, though, or you'll trap moisture – which in turn encourages nasties to take up residence, not to mention making the wood swell and warp.

33. Carbon care

Carbon steel knives are fantastic for the way they hold their edge yet hone easily, but they do require a bit of care as they can rust (unlike the rust-resistant stainless steel).

- Wash carbon steel blades immediately after use in hot water and dry quickly.
- When completely dry, smear a drop of vegetable oil on the blade to stave off rust.
- Do not use carbon steel on vegetables that are rich in anthocyanin pigments – red cabbage, purple carrots, beetroot, aubergines, berries and blood oranges. You could end up with a distressingly blue-black dish!

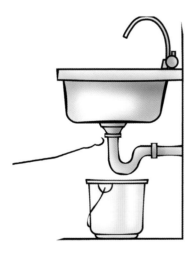

34. Blocked bend?

Kitchen sink filling up fast?

- Try bailing it out and flushing the drain with soda crystals and hot water. If it's still blocked try a proprietary drain cleaner.
- If that doesn't work, the blockage may be in the trap in the u-shaped bend under the sink. Put a bucket underneath to catch the overflow and debris, and open it up. Use the hooked end of a wire hanger to draw out what's blocking the pipe – do *not* push it further in.

35. Rubbish disposal

Some foods can actually be the death of the garbage disposal unit in your sink. It's meant for scraps, really – it's not an all-out refuse handler.

Avoiding pushing through foods that are very greasy, hard or fibrous, such as:

- Raw woody carrots
- Sugarcane stems

- Ears of corn (even if cooked!)
- Uncooked grains or pulses
- Large bones or tough cartilage
- Raw skin from fish or meat, including pork rind (even cooked)
- Oil or fat

Warning: Never put inorganic matter, such as plastic or foil, in the unit.

Kitchen Safety

Precautions for working with water, fire and electricity—all together! How to handle sharp and hot objects—with minimal risk! Emergency action and precautionary measures, too.

■ Safety start-up

36. Non-slip floors

It's all very well to add warmth to a cold hard surface, but a rug that slides on a slippery surface puts you at risk of tripping and falling.

- Restrict the use of unbacked rugs to rougher surfaces such as stone flags, wood or non-slip tiles.
- For high-shine and polished surfaces, use rugs with a rubber backing.
- Avoid rugs and mats in the kitchen; the smallest stumble with a pan of hot liquid can land you in hospital.
- In the bathroom too, avoid loose floor coverings – a mat with rubberized non-slip backing in front of the bath should be the only one here.

37. The family that's safe together...

You need to be sure that the whole family knows the safety rules – one of the best ways of doing this is to gather them together to help make a meal.

- Check their knife technique – chopping food in the wrong way with a knife that isn't sharp enough leads to many accidents in the kitchen.
- Show them how to carry vessels containing hot liquid.
- Teach them how and when to use the fire extinguisher and fire blanket (also *see Tip 39*).
- If anyone has a food allergy, this is a great opportunity for learning about avoiding food contamination and planning meals for special needs.

And, of course, cooking with others also means someone else is watching your back (which may be to the oven or hot-water tap!).

38. Cook's little helpers

Children love helping in the kitchen – you can even include toddlers if you take a few precautions.

- Warn them that the stove and oven are strictly for adults only.
- Make 'lab coats' out of adult shirts with short sleeves (or cut away the sleeves).
- Show them how to measure ingredients, sift flour, mix batters, shell peas and spread toppings.
- Cutting with knives is not for the under fives. Children should start with blunt-tipped scissors – good enough for beans, ham, cheese and even toast!

39. Drop and roll

Fires happen, and they are highly likely to happen in the kitchen.

- Should your clothes or hair catch fire, don't try to run away – drop to the floor on the spot and roll over until flames are extinguished.

Teach children this lesson as soon as they can understand what fire is!

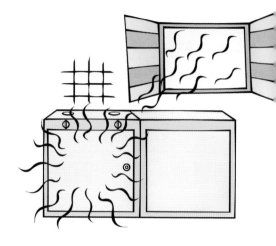

40. Smell gas? Get out!

Gas leaks can be life-threatening.

- Make sure all family members know and recognize the odour of gas.
- If you smell it you should immediately get out of the house and go to a trusted neighbour to phone for help from there.
- On no account should you try to switch on or off any lights or fans, or try to use the phone at home – the smallest spark can provide ignition.

■ Contamination alert!

41. Separate for pets

If you have a pet, be extra careful to avoid contamination between human and animal foods.

- Keep your pet's food preparation equipment away from yours; if possible, designate a separate area of the kitchen for preparing pet food.
- Have a separate can opener, spoon and fork, clearly labelled (or bearing a doggie or kitty motif), so even strangers to your home don't accidentally use them for humans.
- Wash the pet's bowls and other equipment separately, and disinfect all surfaces near the sink thoroughly before bringing your own utensils into that zone.
- When washing, make sure there are no washed 'people utensils' draining or drying near the sink that might get splashed.

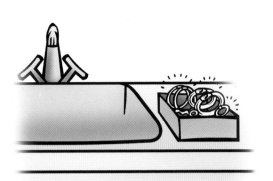

42. Ditch the bling

Top chefs don't wear rings at work. Rings harbour germs that a quick lather and rinse won't get rid of.

- Clean up before you cook – take off watches, rings, bracelets and bangles. Keep a closed basket on the worktop by the door or on the kitchen table, so you remember as soon as you walk in.
- Place a small decorative ceramic box next to the sink – a bright one will remind you to put valuables there before you splash into the soapy water.

43. Safe barbecuing

A barbecue means a lot of alternating between raw and cooked meats, providing ample opportunity for contamination.

- Put a folding table to one side of the barbecue, not too close to the heat.
- Place a large tub of water on the table, with a pump dispenser bottle of disinfectant soap, and a few clean towels.
- Wash your hands after touching raw meat – each time.
- Use a fresh towel every time you dry your hands.

■ Cautious cooking

44. Handles with care

This is especially crucial with young children at home, but even an all-adult household would do well to follow this rule.

- Turn the handles of all saucepans on the hob towards the back.
- Install a protective guard around the hob, to prevent inquisitive little fingers reaching up to take hold of a handle.
- Never keep more than one knife on the chopping board or worktop at a time.
- Rest knives parallel to the front of, not perpendicular to, the worktop so that if you lean on a knife inadvertently it won't shoot outwards.

45. With knobs on!

Children love pressing switches, especially on gadgets that will 'go' – such as washing machines or microwave ovens with turntables.

- If you have small children at home, get safety covers for appliance knobs.
- Even older children should use the microwave oven only under supervision.
- If you can, install a built-in 'appliance garage' unit with a rolling shutter you can lock. If you put a socket strip along the back wall, you can plug in many smaller appliances in situ – waffle iron, toaster, coffee maker, microwave – and have nothing to 'put away' when you've finished.

46. Oil spill alert!

Grease on the floor is a sure recipe for disaster, or at least a painful tumble.

- Throw flour over the grease to absorb it quickly, pressing down and moving the flour around as needed to absorb the grease.
- Now you should be able to brush most of the mess into your dustpan.
- Soap and water should take care of the rest.

47. If there's smoke, there's fire

As in all the other rooms in the house – indeed, even more so – you need a smoke detector in the kitchen. However, this is also the one room that already has an open flame and it could readily get smoky!

Look for a smoke detector alarm with a silencer feature that allows you to hush it up while you chargrill peppers!

48. Fabric and fire don't mix

You can't do without your tea towels and oven gloves, but most fabric is flammable and you're likely to be working with an open flame.

- Avoid having fabric curtains along the same wall as an oven or hob.
- Don't wear long sleeves or loose garments while cooking. Roll up your sleeves and put on an apron, preferably one made of a fire retardant material.
- Never hang tea towels or oven gloves from the handle of an oven that is in use, or behind or above the hob (from a rod along the back of the worktop or from hooks attached to the chimney hood, for instance).

49. Safe plastic and paper

Paper is another highly flammable material, and plastics can exhibit a range of unpleasant reactions to heat.

- Do not keep kitchen paper anywhere near cooking appliances.
- Avoid storing either food or utensils and appliances in paper packaging, even within cabinets. (The fridge is safer, though, being cold.)
- If in doubt about a plastic's capacity to withstand heat, keep the utensil clear of the oven and hob and certainly don't use it when microwaving!
- Avoid using plastic or plastic-lined aprons or gloves – if they melt or catch fire, they will stick painfully to your flesh.

50. Stand back!

Be conscious of how you carry yourself near open flames and cooking appliances.

- Tie back your hair securely while preparing food – it's not only hygienic, but a safety prerequisite.
- Avoid cooking with artificial nails on – not only could they catch painfully while you handle dough or grate a carrot, proximity to heat can cause them to burn or melt while still on your fingers!
- Never allow yourself (or a family member) to fall into the habit of leaning against the kitchen units or worktop as you cook. You might absent-mindedly lean too close to the hot hob or press a knee against the hot oven door.
- Explain to children that touching the oven door is taboo; only the door handle may be touched and that only with gloves on.
- That's a good reason to have the oven at eye level, out of reach of children.

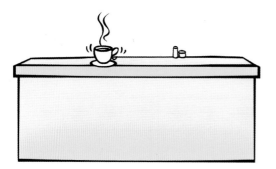

51. You can't stand the heat

Burns are an ever-present risk in the kitchen, so learn to respect heat.

- Never place a hot pot, cup or even a spoon near the edge of the counter. This is especially crucial if you have children or pets. A dog jumping up to grab a dangling spoon could end up with a badly burnt tongue; and even you might accidentally knock the coffeepot over.
- Hanging rods along the backsplash maximizes your storage space. But never hang things directly behind the stove where you might have to reach across bubbling liquids or flickering flames for a ladle.
- If your hob has front and back burners, use the back burners as much as possible. It means a child won't be able to grab a saucepan nor a pet reach into the flame under it – and you won't inadvertently brush against hot utensils (*see Tips 44 & 578*).

52. Food on fire!

Keep a fire extinguisher and fire blanket in the kitchen. Some additional tips:

- If food in a pan catches fire, turn off the hob and place a lid on the pan (to cut off air). Let it cool (about half an hour) before moving.
- If fat catches fire, smother with baking soda – it also helps scour off burnt-on food and grease. Never pour water on hot fat!
- If the fire's in the oven, pull the plug and keep the door closed.
- If the barbecue catches fire, close the lid (or use a large metal bowl). Otherwise scoop some soil over it.

53. Oil safety

Pan drippings make a delicious gravy, but because they have a high fat content, you must take care.

- Never place a pan of drippings or an oil bottle near a naked flame – it could easily be set alight.
- Make it a habit to reach for the oil, pour and replace it in one single, fluid movement.

54. Yellow for danger

If your gas hob is burning with yellowish rather than blue flames, this shows it isn't functioning optimally. Not only is this inefficient use of the gas fuel, it could signal a potentially dangerous problem.

- Get the hob checked and serviced as soon as you notice the problem.

- Always turn on the gas before you put a pot on the hob. That way it flares up faster and upwards, and you aren't 'working blind' (very risky!).

■ Wise up around watts

55. Microwave with caution

- Cook in covered containers to avoid splatters. But uncover carefully – a sudden gush of steam or splash of boiling liquid can cause painful burns. Always open the lid away from your face, easing up the side opposite you first.
- When using clingfilm to cover food, poke vents in it to let steam escape.
- Prick dense foods or those with 'skins' – egg yolks, sausages, cakes of tinned fish or spam, potatoes, tomatoes – to prevent 'explosions'!
- Many unmarked ceramics are microwave-safe. However, if a dish has any metallic trim, do not use it!

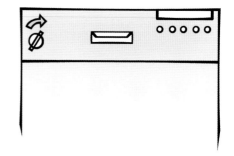

56. Fight the flicker

Flickering oven lights, a sluggish blender or a fluorescent strip that dims when you turn on the dishwasher might all indicate overloaded sockets or faulty wiring.

- Get the electrician in and fix it pronto – nowhere is this more crucial than the gadget-heavy kitchen area.

57. Keep the watts from water

Another kitchen duo that doesn't mix – electricity and water.

- Never operate an electrical appliance near the sink. If it falls in, even while switched off, it could electrocute someone.
- If you ever do drop a plugged-in appliance into water, immediately dry your hands and switch off the power at the mains, then unplug the appliance from the socket before attempting to lift it out.
- Use power sockets equipped with a circuit interrupter that senses any leakage of electricity – from a fault or from immersion of an appliance in water – and switches it right off.

■ Serving safeguards

58. Clear exit

When leaving the kitchen balancing hot food in breakable containers you can minimize the risk of accidents:

- Avoid carrying a tray or container so large you can't see where you are putting your feet.
- Don't have swing doors at the kitchen entrance – it obstructs your view both as you enter and leave, making collisions more likely.
- Install a bright light just inside the doorway if your kitchen opens into a corridor, so that anyone leaving will cast a sharp shadow visible to someone coming up the corridor.
- Avoid having a threshold across the door or a difference of levels that may cause you to trip or lose your footing.

59. Don't freeze those leftovers!

It may seem tempting, but leftovers contaminated with saliva are a health hazard.

- It is especially important not to store the 'leftovers' from a baby's bowl of food.
- You might just get away with refrigerating the remains of your own meal if you will be the one eating it, but even this is risky.
- On no account should you mix food left over from what you set out on the table and what you put away before serving.

60. Don't mix medication and meals

You always seem to have more medication in the house when you have young children.

- Keep a special set of spoons and measures for medicinal substances. That way, no one will inadvertently drink cough syrup from a shot glass!

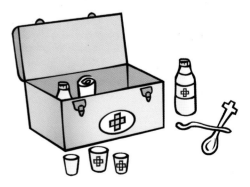

Shopping and Storage

All about food selection and storage. Fruit and veg, dairy products, meat and poultry, fish and seafood – how to select for superior taste and nutrition, and how to keep them at their best in your fridge or larder.

■ Clever shopping

61. You can keep your phone on

Keep your mobile phone handy in the supermarket.

• Use the calculator function to compare unit prices of various brands and sizes instead of guessing or revisiting your mental maths skills. This is not the time!

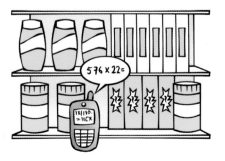

62. Check those expiry dates

Before you decide to bulk-buy that special offer, make sure you'll be able to use it all before the expiry date. Otherwise, it's no bargain!

• Always check the back of the shelf – usually packages from older lots are placed up front and newer stock is stacked at the back. This should have a later expiry date.

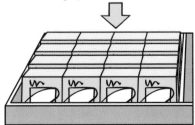

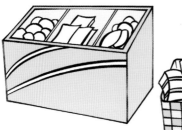

63. Frozen on the final lap

Frozen foods are meant to stay that way – *frozen!* – until you're ready to use or eat them.

- In the store, pick them up on your way out – going to the freezer last thing before paying at the till minimizes the time food spends outside the freezer.

64. Pack clever

As with shopping, so with packing (and unpacking) – there is safety in order. And nowhere more so than with frozen foods.

- Pack all the frozen foods together so that they insulate each other against heat.
- Bring along an insulated cooler bag or box (the kind you take on picnics) to pop the frozen foods in for the journey home.
- Never pack hot food (such as warm bread fresh from the oven or a spit-roasted chicken) together with frozen.
- Never stop to shop for other things or run further errands after you've picked up frozen groceries.
- Put away the frozen food first!

66. Look behind the labels

What goes on front is often a marketing gimmick. The real story's on ingredients lists.

- Marked 'low-fat'? Compare the 'original' – similar calories means extra sugar (to compensate for fat)!
- Your daily fat allowance is 70 g/2½ oz. If a 'diet' snack has 30 g/1 oz, where does that leave the rest of your meals?
- Does it list 'sodium'? Multiply by 2.5 for 'salt' content!
- Manmade trans fats are worse than natural ones in animal products. If it contains 'hydrogenated' or 'modified' vegetable oil, avoid it!
- Don't accept saturated instead of trans! If it reads 'trans fat-free', look out for 'palm'.

65. Partner the perishables

As with the frozen food, you need to get perishables into storage quickly, so it helps if they aren't scattered across several boxes or bags, mixed up with everything else.

- Buy the inert and preserved items first – foil, kitchen paper, detergents and canned and bottled foods.
- Buy fruit, vegetables and fresh dairy products, meat, fish and bakery items on the second-last lap.
- Pack the perishables together.
- Keep raw meat away from fruit and vegetables.
- Keep dairy and cooked items separate from raw foods.

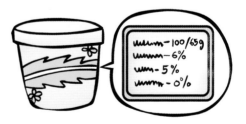

67. Take a pound of impulse

With all the marketing ploys and advertising spots, it's harder for shoppers to avoid impulse buys – indeed, the supermarket is designed to take advantage of human helplessness in the face of temptation.

- Make a list, and do your best to stick to it.
- Always put the impulse buys in a separate handheld basket, not the big shopping cart. That way, the weight will slow you (or your child) down enough to rethink your choices.
- Carry a small amount of ready cash for impulse buys and treats – a pound per person is plenty. Never pay for those with your credit card.

68. Leave the cranky child at home

Avoid taking children to the supermarket when they are not well rested and calm.

- A cranky, sleepy child is high on impulse, low on patience. You will either end up with a curtailed trip, or buy without sufficient thought – which in turn can mean poor nutritional choices and impulse purchases made to stall that tantrum.

69. Don't shop on empty

It may be best to exhaust your supplies before you replenish them. However, there are a couple of ground rules:

- Never shop on an empty stomach. You'll buy things that you really don't need.
- Never do the food shopping with a famished child in tow – that's asking for trouble.

70. Bill foolish?

Always double-check the bill before paying at the till – no matter how long the list.

- You are within your rights to wait to check the receipt – don't let the queue behind dissuade you.
- Remember: computerized is not the same as error-free. Wrong barcodes get entered, specials get left out – cashiers are human after all. However, you shouldn't have to pay for human error.
- If in doubt, ask the cashier to come with you to the aisle and check up – it is not an unreasonable request, and saves time haranguing over what either of you 'thinks' is the case.

■ Smarter shelving

71. Clear out the clear stuff

It's tempting to use clear plastic and glass storage jars – so easy to see what's where. However, heat and light aren't best friends with most foodstuffs – and there tends to be a good mix of each in the average kitchen!

- To protect your edibles, choose metal or well-fired ceramic instead.
- Add a visual label – snap a polaroid of contents and tie on like a gift tag.
- Scribble the 'best before' date under it.

Now you know what's where and how fast you must use it up.

■ Fruit and veg

72. Ripe for the picking?

- Pineapples are ripe when a tugged leaf comes off readily.
- Buy bananas and papayas slightly underripe, firm and greenish. Ripen in a paper bag at room temperature.
- Mushrooms are at their prime for a day, then deteriorate rapidly.
- Go by smell, not softness, for stone fruits. They often have short seasons, so buy some ripe to eat and get enough extras to ripen gradually in a paper bag at room temperature.
- Melons and kiwi are ripe when fragrant.
- Pick fresh figs ripe for the table – they spoil soon after.

73. Too green? Or overripe?

Not all fruit ripens readily on the tree and goes on until rot sets in!

- Pineapples stop ripening once picked. Very handy!
- Some varieties of avocado don't ripen *until* picked, so don't avoid it just because it's hard – it just means it's fresh!
- Tomatoes won't ripen further in the refrigerator – so if you have too many ripe ones, putting them in the salad box may stem the rot.
- Ripe bananas blacken in the refrigerator or freezer, but the flesh is still good to eat – use them for baking or blending.
- Berries will rot rather than ripen after picking. They go mouldy and messy easily – buy them ripe, and store on a layer of kitchen paper in the fridge.

74. Brown but sweet!

Unlike blotches and bruises from poor handling, a matte browning on tree fruits is usually caused by friction with leaves.

- Browning is common on fruits near the tips of branches – and these could actually taste better because they will have had more exposure to the sun!

75. Banana tree

Bananas hasten the ripening – and spoilage – of other fruits if kept together in the fruit basket.

- You could pile them in a separate fruit bowl; but again, if they are stacked more than one deep, they'll rot quickly as the gas rises up between layers.
- A banana tree will allow air to circulate and will keep the fruit fresh for longer.

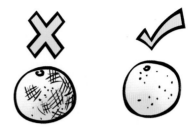

76. Citrus bright?

Don't go by colour when buying citrus fruit.

- Citrus varieties vary widely in terms of colour.
- Ripeness doesn't necessarily result in bright yellow or orange fruit! Green patches or paler hues of yellow-orange are characteristic of some varieties.
- Look instead for smooth, shiny peel – even unwaxed organic fruit won't be matte unless it's past its prime.
- Very brown fruit should be avoided. A few shallow 'scars' are fine though (*see Tip 74*).
- The fruit should have a thin skin (taking the variety into account – limes are usually thinner-skinned than lemons, so compare individual fruit of the same variety). Thicker-skinned fruit can be less juicy.
- The fruit should feel firm and heavy for its size. Avoid dents and gouges. However, loose-skinned fruit such as tangerines will be less dense than grapefruit.

77. Time for tomatoes

Tomatoes crop up in recipes all year, but are at their best in summer.

- During a glut, bottle your own concentrated purée (sealed with a layer of oil) and passata; or oven-dry.
- Off-season plum tomatoes are meatier than beef tomatoes and Hollands.
- Cherry and pear tomatoes are always sweet.
- Usually, yellow tomatoes are sweeter than red!
- In winter, canned – especially peeled whole – tomatoes in juice, no added salt, is a better buy (and cheaper) than hothouse or tropical produce.
- Purée is better than sauce for pizza or crostini toppings, when ripe (uncooked) tomatoes are scarce.

78. Greens are good

It's good practice to buy root vegetables with the greens still attached.

- Beetroot, carrot, turnip and radish greens are all extremely nutritious (not just iron, they have calcium and carotene too) and tasty.
- Fresh greens prove the roots are freshly harvested and in their prime.
- When storing, wrench the greens off and store them separately from the tubers – otherwise the tops will draw moisture out of the roots and turn them woody.

79. Beetroot greens? Stop if red!

Mostly you can tell if your greens are fresh – likewise any root vegetable attached to it – by checking for wilting, yellowing or pale spots. Those are the plants that are too old to be nutritious. Signs to look out for:

- Beetroot greens go red at the tips as they mature!
- With thick-stemmed greens such as kale, thickened veins and woody stems indicate age.
- Ageing mustard and spinach are also identified by coarse stems – they aren't bad to eat if you stew them, add cream and pass through a strainer.

80. On the shelf

It's not ideal to keep salad leaves for more than a day. But if you must:

- Cleaning out the muck and discarding inedible bits can prolong refrigerator-life – as long as you dry well after washing!
- After putting them through the salad spinner, tie up loosely in a clean tea cloth before popping in the crisper drawer.
- Poke holes in a plastic bag, line with kitchen paper and put the leaves in, leaving them plenty of breathing space.
- Use within 3–4 days.

81. Play snap!

When buying okra or celery, make sure it isn't old and fibrous, or limp from long or improper storage.

- Celery stalks should break crisply and sharply.
- Discreetly snap the tips of okra – if they break crisply and fall right off, that's a pod you want. If it bends rather than breaking, leave it.
- Hold asparagus stalks at either end and snap to break – the point of breakage is always the point at which you should trim the stem, separating woody growth from tender tip. Then pare away the tough peel before cooking.

82. Edible flowers

Edible blossoms make a pretty addition to green salads as well as a great garnish for various other dishes. Grow your own – or contact a reputable nursery or farmer who will find you pesticide-free flowers for the dining table.

Good, easily available choices:

- Rocket blooms
- Borage
- Nasturtiums
- Pansies
- Blossoms of all edible herbs – from chicory to fenugreek to tarragon
- Marigolds
- Honeysuckle
- Day lilies – very good frittered!
- Roses, violets and lavender, of course.

83. Listen to your artichokes

Yes, that's right – it's fresh if it talks to you!

- To choose tender young artichokes, hold them up to your ear and squeeze.
- If they have nice moist flesh, the leaves will squeak together.
- A hollow whisper means it's drying out.

84. Little green sputnik!

It's common for the kohlrabi to be likened to an alien!

- A relation of the common cabbage, kohlrabi is milder tasting, slightly nuttier and sweetish when young, and can even be eaten raw.
- It's also surprisingly resilient to pest attacks and so it's easy to grow without pesticides.
- Choose bulbs that are less than 7.5 cm/3 inches in diameter. The bigger heads may have woody bits that need trimming.
- Diced, they make a lovely addition to stews.
- Cook any young and unblemished leaves along with the bulb – this intensifies the flavour.

85. Sweet summer's marrow

The warm-weather squashes such as courgette and pattypans should be harvested while still quite young, so that the rinds are edible and seeds immature.

- Look for smooth, unblemished skins – avoid any black or dark spots, as well as any browning near the tips.
- While not hard like winter marrow, summer squash too should be firm. Yet the rind should be easy to pierce (if it's too tough it's too old to eat).
- As with oranges, squash should feel heavy for its size – this means tender, dense flesh that hasn't turned fibrous or lost moisture.
- Ideally, courgette and yellow summer squashes (such as crooknecks) should be picked no more than 15 cm/6 inches long. The fingerling sizes are best to eat.
- Pattypans should be no more than 10 cm/ 4 inches across.
- Refrigerated in a perforated polythene bag, tender squashes will keep for 3–4 days. Any longer and you risk spoilage.

86. The whole squash

Winter marrows include pumpkins, butternut, acorn and spaghetti squash.

- Winter squashes should have hard rinds – knock on them to check.
- Cracks indicate poor handling or storage, so the flesh may not be sound.
- Green-skinned squashes may have lighter flecks, faint stripes or orange patches. But avoid pale patches and brown spots.
- Butternut squash should be glossy tan, like an egg.
- Pumpkins should be bright orange.
- You needn't refrigerate winter marrows. Stored whole in a cool, dry place where air circulates (turn often or hang in a net bag), they'll last up to two months!

87. Pickle-free pumpkin preserving

Pumpkin is a hardy vegetable if kept dry – lucky for you, given the sizes they can grow to.

- However, once cut, they last better if left in a cool spot – minus their seeds! Which means scooping them out (*see Tip 28*).
- When you take the 'lid' off, slant your knife tip inwards so that the lid will sit snugly but not fall in later.
- Discard the stringy bits (you can save some seeds to toast with salt or sugar). If you need to store it for more than a few days, apply a light coat of petroleum jelly to the cut edges and rub some into the skin to prevent loss of moisture!
- Wipe clean before cooking – just to help flavours penetrate.

88. Basket by basket

Onions, garlic and potatoes are the most common veggies to be left out of the refrigerator. However, they do like a well-ventilated basket and keep best when separated from each other.

- A stacked bamboo steamer is perfect for the job and neat enough to sit on the most streamlined worktop.

90. Soggy in the salad box?

Yes, fresh vegetables and fruit need to retain a certain amount of moisture if they are to stay fresh. However, every time you open and close the fridge door, precipitation and condensation can add more moisture than is strictly healthy. And certain vegetables, such as salad leaves, often turn limp quickly.

- Place a layer of kitchen paper at the bottom of the salad box before you unpack the groceries.
- Wherever possible, discard polythene bags and plastic wrappings.
- Wrap individual vegetables or fruit in more kitchen paper, particularly if there are leafy greens in there.
- Do *not* store mushrooms in the salad box!
- Avoid throwing soft-stemmed herbs there too – they are better off in a jar of water in the fridge door (*see Tip 113*).

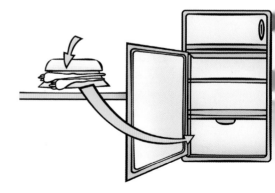

89. Cool new potatoes

Most potatoes keep better in a dark place outside the refrigerator. Strangely, it's not true of the bite-sized cuties!

- As befits their youth, baby new potatoes like to stay 'chilled'! Otherwise the warming, humid air of returning summer tends to make them go soft and ooze.
- Put them in the refrigerator – but no plastic, please, and keep the humidity low.
- A sheet of kitchen paper will soak up any excess moisture from other vegetables as well as keep them in the dark when you open the fridge door.

■ Grains and legumes

91. The hard and soft of flour

When it comes to baking cakes and bread, not all flour is milled equal.

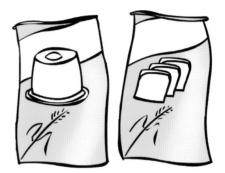

- For a truly light-as-air texture – especially for fat-free sponge and angel food cakes – it's worth seeking out cake flour or a plain flour labelled 'soft' or 'fine' instead of regular 'self-raising'. (You can always add in baking powder separately – *see Tip 237*).

92. Pasta puzzle

Should you buy fresh and turn up your nose at dried boxes of farfalle? Should you penny-pinch over plain Jane everyday pasta instead of the fancy shapes? The answer really depends on what you intend to do with it:

- In a creamy or buttery sauce, softer fresh pasta lends silkiness.
- Oil-based sauces gain heft from the dried semolina.
- Seafood and meat sauces, and even chunkier vegetable sauces, are best off with dried pasta, ideally in a shape with ridges or hollows to 'grab' the sauce.

93. Corny but sweet!

Fresh sweetcorn is a delicacy to treat with respect. The sugar in each ear of corn starts to change into insoluble starch as soon as it is picked off the plant.

- Which means you should store them for no more than a day – if you can't eat at once, it's a good idea to boil, butter (or oil) and refrigerate for a couple of days more.
- When buying, check for freshness by examining the husk first – you want tight, green wrappers and soft silk.
- Now check both ends – look for a moist yellow (not pale or browning) stem at the stalk end, firm plump kernels at the top.

94. Get gritty with grains

Pasta, rice, oatmeal, polenta… Add to the New Age granary bin:

- Amaranth: Super-nutritious; nutty with a mild pepperiness – no seasoning needed. It turns creamy when cooked in liquid; pops lightheartedly over dry heat.
- Millets: Rich in iron. Substitute for rice, wheat, barley or oats. A steamed pilaf is especially nice.
- Quinoa: High in protein, with more calcium than milk! It cooks creamy, making quinoa porridge a great breakfast for the lactose-intolerant.
- Wild rice: Doesn't keep well; expensive too. Use sparingly to perk up humbler grains (such as plain brown basmati rice).

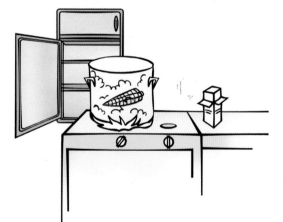

95. Long live legumes

Legumes are less prone to rancidity than grains, so they're well worth buying in bulk.

- Dried lentils and beans, in fact, keep well for up to 2–3 years – much longer than many canned foods.
- The older ones will just need longer cooking, so an overnight soak followed by pressure cooking or a spell in your slow cooker should soften them up nicely.

96. The cost of a can

How much do you actually get from a can of beans after draining and rinsing?

- Well, the typical 400 g / 14 oz can should yield about 240 g / 8 ½ oz of beans such as chickpeas or kidney beans. With some lighter pulses, such as lentils, you might get a little less.

■ Dairy and eggs

97. In defence of dairy

Always keep dairy products and eggs airtight against foods with strong aromas, as they absorb odours easily.

- Make sure yogurt, cream and milk are in tight-lidded containers; if not, wrap the top closely with foil or decant (but *see Tip 301*).
- Eggs should be fine in their carton; if you've thrown away the carton, you'd better pop them in a lidded plastic tub. Keep them on the top shelf of the fridge, not in the door.
- Cheese actually likes to breathe, so keep it away from the aromatic stuff; if you can't, putting it in a cardboard box is a compromise that will work as long as you use it up quickly.

98. Farm fresh eggs?

Yes, we've all heard about floating eggs in water to check their freshness. But we doubt the supermarket's offering you a bowl of water to play with.

- Inspect the shell instead – if it looks chalky, even a little bumpy like fresh plaster, that's a good indication of recent laying.
- A waxy smooth shell, attractive as it might seem, is likely to have been hanging around for too long.

99. Fresh in the whey

Buying fresh white cheese, such as mozzarella or cottage cheese?

- The kind packed in whey keeps fresh longest.
- Don't throw away the whey – it's great for kneading bread dough with. It makes for really soft, tasty, extra nutritious (whey has protein) bread.
- Just be aware that whey will stain (actually, bleach) fabric readily, so get the apron on while cooking. And double-wrap for transporting and storage.

■ Meat and poultry

100. Choosing chicken

If you're making curry or stew rather than a fancy grilled dish, don't bother getting prepared chicken breasts or thighs.

- Just ask for a fresh, whole chicken to be jointed for you, and ask for the giblets to be bagged for your stock pot.
- Don't forget to pick up a few hefty carrots and a couple of celery or leek stalks on the way out. Throw them into the pot to boil with the giblets and a bag of bouquet garni while you cook dinner.
- By the time you've eaten, the stock should be ready to strain.
- Freeze the stock and bag it for soup. There, two dishes for the price of one!

101. Lean loins

An easy guide to shopping for low-fat and lean(er) meats:

- The more marbling, the more tender and fattier. Choose less visible fat and factor in extra marinating or braising time instead.
- Look for 'round' and 'loin', as well as 'leg' cuts.

102. Humbler ham

If you can't get a whole gammon for the Sunday roast, don't despair.

- Ask for a rolled loin of pork instead – it's just as delicious, and not as salty.
- It's easy to turn into a posh roast, too – unroll and stuff with a handful of fresh herbs (pork especially likes sage), or a traditional onion stuffing, or even a few chopped prunes. Roll up and secure again.
- Either lay strips of bacon on top to keep it moist, or have some apple sauce handy for basting.

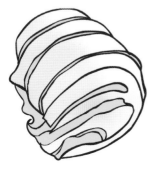

103. Superior steaks

If a great grilled dinner begins with a perfect juicy steak or plump chicken breast, the second step is the marinade.

A good trick is to marinate *before* you refrigerate:

- Put each steak into a freezer-proof polythene bag along with a portion of marinade.
- It will marinate until it freezes, and then once again while you thaw each steak in the refrigerator before cooking.
- Then all you need do is heat the frying pan, pull open the bag and slide it all in…Dinner in 10 minutes!

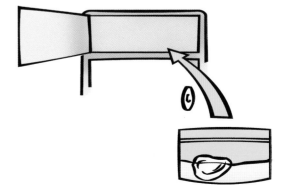

104. Frozen for choice

We're all for convenience; but not at the cost of, well, cost!

Why buy expensive ragù-style meat sauces for pasta when all you want is a meaty sauce for spaghetti?

- Keep some frozen meatballs or fresh coarse sausages in the freezer.
- To serve, thaw till you can mash them or crumble from frozen.
- Heat up with canned tomatoes, some herbs and a couple of chopped onions, and pour over pasta.

105. The value of veal

Because it comes from young calves, veal is leaner than hefty cuts from full-grown beef cattle.

- Typically it has a third less fat, which means it cooks more delicately – cooking techniques and times should be closer to poultry.
- Milk-fed veal is the premium quality – it should be pale pink with hardly any marbling, and with fine sinews.
- The darker veal from grass- or grain-fed calves is cheaper, and not as fine – but it'll still be quite delicate as long as the calf was no more than three months old. Check with your butcher.

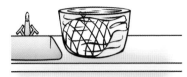

106. Fresh bird or frozen?

We're all for the convenience of jointed frozen poultry, but if it's a whole roast you're after:

- With smaller fowl – chicken – it's fine to consider a frozen bird; it will take minutes in the microwave, or you can simply thaw in the fridge overnight.
- Larger birds – such as turkey or goose –can guzzle up your time. They may be too big to thaw in the fridge, and it would take absolutely ages!
- The quickest way would be to plunge them in a clean basin of tap water, wrapper and all. But even then, it's going to take an hour per pound, or two hours for every kilo!

107. Cold chicken?

Do you need to shove the fresh spring chicken into the freezer straight away? No, not if you mean to cook it soon.

- It's fine to let poultry sit in the fridge for up to 2 days. Just make sure it is securely wrapped and covered so that it can't drip a drop on anything else (be very afraid of salmonella!)
- Any longer, and you really ought to freeze it – for up to 6 months.
- If you like, marinate and then freeze (*see Tip 103*).

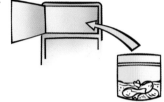

■ Seafood

108. Firm fish, please

Do the triple-test when buying fish – smell, see and touch.

- Fresh fish smells like a fresh sea breeze – briny, then, and not 'fishy'.
- If your environment disguises smells, look closely at the eyes and scales. Loose scales, bare patches and messy fins show signs of too much age. Similarly, gills should be bright red and the eyes should be clear, not milky.
- Finally, feel the fillet. It should be firm, moist, shiny and plump – not soft, saggy or spongy.

109. When frozen is best

If the fresh looks iffy, let alone whiffy, you'd be better off fishing around in the freezer chest.

- Look for 'flash-frozen' – this means that it went from sea to freezer right away, with no time to spoil.

110. The big freeze?

How long fish will 'keep' depends on how fat it is – literally!

- Lean fish, oddly enough, keeps better than oily fish! Oily fish will keep, frozen, for just about 3 months; less oily cousins can hang about twice as long.
- Whole fish, unsurprisingly, last better than cuts.
- Don't store any fish in the refrigerator for more than a day.
- Whatever the type, wash it (even if it has been 'cleaned') when you get home, pat dry thoroughly and wrap in greaseproof paper before bagging.

111. Shell open, shell closed?

For mussels and oysters, it's not just whether they are open or closed that indicates freshness. The question is: when are they open and when are they closed?

- When buying fresh mussels, give the shells a tap – if they promptly clam up, that means they are alive, and good to eat.
- Trawl through the pot again after cooking, though. Any that still stay shut should be tossed away!

■ Spices and condiments

112. Spice labels

Putting spices in identical jars is neat; but if you keep them on a shelf, you won't see beyond the first row to what's at the back. They all look the same until you move the first row out of the way.

- Keep your spice jars in a shallow drawer, rather than that favourite place, a shelf over the hob.
- Tape labels across the lids instead of on the jars.
- They'll keep better too, since heat rising from the hob won't affect them.

113. Water for long herbs

Got a big bunch of fresh herbs and can't use them up at once?

- If they've got their roots or are long in the stem, soft herbs such as basil, coriander and dill can be kept on a cool worktop or in the fridge for several days – as long as they are well watered.
- Immerse the roots or stems (picked clean of lower leaves) in two fingers of water in a tall glass or jar.
- Place a plastic bag over the top and secure at the rim to minimize moisture loss.

114. Wraps for short herbs

For fresh herbs with short stems, or just leaves (such as sage), the watering approach won't work. Yet, left to themselves in the fridge, they will wilt within hours. Wrap them up to prevent loss of moisture.

- Dampen a clean piece of muslin or a tea towel with cold water.
- Place a few leaves or sprigs at one end and roll up loosely.
- Refrigerate and use within 2–3 days.

115. Dry your own

You can dry your own fresh herbs, as long as you buy them with the stems.

- Bunch herbs together by the stems into loose posies.
- Pop the 'heads' inside a perforated paper bag to protect from light and dust and tie them together by the stems, leaving a loop to hang by.
- Hang in an airy place away from direct sunlight for 2–3 weeks to dry.
- Store whole posies in a canister or slip them inside polythene bags and tie at the base.

116. Toasted and hammered

Many spices such as cumin, coriander, chilli and cardamom – as well as dried woody herbs – release maximum flavour when dry-roasted whole and ground in a mortar and pestle.

• Grind only when ready to use.

117. Best not dried

It's on the shelf, but it's possibly best avoided:

• Dried basil
• Dried chives
• Dried dill
• Dried fenugreek
• Dried parsley

118. As good or better dry

Some herbs are actually better dry, or as good and cheaper than fresh:

• Oregano
• Thyme
• Mint (but don't keep for too long).

119. Hot green corns

White pepper is known to be milder than black. And fresh green peppercorns are gentler than either.

- Use them in the mix of ingredients for steak au poivre.
- Partner them with more delicate foods such as really fresh fish.

120. Chilli gone cold?

Chilli sauce and condiments flavoured with the spice keep better than the powdered pepper!

- Chilli powder doesn't lose potency but goes musty and risks spoilage.
- Don't buy more than a couple of months' supply at a time.
- Store tightly closed in a cool, dry place – but not the fridge either!

121. Horseradish hot

Unlike many spicy condiments – such as mustard, salsa and harissa – horseradish paste and sauce lose potency pretty fast.

- Use within a few months.

- Whole dried chillies, though, are happy to stand in the sun.
- Growing your own? Chilli loves sunlight – so move it out of the shade and leave well alone in dull grey weather.

122. The big daddy of cardamom

The cardamom pods you typically buy are pale green in colour. However, it is worth seeking out the larger (about twice the size), dried black cardamom pods for some dishes.

- Any dish with a slightly sweet base benefits from the stronger zest of this spice.
- Use only the seeds, crushed, discarding the pod itself – it's too astringent.
- Try it in coconut-based curries, pumpkin stew, roasted parsnips and carrots, rice pudding and chocolate desserts.
- It also makes a lovely palate cleanser to chew on after a meal. Offer a single pod, pressed open to expose the seeds, with an after-dinner cuppa.

123. Chilled seeds and nuts

Both sesame seeds and oil are frequently used in Eastern cooking.

- However, sesame goes off quickly. It's best to store it in the refrigerator.
- Do the same with peanuts and tree nuts that haven't been roasted or toasted.

124. Vinegar – plain and simple?

Unlike several other condiments and oils, vinegar is not a particularly expensive ingredient on its own. If you're paying a premium, check that you aren't buying 'packaging'!

- Does the vinegar contain expensive inclusions? Exotic fruit, for instance, but not common herbs.
- Does it derive from an uncommon source that is very seasonal, for example raspberries?
- Is it aged? This applies only to balsamic vinegar, which can be casked in oak, cherry, ash, chestnut and whatnot. And yes, this is the one that pares a pretty penny off your purse.
- Can't find just the vinegar your recipe requires? A little citrus or grape juice (for wine vinegars) or apple juice (for cider) will do the trick in most dishes.

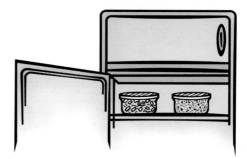

125. Laudable libations

You don't have to break out the Dom Perignon for cooking with. But whatever liquor you use in a dish is there for its flavour (which intensifies as the alcohol evaporates), so do choose a decent bottle.

• If you wouldn't drink it, don't cook with it!

126. Sweet stuff!

• Brown sugar brings extra moisture to your cake! (Which also means clumping – crusts of stale bread and paper towels in the jar help delay the inevitable.)
• Molasses? More moisture still. Expect chewy rather than fluffy results.
• Caster sugar's the stuff for fluff – soufflés, sauces, sponges.
• Icing 'sugar' contains starch, so isn't as sweet! But it dissolves quickly – sprinkle at the last moment for sparkle.
• The darker the sugar, the more complex the flavour. Plain white is best for delicate foods – the bouquet of Darjeeling tea is quite drowned by robust brown beet sugar!

■ Local, seasonal, organic – in order

127. Seasonal specials

Much of our supermarket produce these days is available all year round, irrespective of climate and time of year.

However, some things are still best local and seasonal – not just for the environment, but in terms of flavour too.

128. In spring, savour

- artichokes
- asparagus
- peas
- spring onions
- spring greens and salads

129. Summer specialities

- beans – broad and runner
- corn
- cucumbers
- okra
- summer squash (such as courgettes)
- tomatoes
- sweet peppers
- melons
- fresh figs
- mangoes
- pawpaws
- stone fruit – apricots, peaches, plums and nectarines
- berries – strawberries early on, then blueberries, raspberries and blackberries
- cherries
- rhubarb

130. Autumn glories

- Brussels sprouts
- kohlrabi
- leeks
- parsnips
- sweet potatoes
- swedes and turnips
- winter squash (butternut and acorn)
- apples
- cranberries
- pears
- grapes
- pomegranates
- fennel

131. Wait for winter for

- oranges, tangerines and grapefruit
- kumquats
- coconuts
- beetroot

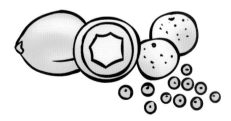

132. Impervious fruit and vegetables?

If you can't buy organic – for reasons of either budget or availability – know where exactly to compromise.

- Any fruit that is thick-skinned and will definitely be peeled (loose-skinned clementines, satsumas, kiwi fruit, bananas) will have less pesticide in the edible parts than a thinner-skinned fruit, especially one you might eat whole (such as an apple).
- Contrast the vulnerable vegetables in Tip 133.
- Anything oily, such as nuts, even if peeled or shelled, is more likely to hold on to chemical residues.
- If you're going to zest citrus fruit, do make sure it is organic.

133. Pesticide pains

What you should buy organic, because they are more likely to be heavily sprayed and/or more likely to hang on to residues:

- peaches and similar stone fruits (apricots, plums, nectarines), both fresh and dried
- berries (strawberries, raspberries)
- apples and pears
- grapes, raisins and sultanas
- cherries
- lemons and limes (because you don't usually peel before serving)
- tomatoes
- potatoes
- celery and leafy greens, including salad leaves and spinach
- cucumbers
- chillies and sweet peppers
- French and runner beans
- carrots
- courgettes and other squashes
- mushrooms

134. Organically ugly?

If you're choosing to buy organic, note that your shopping bag possibly won't look as good as with regular produce!

- Expect produce to look anything but pristine!
- Organically grown vegetables, especially heirloom varieties, will not necessarily have the regular shape, large size and glossy skin of conventional farm produce. Most of the latter are bred for looks, and may have been genetically modified or surface treated to make them more attractive.
- Don't be alarmed by holes in leafy greens – it's most likely safe as long as you wash them well and cook correctly. Even an apple with a worm hole near the stem may not be bad eating – cut and core, and you will probably find that most of the fruit is sound.

135. Poor picks

Organic or not, there are warning signs for all produce:

- Soft vegetables such as tomatoes and fruits may be harbouring the eggs of parasites – these appear as little white or yellowish specks. Not recommended.
- Avoid blotches or bruises (*but see Tip 74*).

Basic Techniques and Standby Staples

This chapter provides preliminary preparation how-tos, including time-saving and trouble-saving hints, ingredient substitutions and larder stocking tips.

■ Preparing fruit and veg

136. No more tears

Stop crying over chopped onions.

- Halve and drop them in a bowl of cold tap water. Leave for 5 minutes before you peel, slice or dice to reduce the pungency. As a bonus, the soggy skin will slip off easily.
- If you're short of time, rinsing the onions under running water for a few minutes will also help.

137. Skinned shallots

Although small, these tiny flavourful onions can also reduce you to tears.

- Top and tail the shallots and drop into boiling water.
- Leave to stand for a minute, then drain.
- Gentle pressure from the fingers should pop the shallot out of its skin!

138. Slicing avocado smoothly

Soft, creamy avocado flesh is easily mushed up – trying to peel and slice is almost always a bad idea.

- Instead, halve and slice while still in the skin (it's tough enough not to break if you go lightly).
- Scoop out the end piece with a spoon, and the others should slide out easily with the slightest nudge of a blunt-tipped paring knife.

139. Peeling ginger? Blunt is best

The knobbly shape of ginger coupled with its thin, papery skin means neither a paring knife nor a peeler will make a clean breast of it – plus you'll lose precious chunks.

- Use the edge of a teaspoon; the curved shape helps it get into the crevices more readily.

140. Dipping Mr Potatohead

When you have a large pile of spuds to peel or cut up, sit down with a big bowl of cold water.

- Drop the peeled or diced potatoes in the water as you work to prevent discoloration.

142. Criss-cross crisps

If you have a mandolin with a 'crinkle cut' slicing blade, you can get 'basketweave' potato crisps.

- Take the first slice off and discard to leave a ridged surface on the potato.
- Now turn it through a right angle for the next slice – it will have a perforated hatched pattern.
- Continue slicing, turning the potato 90° for every slice.
- Rinse off the surface starch and dry carefully on kitchen paper before deep-frying.

141. Grate – No peel!

Don't peel if you don't have to!

- Leave the peel on potatoes, sweet potatoes or carrots that you intend to grate.
- It won't interfere except to add the subtlest hint of texture to carrot cakes or rösti-style potato pancakes.

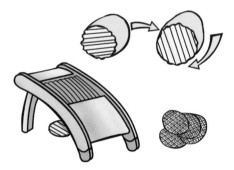

143. Okra on top

The sap inside okra pods acts as a thickener in gumbos. It also makes chopped okra a difficult vegetable to cook, since it gets gluey before starting to crisp up unless deep-fried. However, if you have tender baby okra pods, consider cooking them whole so as not to release the sap and retain all the moisture.

- Carefully trim the top of the stem end, taking off just enough to not puncture the pod through to the hollow core. No leaking sap!
- Of course, you'll have to make sure the tip at the other end is sound too.

144. Seedless pepper

The quickest way to de-seed a pepper:

- Cut in half vertically, along the pepper's natural grooves on opposite sides of the stem.
- Twist gently to separate the halves. The main cluster of seeds under the stem will come away with one half.
- Grasping the stem and seed bundle with your fingers, gently rock to loosen and pull away from the pepper.
- Place the halves face down on a chopping board and tap sharply to loosen any clinging seeds inside so they fall out.
- Finally, trim away any white membranes along the ridges with your paring knife.

145. Pumpkin peeler

If you need your pumpkin peeled and diced for sautéing to add to a stew or soup, cut it before you peel it.

- Whether Halloween monster pumpkin or slender, shapely butternut squash, first slice it up – preferably widthwise, so that you get cross sections with seeds in the middle.
- This may not be practical for a big pumpkin, so cut that into wedges instead.
- Now sit the circles of squash flat and trim off the peel by cutting 'facets' off the rim.
- Halve each circle and scoop out the seeds, then dice.
- For the vertical wedges, first dice so you can lay them on their sides in flat arcs, and peel as described above.

146. Clean greens

Washing salad leaves or other leafy greens?

- Forget the colander – grit that gets moved by the splashing water too easily resettles in the crevices of the leaves.
- Instead, fill a large bowl with clean cold water and plunge the leaves in, pumping up and down or swishing around by hand to rinse.
- Lift out and empty the water – the grit should have fallen to the bottom – and repeat twice.
- Shake off excess water using a salad spinner (yes, you can shake by hand and then pat dry each leaf, but this is so much faster!).

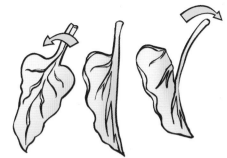

147. De-veining greens

Most greens are better off without the tough central vein. Remove stem and main vein from spinach, sorrel, mustard, radish and kale in one go:

- Fold each leaf along the central vein, glossy upper surfaces inwards.
- Hold them by the leaf margins with the central vein on top.
- Grasping the end of the stem, pull up and away to 'peel off' the central vein from the leaf.
- Cut away brittle lettuce stems before you shred the leaves.

148. Best face forward

When it comes to tight-headed greens such as lettuce, endive and even firm cabbage, many of the nutrients are actually in the outer leaves that see more sun.

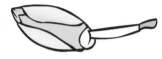

- Try not to lose those outer layers, provided they are smooth, glossy and undamaged.
- On the other hand, the stems of lettuce aren't very tasty and the core of the Belgian endive can be positively bitter. Cut those away before you shred the leaves.

149. Cut to the core

Preparing cruciferous vegetables:

- For cabbages, core as you would a Belgian endive. Unlike bitter endive hearts, cabbage stems are good to eat, though, so shred into the dish a little earlier than the leaves!
- Cauliflower cores are tougher, but you can slice tender parts finely and cook with the florets.
- With broccoli, the skin is tougher – you can keep tender stems after peeling. Slice deep into the stems to help them cook faster (broccoli florets are more tender than cauliflower).
- Cut a cross in the base of Brussels sprouts.

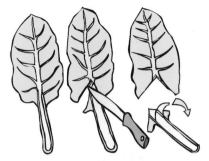

150. Skin the chard

A tough, translucent membrane covers the stalks of Swiss chard. You'll know it's there when the knife slips! But don't wait for accidents to happen.

- Lay each leaf flat, concave surface of the stem upwards, and make a v-shaped incision into the leaf to take out as much of the flat white (or coloured) stalk as possible.
- Cut off the pointed tip of the stalk, but don't cut all the way through the outer membrane. Use the 'tab' top to pull it away, down the length of the stalk.
- Now you can cut it into pieces and cook.

151. Greek stuffed leaves

Dolmades can be made by wrapping a stuffing of rice in cabbage or vine leaves. To make tight, secure parcels:

- Place a spoonful of stuffing near the base of a leaf.
- Fold the bottom edge over the stuffing, then fold the sides inwards over it.
- Roll from the bottom up.
- Cook with the seam downwards.

152. The whole tamale

Yet another leaf wrap, this way of rolling a tamale is easier still than dolmades (*see Tip 151*) and requires no string.

- Place two parboiled corn husks on top of each other, oriented at right angles to each other to make a cross shape.
- Spoon stuffing into the centre – at the crux of the cross.
- Fold as with the dolmades – bottom first, then sides (that is, the ends of the second husk) and finally roll to take up the top.

153. The simplest sorbets

Universally appealing, a refreshing fruit sorbet is so easy to make it should become a freezer staple. The only problem is stopping yourself polishing it off in one go!

- Any juice can be sweetened and chilled – syrup made with about 200 g/7 oz sugar in 300 ml/ 10 fl oz water mixed with 600 ml/1 pint of juice is perfect for a citrus, berry or grape sorbet.
- For naturally sweeter fruit such as peaches, just dilute the juice to taste.
- Leave it to freeze solid and scrape up to serve as a pebbly granita, or wait until it's slushy and beat again for a smoother texture.
- Once it sets smooth again, fold in a stiffly beaten egg white during a second whisking for a creamier sorbet.
- You can also add some chopped fruit, herbs or zest at this point, but don't overdo it.

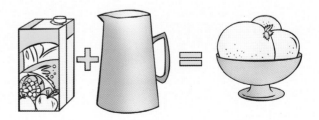

154. Simple sauce for stuffed pasta

- A herbed butter is the easiest thing to toss with some freshly cooked ravioli (*see Tip 190*).
- Add quickly sautéed garlic – do not brown – and fresh herbs if you have some to hand to pep it up.
- A scattering of snipped sun-dried tomatoes would also be good.

■ Store cupboard standbys

155. Larder-aged liqueur

You'll need to lock this up for a week at least to get the flavours going. It will, however, keep for 3 months.

- Thaw 700 g / 1 lb 9 oz frozen blueberries, raspberries or currants and mash with a fork.
- Stir in a bottle of white wine.
- Cover with clingfilm and leave to steep in the fridge for 3 days.
- Sweeten with 450 g / 1 lb of caster sugar and perhaps a couple of spoonfuls of Cointreau or white crème de menthe.
- Strain and bottle.
- Serve cold in shot glasses or top up with sparkling wine in a flute.

156. Melon in a bottle

You can get fancy with the added flavours, but the simplest preserves are just sugar and fruit. Melon jam is the easiest to make.

- Cube your melons – whether cantaloupe, honeydew or musk melon (anything but watermelon will work).
- Place in a large flat dish with enough sugar to cover.
- Refrigerate overnight.
- In the morning you'll find a slush in the dish! If it's too runny to spoon up easily, simmer till just thick enough and bottle.

157. Adaptable apricots

Dried apricots – the leathery hard ones with the stones in, not the plump ready-to-eat sort – have a considerable shelf life. Indeed, they could put any prune to shame!

- Soak them in enough hot water to cover, with a few points of star anise.
- Leave overnight. By morning, they will have swelled and softened.
- Now remove the stones and blend the fruit, with just enough of the liquid to render a sticky paste.
- Bottle and serve with bread and cheese.

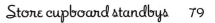

158. Mayonnaise made easy

Preparing your own mayonnaise is well worth the effort. For the lightest, smoothest results, follow the three golden rules:

- Start with all the ingredients at cool room temperature – if they're either too cold or too warm you'll end up sorting out a curdle.
- Add the oil in a slow stream, whisking constantly.
- If you do end up with a curdled sauce, add a teaspoon of cold water and whisk again. Otherwise, another egg yolk added in might help.

159. Versatile vanilla!

Vanilla pods may seem expensive, but they have a long and very useful life!

- Once you've scraped the vanilla seeds into a custard, what is left of the vanilla pod can be snipped in two and kept in a jar of sugar for a couple of months to lend its flavour.
- And it's still got some life left in it! Now you can whiz up the pod with some caster sugar for a second speckled batch.
- The first batch is good for adding just a hint of flavour – for sprinkling on fruit or stirring into your coffee.
- Use the second batch in batters and doughs for a more intense finish and a pretty, speckled effect – not very different from the seed scrapings!

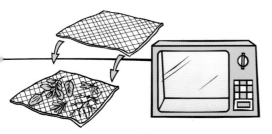

160. Radiant dried herbs

An alternative method for drying your own herbs uses the microwave oven.

- Wash the herbs and pat dry with a tea towel.
- Sandwich between two layers of sturdy kitchen paper and microwave on high, turning every minute, until dry.
- Herbs dried by this method will stay looking vibrant – they don't fade as much as the air-dried kind.

161. Vinegar variety

Make your own flavoured vinegar.

- Use rice vinegar with Asian herbs (lemongrass, galangal, Thai basil); white wine vinegar for European herbs; cider vinegar with spices.
- For 300 ml / 10 fl oz vinegar, use a handful of herbs or 2 tablespoons of spice, pounded or crushed lightly.
- Stronger flavours (ginger, basil) infuse in a week. Subtler herbs (marjoram, tarragon) need two weeks.
- Strain into sterilized bottles. Add a few whole spices or herb sprigs to identify.
- Use within six months.
- If it's a fleshy ingredient (chilli, ginger, lemongrass, mint), refrigerate. Otherwise a cool, dark cabinet is fine.

163. Vodka vroom!

As with vinegar (*see Tip 161*), so with vodka – creating your own cabinet of flavours is both easy and impressive.

- Use a handful of spices or herbs, perhaps even a couple of spoons of fruits (berries give beautiful colour) for a single bottle.
- Steep for at least two weeks.
- Colour will be leached from the ingredients, so strain and add some of the fresh ingredient once well flavoured.
- Keep chilled and serve very cold – from a packed ice bucket – for thick, syrupy shots.
- If you like, rim shot glasses with a coordinating infused sugar or flavoured salt – vanilla with cinnamon sugar, chilli vodka with celery salt, citrus with pepper.
- You can infuse brandy, rum and other spirits in a similar fashion.

162. Aromatic oils

Make your own:

- Refined olive oil and rapeseed oil make the best bases.
- Flavour with spices, seeds, nuts, herbs, onion or garlic, wild mushrooms or nuts.
- Dried ingredients are best; moisture from fresh ingredients hastens spoilage.
- Add 2 tablespoons of robust flavouring (or 4 tablespoons of mild) to 475 ml/16 fl oz oil.
- Heat in an oven at 150°C/300°F for 1 hour 40 minutes. The oil must reach 120°C/250°F (check with a sugar boiling thermometer).
- Strain and bottle, leaving minimal air between oil and cork.
- Use within a month.
- Think sweet too – angelica, vanilla, citrus peel, fennel, saffron and nut oils are excellent with desserts!

164. Trouble-shooting

A couple of odd things can happen when you make your own flavoured oil, vinegar and liqueurs.

- Sometimes the flavoured oil becomes cloudy – this indicates there is moisture present (from the flavouring ingredient). Pour out into a tin, reheat until the cloudiness disappears and rebottle from scratch.
- Many of your flavourings will tend to float into the neck of the bottle. As you use the liquid, longer stalks of herbs or chillies become more exposed. This contact with air can make them spoil, so either use up within a week of opening, or top up the liquid to cover the flavouring ingredient. (This dilutes the flavour slightly, but if you're using the liquid slowly, it will soon catch up – particularly in the case of vinegar or vodka.)

165. Extra special sugar (or salt)

Infuse your own sugar or salt:

- Blitz sea salt or sugar in a blender with pepper, garlic, citrus peel or vanilla pods for the most intense flavour.
- You can get a good flavour over time by lightly bruising the ingredient (vanilla, garlic, chillies, celery or cinnamon) and placing in a jar of salt or sugar. This is useful for large amounts – sugar you intend to bake with or salt to be used as a 'crust' on meat or fish.
- There's little danger of spoilage as both sugar and salt 'pickle' the flavouring ingredient.

■ Kitchen aid!

166. Low-fat spray

Make your own oil spray or mister for low-fat frying.

- Simply mix equal amounts of vegetable oil and water in a clean household-standard spray bottle and shake well.
- Experiment with different oils and ratios of water-to-oil to find what works best for you in terms of flavour and ease of cooking.
- You will need to clean the nozzle of the bottle regularly to prevent clogging. A baking powder solution sprayed through it should do the trick.

167. Clogged sauce bottle?

Got a bottle of ketchup that won't deliver?

- Put the cap on and thump the bottle firmly (but not too aggressively!) on the worktop a couple of times.
- If the sauce has congealed, try pushing a fat straw in and out – that should mix it up nicely as well as let air in (in case a blockage at the neck has 'bottled' it in!).

- If it's really stiff, try adding a small drip of oil and shake to loosen. Do not add water, as this could hasten spoilage.

168. Locked in place

Jars refusing to unscrew?

- Get a (better) grip. A flat rubber band slipped around the circumference of the lid can help.
- Leave the jar in the refrigerator for 10 minutes; remove and run hot water over the lid before you try again.
- Try using a small screwdriver to carefully ease the lid away from the jar – it may break the vacuum. (Replace the mangled lid or decant the contents later.)

■ Less mess, more speed

169. Bag your books

Cookbooks are great, but trying to keep them open at the right page while you follow a recipe can be a nightmare!

- Put your cookbook, opened to the correct recipe, in a clear plastic folder or bag to protect it from smears and splashes as well as keeping the pages from falling shut or flipping in a breeze.

170. Sticky measures

About to measure out sticky stuff like honey, treacle, peanut butter or jam?

- Grease your measuring spoons and cups lightly first, and the ingredients will slip off more easily.

171. It's a wrap!

Avoid getting sticky, greasy hands, rolling pin and worktop dirty from buttery or crumbly pastry, dough, marzipan, even ready-roll icing. Keep the mess under wraps!

- Use either a large polythene bag cut up along one side to resemble a folder or two sheets of greaseproof paper to make the wrap.
- Lay the bag or a sheet of the paper on the worktop. Place your dough on this – centred on the paper or in one half of the bag.
- Lay the other sheet of paper on top or fold the other half of the bag over to enclose the dough.
- Roll as usual. When you need to peel the dough off the worktop, simply lift the paper or plastic!

172. A drop of colour or flavour

Adding flavour concentrates, artificial flavourings or food colouring to a dish? We know all brands aren't made equal – the cookbook's ½ teaspoon may be too much or too little unless your brands match!

- Use a medicine dropper (available at pharmacies) to add the liquid a drop at a time, mixing and checking as you go. It can make all the difference between an appetizing lime green icing and full-on monster goo!

173. Coppered eggs

There is one exception to the rule that you should never prepare, cook or serve foods in unlined copper vessels.

- A round-bottomed all-copper bowl will drastically reduce the elbow grease you need to whisk egg whites!

174. Easy egg-shelling

Shelling hot boiled eggs will often bring away chunks of the white, giving you an untidy result.

- Plunge boiled eggs straight into cold water. This loosens the hold of the shell on the white, so it comes away readily.

175. Eggy garnish

Chopping hard-boiled eggs really small for a salad or garnish gives very appetizing results, but can turn into a chore when cooking for a crowd.

- Give the knife a rest and press the eggs through a metal mesh sieve (the one you use for straining soups) for a pretty mimosa finish on green vegetables.

■ *Flavour savers*

176. Cleaner grater

You couldn't do without your handy box grater. What you certainly could do without is teasing bits of vegetable or cheese out of the holes!

- Unless you're working with something very slippery, add a light coat of oil to the grater. Wipe an oil-moistened tissue down the face or spritz with cooking spray.
- When it's time to clean up, use a baby toothbrush instead of your usual dishwashing brush.

177. Steep the saffron

Saffron is an expensive spice, so you really need to treat it with respect.

- Never add saffron, even crumbled, directly to a dish – you risk making it bitter.
- Soak a few threads of saffron in warm water or milk – not stock! – for about 10 minutes for best results.
- If you need more than a few stamens of this spice (such as the ½ teaspoon some 4-serving recipes call for!), it's time you started shopping around for a cheaper brand.
- Try switching your supply source – go to an ethnic grocery (Indian or Middle Eastern) where it moves off the shelves faster.

178. Bountiful bay!

A few leaves of fresh bay can make a fantastic and unexpected addition to a range of dishes.

- Thread some on skewers, interleaved with vegetables, for barbecuing.
- Tuck a few into pots of cold orange soufflé or ice cream.
- Fresh bay adds a lovely depth of flavour to plain bread sauce.
- A wreath of bay placed on a cake that is intended to mature slowly will bring out the flavours of winter spices and preserved fruit.

179. Limey tang

Don't discard the peels after squeezing lime juice! Make a substitute for Moroccan-style preserved lemons, lovely in roasts and tagines:

- Start with the juice and squeezed halves of one lime in a pickling jar, plus a teaspoon of salt.
- Continue adding squeezed limes and a sprinkle of salt.
- When the bottle's full, give it a vigorous shake and add olive or canola oil to just cover.
- The pickle will be ready to eat in 2 weeks.
- You can pickle whole limes too – layer slices with salt and chilli, then top up with oil.

■ Smart swaps

180. Milk and water

Some recipes call for evaporated milk to be diluted to the consistency of whole milk.

- To achieve the right consistency add an equal volume of water.

182. Low-salt savory

Savory, an old-fashioned herb available in both winter and summer forms, isn't seen often these days. However, it is worth searching out at the farmers' markets for its unusual piquancy.

- Sharp savory makes a good substitute for salt and will be appreciated by those on low-sodium diets.
- Winter savory is more pungent than the summer herb, so use judiciously.
- Savory is very good with legumes – it has even been called the 'bean herb'.

181. Low-fat cream

An all-natural alternative to whipped cream with lots more nutrition for far less fat:

- Just whisk up a can of evaporated milk. It won't hold its fluffy shape for long though, so serve at once.
- Get lovely stiff peaks by chilling the can well and whisking in a chilled metal bowl.

183. A fishy alternative

It's not always easy to keep a supply of fish stock in stock.

- A good substitute is clam juice from a can. Chances are the clams themselves wouldn't look out of place in that stew you're making either!

184. No nam pla?

Here's an easy substitute for Asian fish sauce, nam pla.

- For a tablespoon of nam pla, use 2 teaspoons soy sauce and a teaspoon of mashed anchovies for a very similar salty fish taste.

185. Pesto to the rescue!

Yes, we know pesto is traditionally made with basil and pine kernels. However, an adventurous multi-herb pesto can use up the few sprigs of herbs lingering in the vegetable drawer.

- Taste your mix after adding the nuts, garlic and oil to see if the flavours are intense enough. If not, you can add a piquant extra such as tapenade or sunblush tomatoes, or even a jalapeño chilli!

186. Hot stuff!

Ever wondered how much the heat of a hot pepper sauce compares with that of a whole chilli?

- Well, about ½ teaspoon of standard powdered red chilli would substitute for 16 drops of Tabasco sauce, so a single drop is about the same as $1/_{32}$ teaspoon of chilli powder.
- This is only a rough guide – there are several varieties of chilli peppers that are hotter or milder than the 'average' ancho chillies.

187. Beat the brown

Run out of brown sugar? You can mock up
your own if you have some molasses.

- For 280 g / 10 oz brown sugar, mix a tablespoon of
  thick dark molasses into 225 g/8 oz plain sugar!

■ *As easy as that!*

188. No-cook carbs

When you're too tired even to bake a
potato or don't have any bread at home, try
opening a can of beans for a change.

- Add some chopped salad veggies (tomatoes,
  onions and parsley are easiest) and serve a grilled
  chicken breast on a bed of beans.
- These could be a substitute for mashed or boiled
  potatoes, and are more interesting in terms of
  texture and taste.

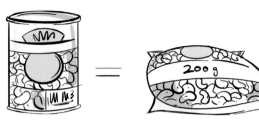

189. Dried legumes for canned

Whether it's chickpeas, haricot or kidney beans – or any other pulses, really – the substitution rule is that approximately half the can weight equals the dry weight needed.

So if your recipe calls for a 400 g / 14 oz can, soak a little over 200 g / 7 oz dried beans overnight and cook till tender.

190. Ravioli wrappers!

You can still enjoy homemade ravioli or tortellini without a pasta machine. It's a bit of a cheat in terms of the dough, though…

- Use wanton wrappers instead of pasta dough to sandwich your fillings. Then brush the edges with a little water before either scoring together with a fork or crimping shut by hand.

Cooking
On the hob, in the microwave

'Meals in minutes', recipe hints, secrets from the pros, common errors and salvaging failures, simple garnishes and serving suggestions – even no cook dishes; plus a section on making the most of your microwave oven.

■ **Chef's confidential**

191. Catch the bouquet!

It's easy to lose sight of that little muslin bag of herbs in your big stockpot, and fishing through it ladleful by ladleful is oh-so-frustrating!

- Use a long string to tie the bouquet garni and knot its other end round the handle of your stockpot. Now all you have to do is tug to retrieve!

192. Bouquet epicerie?

Yes, you use a bouquet garni for a bunch of herbs. But how do you deal with smaller seeds and berries and crumbled dried herbs?

• Tie them in a muslin bag – this will let you crush them with the back of the spoon to release flavours – or use a tea ball, if you have one. Beats chasing after every peppercorn and clove to discard later!

193. Dried in first, fresh in last

For maximum flavour, the same herbs should be added to dishes at different times, depending on whether they are fresh or dried:

• Dried herbs usually need to steep a bit – crumble and add early on, at the sautéing or sweating stage, or when marinating.
• Fresh herbs are more delicate and aromatic – bruise lightly or tear and add towards the end of cooking.
• Woodier-stemmed herbs can go in earlier than soft-stemmed ones, even at the start of a quick-cooking recipe.
• Dried herbs used in a rub can stay in when grilling or barbecuing.
• Marinades with fresh herbs will burn and blacken unless kept moist during cooking by basting or braising.

194. Sweat while you sauté

When sweating vegetables do make sure they soften before browning. This will help the flavours to blend better.

- If you're using a heavy-based bowl – which should mean your vegetables won't catch as easily during frying – put the lid on while you sauté, only uncovering to stir occasionally.

195. Cold water or hot?

When making stew or simmering a soup, you will often find recipes telling you to add hot stock to the sautéed vegetables.

- Cold water or stock will reduce the temperature in the pot, lengthening the cooking time.
- However, if you don't mind the wait, cold water will actually draw out the flavours better.

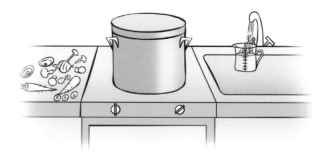

196. Hot or cold soup?

Some soups, such as vichyssoise, can be served either hot or cold, but it's important to decide how you'll be serving yours before you start cooking.

- The seasoning has to be more emphatic with a chilled soup.
- When soup is served hot you can have a lighter hand with the spices.
- If you really can't decide – or intend to serve the same dish in two separate batches – start with less spice and, when serving cold, stir in some fragrant pesto, a little anchovy paste, or a drizzle of flavoured oil and tapenade.

197. Fat disposal

Pouring hot oil down the sink won't do nice things to your plumbing – in fact, it's one of the fastest recipes for clogged drains.

- Drain the fat into a milk or juice carton with a cap. When cool, replace the cap and dispose of the carton.

■ Cereal comfort

198. Perfect pasta

Keeping a little of the starchy cooking water from pasta will help the sauce cling better!

- Leave a little water in the pan – just a couple of tablespoons – when draining pasta.
- If you're using a colander (or two-part pasta pan), add 3–4 tablespoons of the water when mixing in the sauce.
- Alternatively, instead of using plain water, add a ladleful of the pasta cooking water to the sauce when simmering it. Add salt to taste later – the cooking water will already be salted.

199. Springtime pasta

Cheat yourself into springtime exuberance when winter's overstaying its welcome.

- Add a small bag of frozen baby peas to your pasta for the last 5 minutes of cooking time.
- Drain and season with a little lemon zest and juice, freshly ground white pepper and a sprinkling of Parmesan.

200. (Almost) No-stir risotto

Making risotto won't need all that babysitting while you add the stock by the ladleful!

- Measure correctly to begin with. Allow about 1.5 litres/50 fl oz water or stock (total liquid, if using wine as well) for every 300 g/10½ oz risotto rice.
- Add it all to the pan at once, reserving 225 ml/ 8 fl oz to add later if necessary, and bring to a simmer.
- You will need to stir it occasionally to prevent sticking, but it shouldn't need constant attention.
- Stop cooking while the risotto is still slightly runnier than you want the final consistency to be – the starch will 'stiffen' a bit once removed from the heat.

201. Non-stick steaming

Making wontons or dumplings in your trusty bamboo steamer? Most of us add a sheet of foil to prevent a soggy, sticky mess at the bottom – but then the dumpling stops being a pot-sticker and sticks to the foil instead!

- Try using a leaf of lettuce, cabbage or spinach for each dumpling instead. They'll slip off readily, and you can always add the leaves to a side dish of soup.

Dashing dairy, perfect poultry

202. Buttery barrier

If your hot milk is always boiling over:

- Rub the rim of the saucepan with butter or oil to a depth of up to 2.5 cm/1 inch to prevent the milk boiling right over. It will still froth up, but would need to boil very fiercely indeed to breach the butter barrier.

This also works when cooking pulses and lentils, which tend to froth quite a bit.

203. Perfect poaching

Restaurant-perfect eggs Benedict call for perfectly poached eggs, holding together nicely with no straggles of white streaming out.

- Start with a deeper pan – sauté rather than frying. Break the egg into a saucer or espresso cup. Give the water a whirl with a ladle when it's hot, to form a miniature whirlpool in the centre, and then quickly and gently slide in the egg. The centrifugal force pulls the eggs in neatly!
- For multiple eggs, use a flatter pan. Place round biscuit cutters in the pan so that the water almost reaches the rim but the bubbles can't quite break over. When the water's hot, break the eggs into their individual biscuit-cutter bastions.

204. Softly scrambled

Problems getting your scrambled eggs right?

- For soft scrambled eggs that are cooked through but not rubbery firm, mix a tablespoon of natural yogurt into every 4 eggs.

■ Fine fish (and flesh)

205. 'Blackened' bream, or bass, or...

Cajun-style blackened fish gets its flavour from a spice mix that's now easy to buy at any supermarket. Its charred appearance, however, is a spot of culinary deception.

- Do not overcook the fish to 'char' it!
- Instead, dip the fish pieces in melted butter and then press on a plate of the seasoning mix to coat.
- Heat a cast-iron griddle to a high temperature – a drop of water should sizzle on the surface – without any oil.
- Now sear the fish directly on the dry griddle for about 2 minutes on each side, until it looks lightly charred.

206. Slash and grill

When searing or griddling meat and fish, here's how to prevent it 'curling' as it cooks:

- Cut a few diagonal slashes in the flesh – on both sides for a cut of meat and on the skin side for fish. For sausages, a few good pokes through the casing should do it.
- While cooking, use your spatula or fish slice to press the fillet or cut down lightly against the pan to help it cook evenly.
- For very tender cuts of meat such as veal escalopes, instead of slashing, just score the flesh lightly with the back of a heavy cleaver or knife.

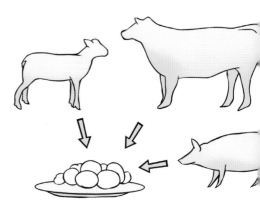

207. Meatball medley

To deepen the depth of flavour in dishes using chopped or minced meat, divide and double up!

- For meatballs and sauces for pasta, consider using a blend of lamb or beef and pork mince.
- You can do the same for pies, casseroles and terrines.
- For fish, which cooks faster, add a cured meat – try a little chopped ham in a seafood mould, for instance.
- However, don't try this with dishes that require only brief cooking – burgers, for instance – as not all meats cook at the same rate.

208. For the juiciest burger

For burgers that stay moist even when well done:

- Provided the weather is cool and you're not cooking outdoors, allow the mince to rest outside the refrigerator for up to an hour. (Don't do this in hot weather, though, as the risk of bacteria multiplying is too great.)
- While making up the burgers, mix in a tablespoon of ricotta cheese, soft cottage cheese, or apple sauce, into each burger.

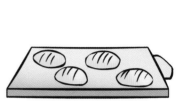

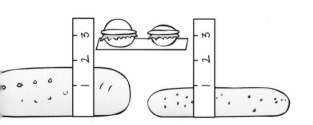

209. Fat or rare?

How thick should your burger be? Well, rather than aesthetics, you should rely on physics.

- If you intend to cook it rare, a thickness of as much as 5 cm/2 inches is fine.
- If you want it well done, though, a burger that thick will dry out and get crumbly on the outside before the inside is cooked. It should be about 2.5 cm/1 inch thick.

■ Valuable tips for vegetables

210. Mash made moreish

This is a good way to sneak vegetables onto the plates of picky eaters.

- First, replace about a third to a half of the potatoes with turnips, celeriac, swede and/or carrots.
- You can boil them in the same pot with the potatoes, adding more tender veg later (baby carrots and young turnips don't need long cooking.)
- Beetroot are nice too, but the colour will be a dead giveaway, so avoid them if you're trying for camouflage!
- Add even more flavour with a little grated nutmeg, a dab of tomato paste or some chopped herbs (rosemary and parsley are both good partners for potatoes).
- Leave it in the refrigerator overnight.
- When you're ready to serve, use a good, fruity olive oil to loosen the mash after reheating.

211. White as a cauliflower...?

Cauliflower can go a bit yellow during cooking.

- To keep the head snow-white as you boil it, add about 200 ml/8 fl oz milk to the cooking water and then pop the cauliflower in head downwards.

212. Best cream of vegetable

Forget the floury roux and the dollops of cream that were once used to give a smooth soup body!

- The easiest method is to add some creamed rice or potatoes, and adjust the seasoning – both kinds of starch tend to soak up the salt in the broth.
- Otherwise use a milder non-tuber vegetable – mushrooms offer a rich flavour boost as well, but caramelized onions, roasted pumpkins and 'melted' leeks all work brilliantly when puréed in the blender.

213. Enokitake

The flavour of most mushrooms intensifies when they are dried or fried. The one exception is the long-legged spidery enoki mushroom. This crisp fungus is nicest raw and cooking for anything more than seconds compromises its delicately sweet flavour.

- Add them towards the end of cooking as you would a garnish of fresh herbs. Or simply sprinkle them on to your salad like any crisp vegetable.

■ Timer-tricking 'traditionals'

214. Faster pasta

Cooking tomato sauce from scratch takes time; ready-made pasta sauce is pricey. Find your comfort zone mid-way.

- Roast a whole trayful of tomatoes when you have a few spare minutes and freeze them in small tubs.
- Roast a whole head of garlic and bottle the creamy contents of the cloves.
- While you cook the pasta, grill some well-seasoned sausages.
- Heat some of the frozen tomato mixture with the creamy garlic and some chilli flakes. Stir in some sage and sliced sausages.
- Tip in the pasta and serve with cheese.

215. One-pot pasta

This calls for cooking pasta as though it's risotto!

- Sauté some onions and/or garlic and any dried herbs you want to use. Add the pasta and stir until glistening.
- Again, take a shortcut and strain some canned tomatoes rather than buying passata.
- Add an equal quantity of stock and bring to the boil, seasoning to taste. Cover and cook until the pasta is tender, but still firm to the bite, adding a little more water if the sauce gets too dry before the pasta is done.

Just one pot to clean!

216. Spaghetti shortcuts

Boil the spaghetti in salted water – and cook the other main ingredient at the same time!

• Add some eggs or blanch some baby spinach. Drain and toss it all together with a little ricotta and a grinding of nutmeg.

Dinner is served!

217. Beans and soda?

Sometimes it seems as if those dried beans will never finish cooking!

• Add a small pinch of bicarbonate of soda (also known as baking soda!). This will soften the tough skin and get them cooking faster.

■ Modern meals in minutes

218. Twice as nice!

You can often cook two foods with different cooking times together if all you're doing is boiling or steaming.

- For instance, you can cook most vegetables along with rice and pasta. Just put the vegetables in a colander and sit it on the rim of the boiling saucepan, so that they come just under the water line.
- The more tender vegetables, such as spinach, broccoli, asparagus or peas, should be balanced just above the level of the water.
- Cook some prawns or mussels the same way on that boiling pot of soup or stock.
- Or boil some eggs to keep in the fridge for later!

219. Asparagus soldiers

An elegant supper doesn't get any easier. Make sure you have plenty of crusty bread to go with it.

- Blanch the asparagus spears and simply serve with a runny egg to dip into, with a few curls of Parma ham and some shavings of pecorino cheese for company.
- Or dispense with the ham and cheese; drizzle over a little truffle oil instead.

Wine with that?

220. Meat, veg – and sauce too

A well-rounded meal needn't mean slaving over the stove all evening.

- Microwave a bag of mixed vegetables while you grill some pork chops.
- When those are done, add some cream and mustard with a splash of wine to the pan drippings.
- When the sauce is bubbling hot and thick, pour it over the chops and vegetables.

Now wasn't that quick? All griddled or roasted meats will yield a delicious gravy or sauce – some stock or cream to dissolve the drippings, a little seasoning, a touch of wine, and you're set.

221. Pre-curry prawns

These bite-sized appetizers are perfect with beer before a curry dinner.

- Stir-fry peeled prawns with Thai-style sweet chilli sauce and toasted white sesame seeds, adding a handful of curry leaves if available.
- Zap mini poppadoms in the microwave with a sprinkling of water until crisp.
- Lay a prawn on each poppadom with a blob of soured cream, a bit of mango chutney and a pinch of cayenne pepper.
- Serve at once; you can't assemble them beforehand as the poppadoms go soft, but you can prepare prawns and poppadoms separately before guests arrive.

222. Quickest curry

This South-east Asian dish practically cooks itself – all you need to keep an eye on is the rice.

- For the curry, mix a carton of coconut milk with the same quantity of stock, a pinch of sugar and 1–2 tablespoons of Thai curry paste – red, green or yellow: you choose!
- Bring to the boil and add some sliced steak or chicken breast.
- Simmer till tender and add a packet of pre-sliced stir-fry vegetables. Heat through and serve with plain steamed rice.

223. Rapid-fire wok dinner

A simple yet sumptuous supper for those days when you simply have no time!

- Stir-fry some peeled prawns on a high heat with just a single green vegetable, such as broccoli, baby spinach or bok choy, then add some teriyaki, black bean sauce or sweet chilli sauce.

■ It's hardly cooking!

224. Lettuce-leaf wraps

This very quick snack or light lunch relies on ready-roasted chicken.

- Shred the meat, lay it on lettuce leaves, add a little coleslaw (minus the mayonnaise) and a drizzle of sweet chilli sauce. Roll up and secure in a serviette.
- For a lunchbox, pack the filling and leaves separately. Spoon into the 'wrap' and eat taco fashion.

225. Stir-fry and... beans?

Canned beans are not only an easy, inexpensive substitute for potatoes or rice (*see Tip 188*):

- They work as a replacement for noodles, too, in stir-fry recipes.
- However, it helps if you can marinate the beans for half an hour in the sauce or dressing ingredients to let the flavours seep in.

Penny-pinching plate-wise

226. Treble the tuna

Canned fish will go further if heated up with lots of extra vegetables. It also reduces their high sodium content.

- The 'stretching' ingredients depend on the kind of fish and seasonings in the can. Tomato goes best with mackerel, herrings wouldn't mind a dollop of crème fraiche instead, while sweetcorn and celery are old friends of tuna.
- First sauté some leeks or onions, some fresh herbs or spices if you like, and the sauce base – tomatoes, stock, orange juice (eerily good with sardines!) or cream. Simmer till bubbling and thick, then stir in the fish.
- A cream sauce from scratch is great with smoked fish such as salmon or kippers too. Serve with toast or toss with pasta.

227. Keep the peel

Not all peelings are for the bin!

- Cauliflower stalks, turnip tops and celery leaves are good additions to the stock pot. Indeed, you can cook, purée and strain them into soup!
- Turnip and radish greens are good braised with a pinch of cumin seeds.
- Broccoli and cauliflower greens are nice in a stir-fry.
- Reserve outer leaves of cabbage for cooking fish – pan-roasting on a leaf prevents sticking.
- Unblemished watermelon rinds make lovely pickles – treat like cucumber.
- Tender butternut and pattypan squash can be eaten skin and all – best baked!
- Drop hard cheese rind into a pot of creamy soup for enhanced flavour.

■ Smart swaps

228. Fresh out of crème fraîche?

- Try soured cream or single cream with a squeeze of lime. However, crème fraîche is made from higher-fat double cream and doesn't curdle on heating; soured cream isn't quite so resilient. So substitute only if your recipe allows you to take the dish off the heat and stir it in at the last minute.
- If you must cook with it, try reducing the heat and using beaten natural yogurt (full-fat or Greek-style) with a spoonful of flour to stabilize. You may need to adjust the seasoning as the yogurt can add tartness.

229. Pour the lemon

Pale white lemon drizzle looks so refreshing on a cake. To get that same tangy-sweet flavour alongside a hot dessert, make this creamy lemon 'custard' super-quick!

- Gently scald some pouring cream.
- Remove from the heat and stir in an equal quantity of lemon curd.
- Whisk and strain into a milk jug to serve with steamed puddings, fruit compôte, warm pies and fresh crêpes.

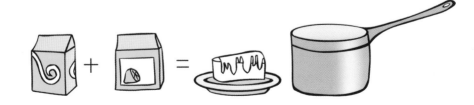

■ Smooth saves!

230. Smoothie too smooth?

If your breakfast smoothie hasn't got enough 'heft', it could be that the fruits you chose were very juicy and there was nothing fibrous enough (such as peaches or wheatgerm) to give your body sustenance. Kiwis, watermelon and similar fruit with a high water content can cause this problem. Or maybe you just added too much juice or ice?

• Add a frozen banana and blend. This is a good bet when you want your drink chilled, but not icy.

231. De-grease a casserole

It's easy to get rid of the greasy bits on a light soup or stock with a skimmer. But that's not so helpful for more chunky soups (such as a chowder) or for stews, casseroles and curries.

• Plop a large flour tortilla on the surface instead; when it starts to soften, lift it out (don't let it get too soggy!). Most of the surface grease should come away with it, but you can repeat if necessary with a fresh one.

232. Peaches and... yogurt?

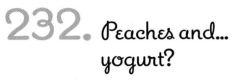

A great solution for overripe fruit:

- Place in a saucepan with just enough water to cover or a splash of wine.
- Poach until soft and mushy.
- Stir into yogurt or muesli.

233. Deflated!

Many people avoid fibre in the form of beans or cabbage because of embarrassing flatulence. However, traditional ethnic recipes have long known how to neutralize it.

- For cruciferous vegetables (cabbage, Brussels sprouts, cauliflower), beans or lentils, add a tiny pinch of asafoetida to the cooking liquid.
- If sautéing or stir-frying, add a spoonful of anise, coriander, caraway or cumin seeds, or a little fresh ginger.
- Onion and garlic help as well, and go with most things.
- Many herbs counteract flatulence – dill, oregano, marjoram, thyme, coriander, celery, lemon balm, basil and mint.

■ Microwave mettle

234. Wave, space, density

Different textures of food behave differently in the microwave. And the same food cooks differently based on position!

- Porous, light foods cook faster than dense ones. So bread heats up faster than a potato of similar size or weight.
- If reheating a mixed platter of foods, place denser foods near the edge and the less dense in the centre.
- Juicy foods heat faster than dry. The moist filling of a pie may get hotter than its crust!
- Hot spots are more likely near the edges, so draw food from the periphery towards the centre when stirring.
- For uneven shapes, such as carrots, arrange in a circle alternating thick ends and thin tips. Halfway through cooking, switch tops and tails around.

235. Zap or simmer?

The speed of a microwave is offset by the need to double cooking time when quantity doubles.

- Food for the average family of 4 can be microwaved faster than it can be baked or simmered on the stove. Any more, and it takes as much time or more!
- Any recipe that concentrates flavours by reducing liquid (sauces, stews, soups) takes longer and yields poorer results in the microwave. If you must, start with less water.
- Faster cooking means aromatic ingredients retain more flavour (lost by evaporation in conventional methods). So add a smaller amounts of herbs, spices and garlic.

236. Citrus curd in a zap

Speed up lemon curd in the microwave!

- Combine juice and zest of 1 small lemon, 125 g/4½ oz butter and 100 g/3 ½ oz caster sugar.
- Microwave on full power for 2-3 minutes; stir to dissolve sugar.
- Meanwhile, whisk 3 eggs and strain.
- Add a little of the lemon mixture to the eggs, whisking constantly.
- Now whisk the eggs back into the lemon mixture.
- Microwave for 2 minutes, stirring once or twice.
- Whisk briskly. Stand 2-3 minutes; whisk again.
- Cover with clingfilm and cool before bottling. (If it curdles when eggs are added, a whirl in the food processor while warm renders it smooth.)

Baking, Grilling, Roasting

Tricks for better treats; pointers that take the pain out of pastry; assemblage and presentation maneouvres; recipe rescues; one-dish dinners and barbeque specials.

■ Basic baker's dozen

237. Get a rise out of plain flour

If you run out of self-raising flour just as you're about to get down to a spot of baking, use plain flour – you can add extra baking powder to compensate.

- About a teaspoon for every 125 g/4½ oz flour should do it. Sift thoroughly – maybe even twice for a sponge cake – to distribute well and add lightness.

238. Milk gone sour?

Don't throw out soured milk! Unless it's actually curdled – that is, the whey and solids have separated – it's as good as buttermilk for baking!

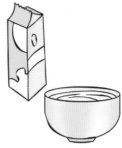

- Use in biscuits, breads, scones and pancakes. It's especially effective when you're using bicarbonate of soda rather than baking powder to leaven.

239. Paper or parchment?

Keeping cakes and sweet rolls from sticking calls for a lining of more than grease and flour for foolproof turnouts.

- Silicone bakeware makes it easy – but it's expensive, the options are fewer and you don't want to throw out your old faithfuls.
- Your best bet for baking flat on a tray or sheet is baking parchment – the silicone-coated surface mimics the non-stick properties of silicone baking sheets and has the same flexibility, making for an easy lift-off for scones and biscuits. And no greasing required!
- For lining a tin, though, you're better off with greaseproof paper, but you should brush it with oil to make sure it peels away easily.

240. Think inside the box

Unlike a round cake tin, a rectangular or square baking tin doesn't need to have paper cut separately for base and sides.

- Cut greaseproof paper a couple of inches larger than the tin on all sides.
- Snip diagonally into the corners.
- Grease both tin and paper, and lay the paper in the tin.
- Fold the snipped corners over each other to fit snugly.

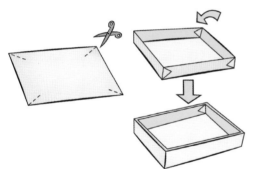

241. Frigid pastry!

If you forgot – or mistimed – the thawing of your ready-to-roll pastry log, you may not be able to make the fancy shapes you wanted.

However, you can still bake a basic open pie or tart shell with it!

- Simply use a sharp knife dipped in hot water to slice rounds of pastry off the log.
- Lay them in the base of the pie dish with the edges slightly overlapping.
- Once you've got it covered, use your fingers to mould the pastry rounds into each other along the 'seams' to finish up with a single 'sheet' – don't worry if it's a bit uneven.
- Blind bake for 3-5 minutes, then add your filling and proceed with your recipe.

242. Heat wise!

These days, we're all looking for energy-saving solutions, so it's time to explode a couple of myths about oven heating.

- You can safely skip preheating the oven for foods that cook slowly over a longer time, such as roast meats, oven-dried tomatoes or baked vegetables.
- You can also switch off the oven a few minutes early, especially when baking at a higher temperature (above 200°C/400°F/Gas Mark 6), if you leave the oven door closed. Obviously, don't do this with more sensitive foods such as soufflés or bread, or when cooking quickly (grilled fish).

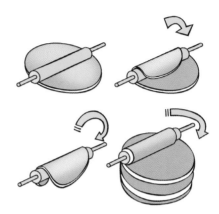

243. Pastry lift

It can be quite a task to lift a round of rolled-out marzipan or sugar paste onto a cake to cover the top. Rolling pin to the rescue!

- Lay the rolling pin down in the middle of the marzipan circle (or square, if that's your shape).
- Pull the end of the sheet furthest from you over the rolling pin, folding it in half.
- Now lift the draped rolling pin, with a gentle half-turn towards yourself as you peel the marzipan upwards.
- To place on the cake, let the nearest end fall on the cake first; then move the rolling pin backwards over the cake to cover, unrolling the flipped-over icing or marzipan to go over.

244. Help for plummeting plums!

Fruits and nuts added to cake batter have a tendency to sink to the base of the tin for all but the heaviest mixes.

- Dredge the fruits with flour and fold gently into the batter last. Do this even for alcohol-soaked fruit.
- The air trapped by the flour will help them 'float' until the cake cooks around them to support their weight!

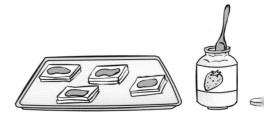

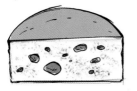

245. Pastry puffs

Left with pastry but no more filling to make a tart or pie?

- You can brush a little preserve or jam on squares of sweet pastry and bake for a quick sweet treat.
- Or brush with fruit juice to glaze and sprinkle on some chocolate chips.
- For savoury pastry, grate some cheese on top for 'open puffs'.
- Or add a layer of pesto, tomato paste or tapenade to flavour more intensely.
- Alternatively, glaze with beaten egg and press in some herbs – chives or tarragon stand up well to the egg.
- Or try a smear of melted butter and a sprinkling of your favourite spice mix.

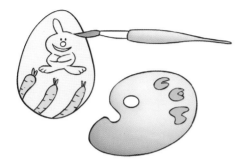

246. Colour me sweet

You can buy coloured icing in a range of shades these days. If you're making your own, though, here are a few pointers.

- All food colouring is very concentrated – add in very small amounts (*see Tip 172*), and mix well before adding more.
- Liquid colour is easiest to work with for pastel shades, for colouring sugar or shreds of desiccated coconut – powder won't mix and paste can obscure the texture – and for painting directly onto rolled-out icing in the pattern you want (make sure your brushes have been used *only* with edible paints!).
- Powder is best if you're after a mottled or marbled effect as it doesn't spread too fast and is easier to control.
- Paste is probably the most versatile. And it's also the best when you want a deep, intense shade.

247. Stop that sliding gâteau!

You've got your three-layers nicely assembled when – horrors! – they begin to slide… Next time, hold them in place with a couple of nifty anchoring techniques.

- If the entire gâteau threatens to leave the platter or cake board, add a blob of royal icing at the base. It will harden as it dries, holding the cake board and lowest layer firmly together.
- If the higher layers are the problem, it could be that they aren't perfectly even – and that's almost a certainty. Use a fork to mark the side of the cake before layering, so you have reference points for lining them up.

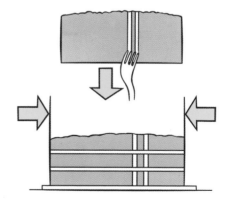

248. No-mess muffins

Muffins – so simple, so versatile, such a comfort. But teasing them out of their tray can be a fiddle. (Not to mention getting the burnt-on dribbles of batter off without bending the cups out of shape!)

You could switch to silicone; but it's pricey and has its own drawbacks (*see Tip 4*). Or you could just put your trust in foil.

- You'll need a sheet about 1½ times the length of your tray.
- Lay it directly on the tray and, starting at one end, scrunch the foil in to line the cups as you go.
- Slip the paper muffin cases in, spoon in the batter and bake.
- When cool, ease up the foil and out pop the cakes!

■ Piecrust promises

249. Nimble pie

It's possible to prepare a pie dinner for four in less than 30 minutes – with leftovers for a packed lunch!

Apart from larder staples, you will need:

- 4 grilled chicken breasts
- 100 g/3½ oz smoked ham or cured bacon
- 140 ml/4½ fl oz cream
- 90 ml/3 fl oz stock
- 250 g/9 oz ready-to-roll puff pastry

Method:

- Preheat the oven to 200°C/400°F/Gas Mark 6.
- Dice the chicken and the ham.
- Mix the chicken with the cream, adding some dried herbs (rosemary or tarragon), the stock, a teaspoon of cornflour and a little mustard powder. Season to taste and pour into a pie dish.
- Roll out the pastry and lay on top, trimming to the rim of the dish. Lightly moisten the edges and press firmly to seal.
- Brush the top with beaten egg for a golden glaze and cook until the pastry is puffed and crisp.

Serve with some blanched haricot beans.

250. Pie-crust plight!

Singed pastry case?

- Scoop the filling carefully out of the scorched case and set aside.
- Get a bag of ready-roll pie crust and roll it out – don't worry about getting a neat round or square.
- Lay the pastry on a greased baking sheet and pile the filling in the centre.
- Now simply draw up the pastry 'sides' and scrunch together the edges to close.
- Bake and slice into wedges – think of the irregular shape as rustic chic!

251. Cheat's mince 'pies'

No fiddling with crusts and tart shells!

- Preheat the oven to 200°C/400°F/Gas Mark 6.
- Lightly grease the cups of a mini-muffin pan.
- Cut some filo pastry sheets into squares big enough to lap out of each cup, and line each cup with 2–3 squares. Brush with melted butter. Bake in the preheated oven until golden.
- Mix store-bought mincemeat with an equal quantity of grated apples. Add an extra pinch of cinnamon and a small splash of orange juice if the texture is too dry.
- Plop two spoonfuls into each pastry 'cup' and bake for a further 2–3 minutes.
- Serve with pouring cream or brandy butter.

■ Lively loaves

252. Too cold for warm bread?

A kitchen that's not warm enough won't allow bread dough to rise – not even if you've kept it clear of draughts. This isn't a problem in professional kitchens where they use dedicated proving boxes or cupboards. However, for small quantities of dough you can make do with the microwave oven.

- Bring a large mug of water to boil in the microwave.
- Zap the dough in the microwave for 5–7 seconds on High along with the water.

253. Trusty trick for crusty bread

It can be hard to get that shiny crust on homebaked bread.

- Spritz the inside of your oven with a weak vinegar-water / solution and brush some over the loaf before you quickly shut the door on it.

254. Fresh from the oven, again!

Day-old (or two-day-old) bread in need of a bit of oomph? Here's a trick that'll get it warm, crusty and yeasty fresh again.

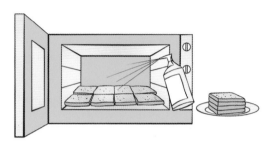

- Preheat the oven to 180°C/350°F/Gas Mark 4.
- Spritz the loaf with water and place in the oven for 10 minutes to revive it.

255. Crumbs!

Jazz up fried fish or breaded chicken pieces by adding an extra green edge to the breadcrumbs.

- Whiz some dry bread in the blender with a small spoonful of herbs.
- Mix in some pepper and salt.
- Coat the meat or fish in the breadcrumbs for a zestier flavour and a fresh green-speckled look.

■ Trouble-free tortes

256. A right roll-up!

Getting the Swiss roll right is just a matter of planning ahead.

- While the cake's in the oven, soak a clean tea towel in hot water and wring out well.
- Lay flat on the worktop with the shorter end facing you.
- Place a sheet of greaseproof paper over the cake tin and turn out the cake, sandwiching the paper between cake and towel.
- Tuck your thumbs under the tea towel and begin lifting it off the counter, rolling up the cake as you 'walk' your fingertips along the back of the Swiss roll to pat and prod the roll firmly into shape!

257. Sunken sponge?

If your sponge cake fell flat, don't waste it, use it to make a gâteau!

- The cake probably isn't as light and airy as it should be, so split it into two or three layers.
- If it looks very dense, soak it in light syrup. If you have a can of fruit, use the liquid from that, or use a sweetened fruit juice.
- Sandwich with some cream cheese flavoured with citrus zest and icing sugar, and slices of fruit.
- Tumble some fruit or frozen berries on top to fill the 'crater'.
- Dust with icing sugar and add a scattering of chocolate shavings or flaked almonds.

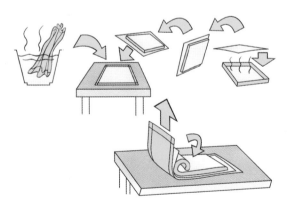

258. Tough torte!

Another solution if your sponge hasn't risen or your cake is rock hard:

- Serve a fruit salad. You can use canned fruit heated in water or poach some dried fruits in water with a splash of juice and citrus zest. Top with the diced cake.
- Chop up the cake and serve with a fondue-style hot sauce – melted chocolate, a plain custard or even a thick fruit coulis (especially something naturally sweet, like sieved berries or mangoes).
- Slice the cake into thin slivers and serve with a hot custard swirled with a dessert wine or fruit purée.
- Serve the slivers with a liqueur-infused whipped cream topped with a matching decoration.

259. Carrot cake with a twist!

Substitute one of these equally nutritious vegetables in your carrot cake recipe.

- Grate some sweet potatoes (the orange-fleshed kind), yams or a firm-fleshed pumpkin (or other winter squash).
- With parsnips, the result is subtler and a little nutty.
- Or use something a bit blander, such as apples or courgettes.

■ Cake toppers!

260. Muffin madness

Turn your muffins into a real treat with this rich frosting.

- Mix together 125 g/4½ oz smooth peanut butter with 40 g/1½ oz sifted cocoa.
- Add 200 g/7 oz icing sugar and 100 g/3½ oz redcurrant jam, with just enough single cream to loosen to the consistency you want – you shouldn't need more than 150 ml/5 fl oz.
- Spoon into or pipe onto rich chocolate muffins.

261. No-fuss icing

Dress up store-bought muffins in a jiffy with some chocolate mints (or other individual chocolates).

- Place the chocolate mints on the muffins.
- Place in the microwave oven and cook on High for 15-20 seconds.
- Spread the softened chocolate mint over the top of the muffin and serve.

262. Spoonfuls of swirls

So many recipes tell you to swirl frosting on a cake attractively using a palette knife. Easier said than done!

- Use the palette knife to slather on the icing and then switch to a spoon. Using the back of its 'bowl' prevents you scraping off the icing you've carefully applied!

■ Dinner's in the oven!

263. Toads and Yorkies for one

If you're making Yorkshire pudding or toad-in-the-hole for a young family or a special dinner, consider making single-serve portions.

- Oil the holes in a muffin tin and place a spoonful of the batter in each one (with a piece of sausage in each of the 'Toads').

This is far less fiddly than dropping spoonfuls of batter and hoping they hold their shape.

264. Bite-sized 'cannelloni'

Use conchiglie when you run out of the fat cannelloni tubes.

Stuffing the individual shapes may seem fiddly, but they look pretty and are not as messy to eat – which can be a consideration when serving younger children.

- Fill them with diced sausages, curried lentils or sautéed mushrooms or use stuffing recipes which include mince or breadcrumbs.
- Line a shallow dish with the stuffed pasta and bake in a herbed tomato concassé.

Serve with salad, for a smart supper.

265. Speedy spud skewers

Jacket potatoes can seem to take forever to cook! Here's a way of saving as much as 15 minutes' cooking time on a medium potato.

- Push a sturdy metal skewer through the potato before putting it in the oven.

266. Tropical beach jacket potato

Jazz up the humble jacket potato filled with tuna out of a tin, coleslaw and mayonnaise – by upgrading to a more exotic topping.

- Mix together cooked peeled prawns, diced mango or canned pineapple, some soured cream and a little chopped dill.
- Cut a cross on top of a foil-baked barbecued potato, push the sides gently inwards to ease open, and spoon in the topping.
- For an even more luxurious touch, substitute smoked salmon for the prawns, cream cheese for the soured cream, and a couple of capers instead of the fruit. Add a good grinding of white pepper.

267. Pungent purée

Baked garlic has a surprisingly mellow, buttery flavour. It's worth your while baking several heads at once and refrigerating.

- Wrap 24 whole bulbs of garlic into a single foil package and bake at 180°C/350°F/Gas Mark 4 for about an hour.
- When cool, separate the cloves and gently press – the pod will ooze or slide out readily.
- Purée by passing through a sieve or process with 2 tablespoons of olive oil and some salt.
- Place in a jar and add more oil to cover.
- Refrigerate for up to three months, topping up the oil as you use the purée.
- Use a little on croûtons, in salad dressings and to accompany roasted meats.

268. Whole roast marrow

You don't need to peel, clean and slice medium-sized winter squashes and marrows before cooking. Baking them whole makes them easier to prepare.

- Rub all over with olive oil and bake for approximately 1 hour (or till the skin yields easily to a fork) at 200°C/400°F/Gas Mark 6.
- You don't even need to peel them – just cut them up, discard the seeds and serve, with a drizzle of seasoned soured cream or oil.
- You will have no trouble separating the soft, sweet flesh from the peel with knife and fork.

A nutritious – and different – alternative to jacket or mashed potatoes with a hot casserole or grilled meat.

269. Roasted Mediterranean vegetables

Roasted vegetables needn't be restricted to lazy winter evenings. Try a less starchy selection for a sprightly summer supper.

- Thinly slice some aubergines and dice some courgettes and onion wedges.
- Toss with whole garlic cloves (skin left on).
- Roast for 20-30 minutes at 200°C/400°F/Gas Mark 6 with a drizzle of olive oil to make a Mediterranean feast.
- A spoonful of balsamic vinegar and a scattering of fresh basil on the vegetables as they leave the oven make them extra special.

270. Quick ham & leek surprise

Choose a dozen very tender baby leeks – or asparagus spears – for this recipe.

- Preheat the oven to 200°C/400°F/Gas Mark 6.
- Wrap a 'sash' of Parma ham around the middle of each leek. Place in a roasting tin, pouring in 125 ml/4 fl oz hot water and a tablespoon of olive oil.
- Roast for 15 minutes or until almost tender.
- Sprinkle over a mixture of breadcrumbs and grated Parmesan.
- Continue to cook until crisp on top.

Serve alone as a starter, or as a side dish with some grilled or poached fish.

271. One-foil fish

Fish cooks quickly; it's usually the vegetables and starchy accompaniments that take more time. Enclosing the vegetables in an airtight packet helps trap the steam in and tenderizes them faster.

- Preheat the oven to 200°C/400°F/Gas Mark 6.
- Construct your own container with a sheet of foil laid on a baking tray.
- Pile some noodles, sliced new potatoes, wedges of sweet potato or some diced pumpkin (or other winter squash) into the sheet of foil.
- Toss in sliced onions or spring onions, green vegetables (beans, broccoli or fennel)*, any herbs or whole spices you want to use, some salt and a drizzle of olive oil.

- Lay the fillet of fish on the vegetables, season well and crimp the edges of the foil square together to close.
- Bake in an oven at 220°C/425°F/Gas Mark 7 for 15-20 minutes (depending on the chosen vegetables and the thickness of your piece of fish).

*If you prefer a more tender green, such as young spinach or asparagus spears, pop them into the packet for the last 5 minutes.

272. Pork & orange rosemary skewers

You know pork goes beautifully with apple sauce or with grilled pineapple. Now try it with oranges.

- Thread diced pork fillet rubbed with salt on rosemary skewers, alternating with chunks of oranges (peel left on).
- Grill or barbecue, basting with orange juice and olive oil.

Serve with a simple bean, red onion and black olive salad dressed with balsamic vinaigrette.

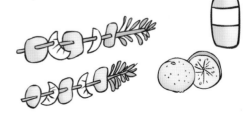

273. Baked wheels of Brie

An interesting turn of the cheeseboard for winter.

- Stuff a whole wheel of mild Brie or Camembert with honey, dates and pecans – just push them into the soft centre. Bake in the oven at 200°C/400°F/Gas Mark 6 until golden and just starting to ooze. Accompany with oat biscuits.
- Insert snipped sun-dried tomatoes into the cheese and smear with pesto. Then parcel up in filo pastry and bake till the crust is done.

274. Not-so-humble crumble

Dinner table trends are now moving away from posh nosh to home bakes with a rustic touch. Fruit crumbles will always be a favourite.

- Dice fruit and macerate with sugar for 10-20 minutes – or as long as it takes to heat the oven to 200°C/400°F/Gas Mark 6 and make the topping.
- How much sugar you use depends on how sweet your fruit is. For instance, tart berries will need more sugar than sweet apples.
- Consider mixing fruits for a colourful result – pale pears and apples get a lovely kick of colour from berries and cherries. Cover with flour rubbed into cold butter till it resembles breadcrumbs and then mix with sugar if your fruit is really tart, or use spoonfuls of rolled oats or muesli sprinkled and dot the top with butter.
- You can add crushed or flaked nuts to the topping, if you like.
- Bake until the top is golden and the fruit is visibly bubbling around the edges.

■ Bravo – biscuits!

275. Drop the ball

Getting perfect portions of the sticky dough for biscuits on to the baking sheet can be quite a trick – and can result in a headache-inducing number of sticky spoons!

- Get out your small ice-cream scoop, and use the usual method of cold-water dips between drops.

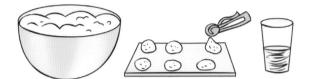

276. Biscuits that crumble!

You baked them chewy, but now those yummy oatmeal-raisin discs have hardened into frisbees.

- Pop them in the microwave for 10 seconds.
- If this doesn't work, brush them with hot milk and place in a cool oven (about 110°C/225°F/Gas Mark ¼) for 5 minutes.
- If you're storing the biscuits in the refrigerator, you might leave a chunk of baked apple in the tin with them to provide some moisture!

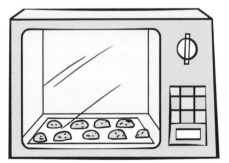

■ Barbecue cues

277. Don't shuck the corn

Leave the corn husks on when barbecuing.
- Soak whole ears, husk and all, in water for 20 minutes before throwing on the barbecue.
- You won't have to worry about soot on the ears or charring.
- Peel back the charred husks, discard and serve – the corn will look as clean as boiled and yet have that smoky barbecue flavour.

278. From freezer to flame

It's great to have frozen burgers or meatballs on hand for a quick dinner, but they spit and stick when you try to brown them in a frying pan.

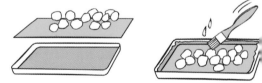

- Lay them on a baking tray, on the greaseproof paper used to wrap or interleave them.
- Brush with oil and place under the grill to brown.
- When one side is done, switch off the grill and wait for the splatters to subside before removing, turning and basting on the other side. Heat the grill again, and finish cooking.

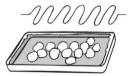

- Do not attempt to thaw frozen mince or mince products in the microwave if you intend to brown them. This makes them give up their water and become even soggier.

279. Chargrill chequers

Want that restaurant-perfect 'netting' of char marks?

All you need is your ridged griddle pan or your barbecue rack.

- Halfway through the cooking time for each side, pick up the vegetable or meat pieces with tongs and turn them to lie at right angles to their original position.
- Do the same on the other side, and you will have the criss-crossing of char marks on both sides!

280. Soaked satay skewers

Before you make a batch of satay, remember to soak your wooden or bamboo skewers.

- They need to be soaked in water for 10 minutes before cooking to prevent them burning or charring.
- This means that while you can marinate the meat well ahead of time, you shouldn't put them in the fridge pre-skewered.
- Thread the meat on to the soaked skewers just before cooking.

Freezing and Refrigerating

Put precooked foods and partially prepared ones on ice; manage your stocks and garnishes better in the icebox; learn to make your own dips and marinades to have on hand – ready in less time than you need for a grocery run. Pack prettier; thaw without ado; what not to freeze… There's even a superior, no-drinks-dilution trick for ice cubes!

■ Icy cool!

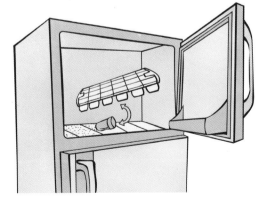

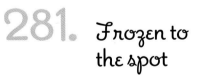

281. Frozen to the spot

If you've ever struggled to lift an ice cube tray out of the freezer:

- Sprinkle some salt onto the metal bottom of the freezer to prevent ice trays from sticking in place.

282. Artful ice

You can add some fun to regular ice cubes even without fancy shaped trays.

- Consider adding citrus twists, olives, capers or maraschino cherries – a nice touch for drinks.
- Non-traditional decorations suspended in ice can add quirkiness to a drink without affecting flavour – sunflower seeds, star anise, yellow pear tomatoes, a knot of liquorice…
- If you are watchful, you can keep an eye on the ice tray until the water is 'slushy', then add a pip of food colouring paste or syrup. It will spread partially if you quick-freeze, giving you Impressionist ice!

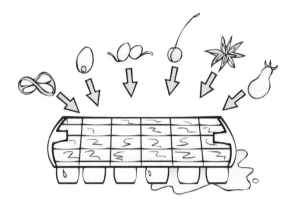

283. Nicer than ice!

Ever notice how ice tends to dilute a fruity punch or lemonade, even iced tea, as it melts?

- Keep your beverage at full-strength by freezing diluted fruit juices (half water) in ice trays, then bagging like ice.

When an orange cube melts in your lemonade, you'll call it a cool St Clement's sip!

284. Cold cups

Make your own pretty ice bowls to serve iced desserts on a warm day.

- You'll need two plastic bowls, one a size smaller than the other.
- Suspend the smaller bowl in the larger by taping the rims at 'quarter points' so that they are at the same level (which means the bottom of the small bowl doesn't touch the base of the large one and the gap between the rims is 'bridged' by the sticky tape).
- Add water between the bowls, filling up to 2.5 cm/1 inch from the rim, and freeze.
- To release, pour hot water into the inner bowl and lift it out as soon as it loosens.
- Now briefly plunge the outer bowl in warm water to lift the 'ice bowl' free.

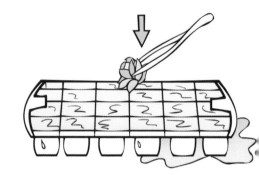

285. Frosted flowers

For desserts and drinks, edible flowers add a lovely twist. Here's a refreshing change from the usual sugar-frosted violets or rose petals.

- Using a tweezer, carefully push the flowers down into the compartments of an ice tray filled with cold water. Freeze to suspend the flower. (This is not very different from the ice garnish trick in Tip 282, but you need to start with chilled water to preserve and embed the blooms properly.)
- You can also use the tweezer to insert flowers or petals between the plastic mould bowls in the 'ice bowl' tip (*see Tip 284*) for a more picturesque serving idea.

■ Preserved in ice

286. Frost-fastened metal

Metal containers withstand freezer temperatures well, and it's a great way to bake from frozen. However, if there's a metal lid as well, chances are it'll freeze fast.

- Try adding a layer of greaseproof paper before putting the lid on. The edges of the paper should stick out beyond the rim.
- If you already have a frosted-up container that needs opening, wring out a tea towel in hot water and wrap around the top to loosen the lid.
- Next time, you might just use a layer of clingfilm followed by foil instead of a lid.

287. Freeze some cream

Cream is not a store-cupboard staple that you can easily hoard. However:

- Thanks to its very high fat content, clotted cream freezes beautifully.

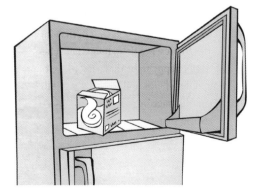

288. Cheese freeze!

If there's more cheese in the refrigerator than you can use over a couple of weeks, it might make sense to freeze it.

- You can freeze most hard cheeses as long as they are full-fat.
- When you thaw it in the refrigerator, wrap in a double thickness of kitchen paper to absorb moisture, then discard the paper and replace with greaseproof paper. Use within a week.
- If you're going to grate the cheese for use in cooking, you can either do so from frozen or grate and freeze in spoonfuls on an open tray, then bag the lumps to use as needed.
- Soft cheeses won't respond well to thawing, so it's better to preserve them in oil. Feta cheese is especially happy to be dunked in olive oil flavoured with herbs and spices – try chilli, cumin, garlic, sage or rosemary for extra flavour.
- You can also shape creamy cheeses such as fresh curd cheese or cottage cheese into balls and keep in oil the same way.
- Camembert and Brie, if not too ripe, freeze magnificently.

289. Frozen-stiff yolks

Eggs can be frozen! As long as you separate whites and yolks, that is.

- If you end up with excess yolks, it's better to freeze them as refrigeration will quickly dry them out (they'll be fine for up to a day if you cover them with cold water) and they will develop a 'skin'. Use within three months.
- Depending on whether you're going to use them in a sweet or savoury recipe, you can sprinkle a little salt or sugar on them before freezing.

290. Frozen rolled bacon

Yes, like most meats, bacon will keep longer if frozen – and that's good news if you've just bought the economy pack. However, it's almost impossible to peel off a slice of ham or bacon once you've frozen the package.

- Peel each slice off and roll up, then pop into a freezer bag to freeze. Now you can just take out as many as you want to thaw each time.

291. Nutty but nice

Nuts, like flours, will stay fresh longer – most of them for a couple of months – in the refrigerator. However, the freezer is a better bet.

- It can put a stop to any tendency towards rancidness.
- Nuts can be frozen for about a year.
- They won't develop icicles if stored in an airtight container.

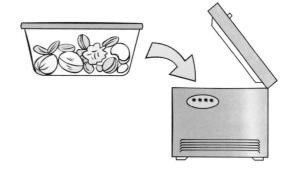

292. Mushrooms at their best

Fresh mushrooms should be cooked the day you buy (or pick) them. If you can't do that, freezing is next best – you won't be able to fry them or grill them from frozen, but they'll still be good in a stew or sauce.

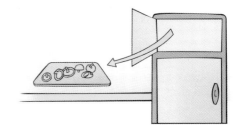

- Firmer varieties withstand freezing better than spongier types – shiitake, chanterelle and closed field mushrooms are better bets than open button mushrooms or soft-stemmed enoki.
- Bring a saucepan of salted water to the boil.
- Line a baking sheet with greaseproof paper.
- Wipe the mushrooms clean of grit with kitchen paper, trim and slice thickly.
- Simmer in the water for 1 minute, then drain.
- Lay out on the baking sheet and open freeze for 30-40 minutes.
- Working quickly, peel off the paper and transfer into a plastic freezer bag; return to freezer.

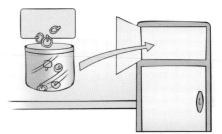

293. Soft fruit? Sorbet!

Berries or stone fruits (such as peaches) looking a little squidgy around the edges?

- Purée and freeze them with half the quantity of juice for a quick sorbet or granita.

294. Citrus slices

Orange or lemon glut?

- Freeze the excess for cooking or garnishing.
- Slice thinly and lay in a single layer on a baking tray lined with baking paper to open freeze.
- Peel off carefully and bag to store, arranged one on top of the other like a tower and interleaved with squares of greaseproof paper.
- Use in punches and sangrias straight from frozen.
- Line a cake tin with them for a pretty top (when you upend the cake on a serving platter), layering with a slight overlap before pouring in the cake mixture.
- You can line ramekins or dariole moulds in the same way for steamed puddings.
- Just add to water instead of ice cubes by way of a refreshing summer drink.

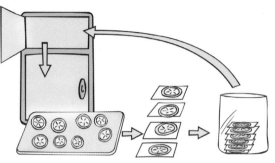

295. Fresh fruit – from the freezer

Hunting down a single piece of citrus fruit just for a recipe can be a pain, so make sure you always have some on hand instead.

- When oranges and lemons are in season, get a large bag of each.
- Zest the fruit and then juice it.
- You can freeze zest and juice separately in ice trays, and then transfer to a bag.
- The juice can be used from frozen in sauces and smoothies (instead of crushed ice, which can dilute fruit flavours).
- The zest can be thawed a cube at a time for flavoured butters and cake mixtures.

296. Easy slushes

Make use of your freezer to make slushes the easy way:

- Freeze juice – from a single fruit or a blend – until its texture goes grainy, at which point it has legitimately become slush.
- Scoop into glasses, filling halfway, and douse with chilled ginger ale.
- Provide a crochet sleeve for the glasses so the juice doesn't melt from your body heat and insert a straw to sip.

297. Herbs on ice

All too often, half that bunch of fresh soft herbs wilts before you can use it.

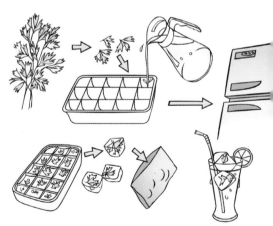

- Snip the herbs into small sprigs as soon as you get home, then pop them into ice trays.
- Fill with water and freeze as usual.
- Once frozen, you can pop them out of the tray and bag them in a freezer-safe pouch.

Now you just need to pull out a bag of mint cubes from the freezer to flavour stews, soups, casseroles or lemonade!

298. Sprightly sprigs

Are the herbs in your refrigerator looking a little tired? It's not too late to freeze them, as long as they aren't black or slimy!

- Purée or chop finely and freeze in ice-cube trays – pack them in tightly, and there should be no need to add water. Use in soups and stews.
- Make a sauce by heating with cream and seasoning to taste.
- Rub on joints for roasting, along with some crushed garlic, lemon juice and salt.
- Use wilting herbs for making your own herb butters (*see Tip 410*).

299. Freezer fiends!

Freezing forms ice crystals, which may not be kind to some foods.

- Starchy vegetables such as potatoes will rupture their cell walls if frozen – the higher the starch content, the greater the loss of texture. So cooked or raw, keep potatoes out of the freezer as far as possible. (It doesn't matter in a soup, though, where a quick blend will sort things out; it will hurt a stew, however.)
- Crisp vegetables such as celery, onion, salad leaves, cucumber and even peppers will go limp!
- Whole raw eggs would crack in the freezer. As for cooked, the yolk should be fine but the white may go rubbery.
- Cheesecake suffers in the freezer unless artificially 'stabilized', so if it is homemade, you'd be best advised to eat it up.

300. Stretch that date!

Open packages of even dry goods can spoil gradually as they come into contact with more and more air in a jar or canister, especially if they contain oils that can go rancid – breakfast cereals, for instance.

• If you doubt you can finish an open packet within a month of opening, put it in the refrigerator rather than a kitchen cabinet.

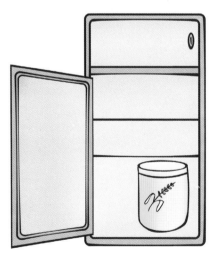

301. Don't decant dairy

When refrigerating non-solid dairy products such as milk, cream or yogurt, it's best not to decant them out of the original packaging unless it's been damaged.

• These foods are especially sensitive to spoilage or tainting, yet are usually consumed uncooked. Changing containers increases the likelihood of contamination or exposure to both odours and microbes.

303. Fridge your own vinaigrette

Making your own salad dressing allows for endless customization – and it can keep at least a week as long as you aren't adding fresh herbs or garlic.

- The basic recipe is 1 tablespoon vinegar and 1 teaspoon mustard to every 3 tablespoons of olive oil (plus seasoning to taste, of course).
- You can vary it with spices and dried herbs – seeds such as fennel, cumin or coriander, chilli and garlic flakes, a little splash of balsamic vinegar, or some crushed dried herbs.
- The basic recipe can take an already-flavoured oil, vinegar or mustard for that extra punch.
- Refrigerate in a screw-top jar and shake well before use. This is the time to add in those fresh chopped herbs, garlic pods, or sun-dried tomatoes if you want.

302. Fish against freeze

You meant to cook the fish fillets and then didn't get round to it. And freezing will ruin the texture…

- Unless you're cooking at once, always place fresh fish on a layer of ice in a box and cover with more crushed ice.
- This way you won't have to thaw very long, yet it doesn't suffer the ignominy of 'freezer flaking'.

304. Dream creams

While leftover cream sits in the refrigerator, waiting to be used up, add one of these magic ingredients to transform it into a luxury sauce for desserts.

This works best with scalded cream – add the infusing ingredient as soon as possible.

- Add a spoonful of rum and a stick of cinnamon.
- Perhaps a spoon of bruised rose petals or dried lavender buds.
- For warm simplicity, a couple of lightly crushed cardamom pods.
- A couple of sprigs of rosemary and a spoonful of ground almonds.

305. Go yellow for keeps

Cooked rice is one of those foods that really isn't keen on sitting around in the fridge.

- If you're not sure you can use it all up, better add some turmeric to the cooking water and turn it yellow – that helps preserve the rice a bit longer, a lot better.
- This trick also works for vegetables and lentils, especially in soups (where the colour can be easiest to disguise if you have tomatoes, carrots or pumpkin giving it a dark reddish hue).

306. Ready to roll, again

Ready-roll icing dries out very fast – after all, it's meant to so that you can save time.

- If you've got some left over, wrap tightly in clingfilm and refrigerate in an air-tight box until you can use it up.
- Knead well before using, adding a few drops of lemon juice or glycerine to loosen if need be.

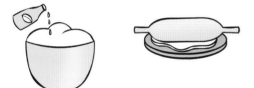

307. Glaze for the future

While not as stiff as fondant, royal icing or sugarpaste, hence not as prone to drying out, glaze-type or drizzle-on icings and whipped frostings have their own problems.

- Icing sugar glazes will quickly develop a skin on top that cracks while a moist pool develops below, trapping air and speeding up spoilage.
- Ganache icings tend to become gritty and lose their gloss if made to sit around.
- As for whipped frostings, they quickly deflate as the sugar picks up moisture from the air and weighs the fluffiness down.
- In all of these cases, put in an airtight container to refrigerate. But first, lightly press a layer of clingfilm on the surface to seal the freshness – and the texture – in.
- Try to use up within 2-3 days.

308. No loafing

One thing you really should avoid refrigerating is bread.

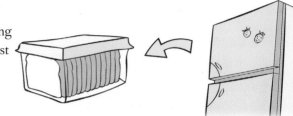

All too often, we think nothing of tossing the bag into the refrigerator to help it last another day. But for once, the humidity (that helps veggies stay fresh) will actually hasten mould in already yeasty loaves and buns!

Store bread in a cool spot in an airtight box outside, or freeze outright.

■ From freezer to fire

309. You only heat twice!

That is to say, you can heat food to cook it and, after freezing, apply heat a second time to thaw – that's it!

- Never re-freeze food that has been thawed.
- When reheating food that was frozen and thawed, make sure it gets piping hot all through.
- If you mean to freeze it, do so as soon as possible – divide into small containers to cool fast and freeze at once rather than refrigerating, dilly-dallying, then freezing a couple of days later. Even if you don't end up with a mess of bacteria, the repeated temperature changes can ruin the texture of meats and vegetables alike.

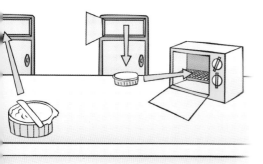

310. Hot from the freezer

Did you know hot baked soufflés can be made up to a day ahead and frozen?

- Prepare the soufflé mixture and freeze it directly in the ramekins you'll bake them in.
- Cover with freezer-safe clingfilm and freeze immediately to prevent the whipped egg whites collapsing. If your freezer has a quick-chill function, use that.
- When ready to bake, remove from the freezer and score a shallow cross on top to allow venting as it thaws.
- Pop straight in the oven and bake for an extra 5 minutes more than if baking fresh.

311. Go hot, go cold

Commercially available frozen vegetables and fruit retain better colour and texture because they have been pre-treated to optimize these properties.

You can certainly freeze your own fresh produce as well, but the results may not be quite the same.

- Fruits can tend to brown in the freezer, while vegetables lose their colour and go yellow.
- To prevent this, fruit needs to be acidulated – finding a freezing recipe for that particular fruit is your best bet (they tend to use ascorbic acid, but the amount varies).
- However, a little change in colour as well as the inevitable mushiness of texture shouldn't matter as much in a smoothie, pie or sauce.
- For vegetables, the best bet is to blanch them quickly before freezing.
- That means they won't need to cook as long later, which is why commercial frozen vegetables can be added to the pot straight from frozen.
- Without the blanching, veggies from the freezer will take a bit longer to cook – you'll have to account for thawing time to return the contents of the pan to the high temperature, as well as the usual cooking time of the raw veg.

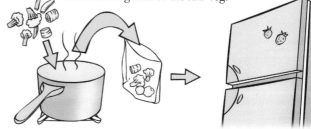

312. Frozen fresh-bakes

Biscuits, like bread, respond rather nicely to freezing – for up to 6 months. But the dough lasts twice as long!

- So roll up a log and leave in the freezer.
- When you want some fresh-baked cookies, just slice off a few roundels with the bread knife and bake from frozen.
- If you pop them in just before dinner, they'll be ready to serve warm with coffee!

313. Slice and freeze!

Unlike biscuits – when you freeze, slice and bake – you need to follow the reverse order for bread.

- Slice up the baked loaf (it'll be a chore to cut up once frozen), then freeze the slices, interleaved with greaseproof paper.
- Later you can toast straight from frozen.

314. Cold coffee

Coffee beans stay at their best longer if they are frozen in an airtight container. You can grind directly from frozen.

- Scoop out just enough to grind for a single brewing each time, and brew right away – letting the beans or grounds 'thaw' at room temperature will attract moisture and encourage spoilage.

315. Frozen in shape

You have only so many containers, so you don't want them sitting in the freezer for months.

- If you make a terrine or pudding that will need to be baked in a specific mould, it simply can't be cooked or thawed in another container.
- So the cooking container must go into cold storage? No! Get the best of both worlds by lining the container in a double thickness of foil with enough excess around the edges to completely wrap over the top. Fill and freeze, then carefully fold up and close the foil package, and transfer the package to a freezer bag.
- Thawing time? Unwrap foil and slip the food, a block of the correct shape and size, into the destined container to cook or reheat. Neat!

Leftovers

Dinner-to-lunchbox 'recycling' suggestions; jazzer-uppers for plain-Jane staples; stretching sides to make a main; and sweet surprises from the remains of yesterday.

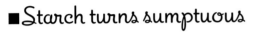

■ Starch turns sumptuous

316. Spaghetti snack

This is great for almost any kind of leftover pasta – just coordinate the vegetables with the sauce you started with.

- Sauté onions and sliced vegetables in a large frying pan.

- Stir the pasta into the pan.
- Beat and season several eggs – enough to cover the other ingredients – and pour over the mixture in the pan.
- When it sets at the bottom, add grated cheese and pop under a hot grill.
- Serve hot or cold.

It's worth making extra pasta just for this. If you start with double the quantity you need, you can also make this frittata with the leftovers.

317. Spiced rice

You should avoid refrigerating rice for more than a day – it spoils really quickly (*also see Tip 305*). However, it can be freshened up for your next meal with:

- Sautéed mushrooms
- Fried onions
- Toasted nuts and pumpkin seeds
- Grated or crumbled cheese
- Sweetcorn kernels and carrot julienne strips
- A can of drained beans or lentils with a pinch of cumin and a pinch of chilli
- Chopped fresh herbs, spring onions or shallots
- Currants, toasted coconut curls and turmeric

318. Stir-fried rice

Cold rice is actually better for stir-frying than freshly cooked because it won't turn mushy. The cold temperature of the refrigerator will have stiffened the outer layer of starch.

- Heat a little groundnut oil or sesame oil.
- Stir-fry some chopped bok choy and peeled prawns with a little crushed garlic. (You could also use spring onions, sweet peppers and sesame; or strips of meat, spinach and peanut butter)
- When the greens wilt, stir in a couple of spoonfuls of teriyaki sauce.
- Add the rice. Heat through and serve.

■ Sides to staples

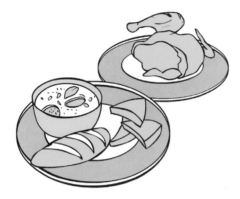

319. Curried chowder

Almost any leftover meat or fish is fantastic in this milky chowder base.

- Sauté a couple of chopped onions.
- Add 2 cans of sweetcorn kernels.
- Stir in 300 ml/10 fl oz milk and 600 ml/1 pint stock.
- Season with dried herbs or curry powder.
- Simmer for 20 minutes.
- Meanwhile, chop up, shred or flake the meat or fish – about 225 g/8 oz is plenty.
- Use a hand blender to liquidize the soup.
- Stir in the meat or fish.
- Serve with Melba toast or some garlic bread made with a small sliced ciabatta or baguette.

320. Keep the beans green

It's not a good idea to just refrigerate leftover steamed or blanched green beans as they will lose their crunch and colour.

- Refrigerate overnight, covered with ice water.
- Drain the beans and stir-fry with some garlic and tomatoes or lemon juice and zest.
- Add a little grated pecorino cheese or Parmesan cheese, or some toasted almonds.

321. Roasted root hot pots

With leftover roasted root vegetables, you don't need much more than some spices or herbs and either risotto rice or pasta.

- If you already added a good helping of herbs or spices to the roasting vegetables, don't add more.
- If you didn't, consider complementing the natural sweetness of root vegetables with pungent spices like coriander, cumin or chilli.
- Rosemary and sage go well with winter vegetables.
- Roasted onions make a great addition.
- Prepare a basic risotto with stock – no wine. Add the vegetables, diced, in the last 5 minutes of cooking. Serve with grated Parmesan cheese or pecorino cheese.
- Or cook pasta adding the vegetables. You could add toasted nuts as well – hazelnuts, chestnuts or walnuts. Stir in some blue cheese or soured cream to bind it all together.
- You can also add blue cheese salad dressing to the roasted vegetables with some crisp bacon bits.

322. Mediterranean vegetable mealmakers

Roasted summer vegetables – courgettes, aubergines, peppers and leeks – can be transformed into one-pot meals just like their winter counterparts (*see Tip 321*).

- For risotto, stir in the vegetables at the end. Add a spoonful of pesto or rouille for flavour.
- For pasta, mix in a vinaigrette made with strong mustard or a bit of pesto. For cold pasta salad, toss the vegetables with a balsamic dressing. Fresh herb garnishes could be mint or basil. If you'd like, add some baby mozzarella balls. Or supplement the vegetables with caramelized onions, grilled corn, or some stir-fried spinach.
- To make pizzettes, use toasted pitta bread for the base and layer the vegetables on tomato paste with cheese and pine kernels or sunflower seeds.
- For minestrone-style soup, bring a can of chopped tomatoes to the boil with an equal quantity of stock, adding some pasta and/or beans along with the vegetables in the last 7-10 minutes of cooking.

323. Cover up with cheese

A good store-brand cheese sauce can turn many a batch of leftovers into a substantial bake. Some coordinates from the day before:

- Strips of roast chicken, ham and leeks.
- Sautéed mushrooms and peas.
- Peas, asparagus, broccoli or spinach with ham or bacon.
- Sausage meat or meatballs with sage, onions and perhaps some chopped apples.
- Pineapple chunks and any meat.
- Refried beans and broccoli.
- Or, indeed, the classic cauliflower, given a twist by the inclusion of some orange segments.
- Throw in some cooked macaroni, and you have a meal-in-a-dish.

324. Curry-style sauce

The meat in a curry is usually demolished while the gravy lingers on. Don't throw it out quite yet!

- You can add chunks of fish and reheat for a quick new curry. Add a squeeze of lime and some coriander to finish.
- Stirring in a can of beans even before you refrigerate it will you give you a new dish. Check the seasoning after reheating, though.
- Or serve the curry base as a sauce with pasta, especially stuffed pasta.
- You can reheat the curry with some chopped green pepper and mushrooms to serve with rice.
- Or, simmer till it thickens and serve over grilled sausages or burgers.

- Consider simmering over a low heat with coconut milk or yogurt for a creamier sauce, and stirring in blanched green beans or baby carrots. Perfect as a soupy dish with egg noodles.
- A neat Indian trick is to halve and brown some hard-boiled eggs in a frying pan and add them to the curry.

325. Sangria fruit salad

Turn leftover sangria or rum punch into a dessert sauce for fresh fruit.

- Strain the sangria, reserving the fruit.
- Simmer the liquid with a pinch of allspice.
- Meanwhile, prepare fresh fruit to supplement the steeped pieces.
- When the sauce reaches the consistency of a thick syrup or coulis, pour over the fruit.
- Serve at once or chill until needed.

326. Pudding-ed ice cream!

Got some leftovers from a dense chocolate cake or plum pudding?

- Crumble it into plain vanilla, butterscotch or orange ice cream.
- You could add a shot of good brandy, single-malt whisky or schnapps.
- No need to break it up completely – a little bit of 'chunk' is fun! Scoop and serve as usual.

327. Rocky river

Here's a shake that no one will ever attach the label 'leftovers' to!

- If you ever have leftover cake, biscuits or brownies that have gone irredeemably dry, blend with ice cream and chilled milk.

Togetherness at the Table

Everything you need to know to bring mealtimes out of the nursery, without teething pains (though we have bite-sized solutions for that too). Age-wise edibles. Less-mess table-setting tricks. Menus for the whole family, from infant to old-timer – out of one dish!

■ Grown-up nursery meals

328. Small but sophisticated

Raise your child to feel at home with the tastes of a world full of choice and variety.

- Offer a meat-free meal from time to time.
- Offer more texture – use slices or small bits of meat instead of sandwich paste or frankfurters.
- Make the colours more intense – red cabbage instead of white; dark green leaves instead of iceberg lettuce; sweet potato rather than plain white potatoes.

- Add variety– a mixed mesclun salad rather than plain coleslaw; different pasta shapes instead of spaghetti.
- Let them try more exotic grains from time to time – couscous instead of pasta or bread.

329. Little grown-ups

While planning meals, treat your children as little grown-ups with some special needs – in the departments of chewing, handling cutlery and complicated finger food, and a few nutritional taboos. The early years are the best time to build good taste.

- Toddlers over the age of two are ready to eat in courses, just like grown-ups. If you and your partner are having a three-course meal, resist serving your child a one-dish mush!
- Making your child a sandwich? Ask yourself whether *you* would eat it. If not, don't give it to your child.
- Serve your child on a smaller plate with child-sized cutlery.
- Never serve your child adult-sized portions, even if it is a favourite dish.

330. Old favourites versus new friends

Children will have their favourites – perhaps your toddler prefers farfalle pasta to all other shapes; but make a game of having something 'new' every so often.

- You can have a 'new day' each week, when you try something your child has never had before, like an unusual fruit. Children like 'new'!
- And just so they know it's good to try something different although they have favourites, let them know you have favourites too! Say, '*My* favourite pasta is spaghetti, but today I'm making pasta twists because this sauce tastes nicer with it.'

331. Fledgeling foodie (out and about)

The best way to encourage a child to experiment is to make the world of food into a big adventure.

- Children, no matter how little, will usually willingly try anything they helped 'pick'. Take children along for pick-your-own farm trips; at the supermarket, have them help you choose.
- Teach them how to shop – to look at simple labels (children old enough to add and subtract can assess price tags) and learn what differentiates a tasty fruit from a bland one.
- Always be up for adventure yourself – don't say no to samples unless you believe they are unhealthy and, if so, explain to your child why you said 'no'.
- When sampling at the farmers' market, offer your children a taste – suggest, don't insist, they try the 'stinky' goat's cheese; ask for their opinion and explain why something tastes the way it does.
- When they suggest an inappropriate purchase, explain why it's not a good idea and suggest a compromise.

332. Fledgeling foodie (at home)

The food adventure (*see Tip 331*) should continue at home, and not just in the kitchen (*see Tip 333*).

- Avoid throwing out food – it's the worst example you can set because it signals that it's acceptable to waste food if you don't 'want' it.
- Shop sensibly, and plan meals based on what's fresh in the refrigerator and how many will be eating.
- Encourage your child to help you plan the menu. Leading questions should help even toddlers make an acceptable choice.
- Offer alternatives as suggestions, and explain why you think spaghetti with tomato sauce would be better than macaroni cheese.
- Consider growing a few easy vegetables at home – tomatoes are really easy – and 'help' your children tend them. If they grow it themselves, they will eat it with pride.

333. Fledgeling foodie (in the kitchen)

Treat the kitchen as the fairground of culinary adventure. This is where all the action and excitement is!

- Even small children can 'cook' with a few precautions and careful supervision.
- Encourage children to have friends over for a make-your-own snack session.
- Let them have a hand in the foods they take to school – even if it's only stirring or throwing in the raisins. They'll glow with pride.
- They can top their own pies and crumbles and stamp out biscuits, as well as help you measure and mix.
- Allow them to experiment! It keeps them hooked, helps them learn and builds confidence. Older children can pick their own sandwich fillings or pizza toppings, for instance.
- If the experiment fails, be ready with words of consolation and encouragement – suggest what you might add or leave out next time.
- Most importantly, let them see you experiment – if you always cook only by the book, then they will soon come to regard cooking as the same as swotting from a textbook (which opens a whole new can of worms)!

■ Baby meals

334. Chubby cheeks

You don't want to encourage juvenile obesity by serving fat-laden food. But don't swing too far the other way either.

- Children up to the age of two need a larger percentage of food to body weight than adults because they can eat only much smaller volumes.
- Fat is calorie-dense and growing takes a lot of energy – the same calories would create a lot more bulk if they came from protein or carbohydrate!
- While this doesn't mean you need to add extra fat to food, don't remove it forcibly either.
- Never give your child low-fat versions of standard foods – so no skimmed or semi-skimmed milk yet and no 'diet desserts'.
- This is not a licence to gorge on fried food, however. Use healthier cooking methods most of the time.
- Shift towards the same lower fat guidelines as for adults when your child starts school.

335. Kiddie carbs

A baby's transition from low-carb milk feeds to complete fibre-rich adult food must be gradual.

- Introduce the first carbs (apart from baby rice) at nine months.
- At this point, you don't want to give too much fibre. So begin with bread, porridge, potatoes, rice or pasta first.
- After a couple of weeks you can start adding puréed root vegetables and blander fruits such as apples or pears.
- Beyond age two, toddlers should be able to digest most carbohydrates, including high-fibre vegetables and fruits, quite comfortably. But not too much of those – they still need their lower-fibre grains. And no high-fibre grains until they're five!
- By the time they approach school-going age, you can start the transition to an adult type diet in terms of the fibre balance.

336. Drink up

A baby's tiny stomach is easily filled by liquids. Too much fluid will prevent the absorption of essential nutrients.

- Avoid offering a drink with a meal until the child is at least two.
- Offer a drink after the meal, though.
- In very hot weather, offer a small sip up to half an hour before meals.
- For toddlers over the age of two, offer a small cup of water, milk or well-diluted unsweetened fruit juice.

337. Safely sterile

It's not just your baby's bottle, bowl and spoon that need sterilizing.

- Also scald any utensils used for food preparation– knife, chopping board, sieve, blender jar and saucepan – in boiling water.
- Placing everything together in a deep roasting tin or stock pot and pouring in boiling water from a kettle is the quickest, least messy way.
- Keep a set of separate utensils for your baby's food, making sure the chopping board and saucepan are smaller in size.

338. Baby batches

Blending your own baby food (*see Tip 357*)? Save time and avoid waste by making several batches at once.

- A baby will typically eat only a small amount of the purée you offer – from a teaspoon early on to 55 g/2 oz while still supplemented by a milk feed.
- That's why a sterilized ice tray produces the perfect portion sizes.
- Freeze and then pop out the cubes to secure in freezer bags or a lidded container. Label clearly.
- Don't keep for more than three months. You should actually use it up much faster because your baby will outgrow the smoother textures quite quickly!

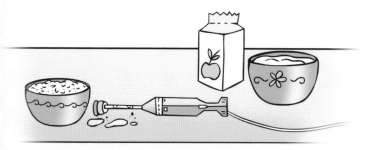

339. First foods

Some ideas for those first purées.

- Don't hesitate to blend more than one vegetable with formula milk. Which ones go together? That's the same as for adults.
- Be careful about adding fruit to milk, as it might curdle. Thin with puréed apple, baby rice or apple juice.
- You can also add a little 'grown-up rice' to a purée.
- When the baby is six months old, you can start leaving the purée a little chunkier, perhaps even process the food to a fine mince rather than blend to a purée. Occasionally you might add a little carefully deboned chicken or white fish.
- Now you can also start introducing stronger flavours – a little red meat, tomatoes, mushrooms, mild hard cheese and a little onion.
- That's when you can start adding tiny pinches of herbs and spices, maybe even a hint of garlic, too.

340. Egg-citement

It's certainly a very nutritious and tasty food, but little babies can't digest egg very well.

- Don't give eggs to babies under six months.
- You should only give them hard-boiled yolks, not the whites, between six and 12 months.
- By 12 months, however, a baby should be quite comfortable with whole eggs.

341. Purée inspiration

Think about your own favourite foods when inventing purée combinations. These combinations are suitable for babies over six months.

- Fruits with custard powder and milk will be very well received.
- Try yogurt with banana or any combination of fruits you might serve in a smoothie or sundae (peach Melba!).
- How about a mix of Mediterranean vegetables?
- Or try a kedgeree-style rice purée – add a little white fish, some peas and a little hard-boiled egg yolk to rice and milk.
- Rice with a few carrots, cauliflower, potatoes and peas is very satisfying.
- Be adventurous with fruit purée mixed with some chicken.
- For purées that include meat, consider replicating the ingredients of a classic stew or casserole.

342. After nine months

By nine months, a baby's teeth are starting to appear, so progress to chunkier food.

- Baby food need no longer be a purée; move to a rough mash or finely chopped meal.
- During teething, babies will appreciate finger foods to gnaw – offer peeled fruit, raw carrots or cucumber sticks, and small pieces of chicken, ham or fish. Not too much ham, though, as it is very high in salt.
- Your child might not mind a little more seasoning at this stage – such as the flavour of stock.

343. I can do it myself!

As soon as your baby starts making a grab for the spoon, you should start providing pint-sized cutlery.

- At first, a bowl and spoon to play with will be enough – you can go on with the real job of spooning in without fear of too many grabs.
- While still giving fine purées, put a little in the bowl for the baby to play with.
- Don't worry if the baby digs in with hands rather than spoon! Just make sure the little hands are clean.
- Once teeth appear, some finger food while you feed – cooked carrot, broccoli or cauliflower at first, then bits of bread or toast – is a good idea.
- Finally, allow the baby to attempt to feed himself or herself – and don't intervene when he or she makes a mess! It's the only way to learn how.
- Put newspaper under the chair as well as the tabletop! Carry some with you when visiting with your baby.

344. Join the table!

When your baby's just starting to feed himself or herself, you will get a chance to concentrate on your own meal for a few minutes.

- This is when the baby can start sitting at the table, at a high chair pulled up.
- Offer chopped or minced food for eating with a spoon. This should be about half the meal and your help and attention will be needed.
- The second course can be finger foods – bread-based, vegetables or toast.
- This gives you a chance to finish your own meal and start tidying up.
- It also establishes the habit of eating in courses!

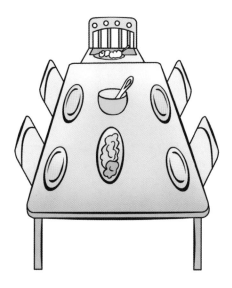

345. First snacks

A baby about to turn one is a natural snacker! After all, young children expend a lot of energy playing and growing, so it's not reasonable to expect three small meals in tiny tummies to last all day.

- Offer simple finger foods at first (*see Tip 342*) and let the baby take his or her time. He or she will stop automatically once full.
- Avoid sugary snacks because once that taste for sugar is acquired, it is very difficult to get a baby to eat a savoury or blander food!
- Now that a little more salt is tolerated, cubes of mild hard cheese, pieces of French toast, chicken nuggets or fish fingers are of interest.
- Gradually move on to offering mini sandwiches or bread with a mild sandwich spread to get the baby used to 'real' food.
- Popcorn and cheese straws are usually popular.
- Don't give whole nuts to under-fives (*also see Tip 346*)!
- Stick mainly to fruits and vegetables, and occasionally dried fruit.

346. Now I am one

Most foods will have been introduced by now and some of the rules can be relaxed.

- Reserve miniature fairy cakes or shortbread as occasional treats.
- It's time for real breakfast cereals, and even sausages!
- Ground nuts can be given to babies over 12 months, but monitor carefully for any adverse reaction.
- Avoid the pudding-after-every-meal habit, otherwise the child will soon learn to avoid or eat less of the main course!
- By now definite likes and dislikes are taking shape, so be wary of snacks – too many will ruin the appetite for meals.

■ Nutrition in the playschool

347. Good for you

As your child develops preferences and gets more active in and outside home, keep an eye on the nutritional content of snacks.

- Snacks of raw vegetables and cheese to end a meal combat tooth decay, which frequent snacking and sugary foods can encourage.
- Children should drink full-fat milk to get the benefits of fat-soluble vitamins. If there's great resistance to plain, offer a flavoured drink (but check just how sweet it tastes and keep it light). Also check with your doctor that there's no lactose intolerance.
- From time to time, reintroduce the 'hated' foods in new forms. Growing children make up their minds afresh all the time!
- Many foods that have previously been spat out will be tried happily if offered as part of an 'experience'. The adventure might be a picnic, a 'camping trip' (in a tent in the garden) or a toys' tea party.

348. Smarter sandwich

Just because all the kids at playschool have sandwiches with mayonnaise doesn't mean you must offer your toddler the same!

- Instead of sad, squishy white bread, rotate different traditional breads for sandwiches. Try pumpernickel, Irish soda bread, seed and multigrain breads, foccacia with tomatoes.
- Or turn the sandwich into a pitta pocket or tortilla wrap.
- Look beyond mayonnaise to pesto, hummus, grainy mustard, mild pâtés, even a good quality ketchup that's not too sweet or synthetic.
- Think of a pizza as an open sandwich – easy on the cheese, more veggies and a wholewheat crust.
- A vegetarian sandwich needn't be cheese by default. Use roasted peppers (very good with hummus), spinach with mushrooms or sweetcorn with sprouts.
- Few children will turn down peanut butter and banana. Make it an occasional treat.

350. Kids' kebabs

Many children will turn up their noses at chunks of vegetables on a plate, but will gladly pop them in if those same chunks are threaded on a skewer!

- Start easy – alternating chunks of salmon and cod for a fish-finger addict or just presenting cocktail sausages on a stick.
- From there, go on to a mix of the familiar and the different – ham and pineapple with cheese, sweetcorn with sausage slices, peppers with fish.
- Once they are happy with that, add one of these – chunks of courgette, cubes of baked pumpkin or sweet potatoes, button mushrooms, cherry tomatoes.
- You can even make fruit kebabs – bananas to begin with (serve a chocolate custard to dip in) and then gradually grapes, melons (balls for the pale ones or dice for watermelons), wedges of peaches or plums, kiwi slices and star fruit.

349. A lunchbox to love

Children are attracted to a wide variety of textures and colours, since they are biologically programmed to be inquisitive enough to learn! And that need not mean smiley faces on everything – not all your child's heroes are clowns, are they?

- Make it interesting to look at and hold as well as taste. Broccoli 'trees' bordering a 'field' of sprouts sewn in a bed of potatoes…
- Keep up the novelty value. Vary the juice box, yogurt and fruit.
- Keep them 'growing'. Don't just opt for the simplest option (banana or grapes) each time – try a new fruit. Such as physalis or cape goose berries.

351. Hide and treat

If the appearance of a new food threatens to put your toddler (or slightly older child) off, adding a favourite to it should induce them to give it a chance.

- Pair fish florentine with dinosaur pasta shapes.
- Serve a wild mushroom sauce on toast with a grilled cheese slice.
- Falafel 'veggie burgers' should quickly banish a reluctance to eat chickpeas.

352. Sweet and sound

Dessert needn't be a nutritional disaster.

- Make frozen yogurt lollies.
- Serve fruit dippers with chocolate custard.
- Instead of bought ice cream (often too sweet and fatty), make fresh fruit sorbets or stir fruit purée into custard to freeze for 'scoops'.

353. Fussy eaters

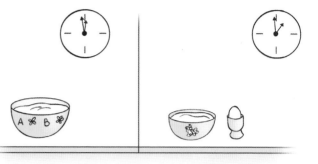

Some ways to deal with a fussy eater:

- Reduce portion sizes.
- Don't make a fuss – if he or she is just playing with the food rather than eating, quietly remove the plate.
- See if it is possible for a favourite adult or a small friend to be present at some meals. Don't draw attention to the child's eating habits.
- Offer new foods when the child is really hungry.

354. Mama's little helper

Get toddlers to play their part in the mealtime ritual early. That sense of participation – rather than being forced to sit quietly (which seems like punishment) – can make a world of difference.

- Ask them to lay the table for you.
- Encourage them to pass the condiments. Expect a mess of salt, pepper and butter initially!
- Setting a place for teddy can be a great incentive.
- Switch to shatterproof dishes for a bit!

■ Everybody eats

355. One-stop meals

You can introduce small amounts of meat, chicken, white fish and yogurt to babies over ten months, so even with a toddler and a baby in the family, plus any older children, careful planning will allow you to cook just one basic meal.

- Of course it will have to be 'finished' differently for various age groups.
- Keep things bland as late into the cooking process as possible – this way, making baby's purée is just a matter of chopping, blending and straining.
- While it cools, you can season the rest – lightly for the toddler.
- Set that out and let it cool too while you add grown-up ingredients to the rest of the portions – the alcohol reduction, the chillies and heavier doses of garlic, sautéed onions, the soy sauce, the curry paste, the whole eggs, the nuts.
- Always check the temperature of children's food before serving.

356. Eating together

Make it a habit to eat together at the table as a family whenever possible – that means no one is excused unless they are not home or there is a genuine crisis.

- Baby joins the table in the high chair and will make a grab every so often – avoid a tablecloth under hot dishes, and keep knives and teapots out of reach!
- Toddlers will sometimes start to fuss over what you choose or demand to eat in front of the TV. Explain that your family eats together. If baby resists, serve food at the table and otherwise ignore him or her. Steel yourself to stay calm in the face of a tantrum. If it gets too distressing, sit the child down in a different room.
- Older family members must set an example by never getting up until everyone has finished eating.
- If the child changes his or her mind and decides to eat at the table, have the whole family sit down again till he or she is finished – this serves as encouragement and reinforces the point that you eat *together*.

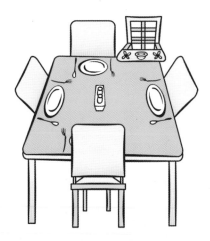

357. Baby blender

A smaller-sized blender jar is one of the best investments you can make for a baby starting on solids.

- You can easily turn any fruit, vegetable, cooked cereal and even a portion of whatever you are eating into baby food that's far nicer than any can or jar you may buy.
- Cut up small portions of everything and blend, adding a little water, milk or apple juice if necessary for a smoother texture.
- Strain to remove fibrous bits, pips and stray fish bones.
- If offering a portion of what you are eating, season your food later.

A baby fed on blended adult food tends to move to 'proper' food more readily!

358. Toned down for tots

Toddlers above the age of two can start eating meals quite similar to your own. However:

- Avoid anything very spicy. Certainly no chilli peppers or hot sauce yet, and keep the pepper down.
- Remember that a concentration of herbs or spices that is perfect for you may be too much for a tiny tummy.
- Tone down the onions and garlic. You can sauté some and add to your own food separately later.
- Season the adult portions at the table – salt should be avoided in a child's diet.
- Anything that contains alcohol or a high concentration of caffeine is out. Even with chocolate, avoid high cocoa percentages.
- Avoid adding too much sugar.

359. All-family smoothies

It's worth buying a blender just for these!

- Whether made with yogurt or milk, smoothies provide a quick, delicious calcium boost laced with fibre and potassium.
- They can serve as breakfast, a side (instead of milkshake) or a snack.
- They're quick to slurp when in a hurry and easy to drink on the go.
- They're endlessly versatile – besides fruit, you can add seeds and nuts as well as some grains (toasted oats, cornflakes).
- They're a whiz to make, and anyone over 12 should be able to make one safely and successfully; even under-tens might do well with some supervision.

360. Mediterranean mini menu

If you're serving lamb chops and roasted Mediterranean vegetables:

- Simply skip the seasoning on one of the chops.
- Process half the unseasoned chop with some vegetables for the baby.
- Slice the other half for a toddler to eat with vegetables and some toast.

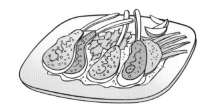

362. Curry for kids

Craving a curry?

- Hold the coconut milk and curry paste until you have cooked the meat or vegetables and have reserved the children's portion.
- For a toddler, you can mix in a little yogurt and serve the 'curry' on a bed of rice or pasta with a piece of naan bread.

361. Hot pot-lets

Making lamb hotpot?

- Prepare the filling and set aside the children's portions in a separate casserole.
- Add some rustic sausages to the remainder, or a little Guinness if you prefer.
- Top both casseroles with potatoes and bake according to the recipe directions.
- Serve with boiled Brussels sprouts.

363. All Greek to us!

Moussaka is easy to manage for a family!

- Cook the mince with a very light seasoning.
- Spoon the toddler's portion into a ramekin.
- Season the adult portion to taste with garlic, salt and extra herbs or spices.
- Top your portion and the toddler's with potato slices, putting less cheese and more breadcrumbs on the ramekin than on your own.
- Leave to cool for a bit after baking. (You can reheat yours, if necessary.)

364. Tex-Mex tots

Does chilli con carne sound unsuitable for small children?

- Hold the spices and seasoning, and cook the mince with more vegetables than is strictly traditional – mushrooms, peppers, peas.
- Don't add any beans yet – the skin of the red kidney bean is tough on immature tummies.
- Put the children's portion of cooked mince in a casserole dish and bake with a few small scrubbed potatoes alongside.
- Season your own chilli with spices, stir in the beans and simmer until cooked.
- Spoon the toddler's portion into halved and hollowed-out potato boats.
- Adults will get a green salad and soured cream on the side, and can melt some cheese on the potato skins under the grill!

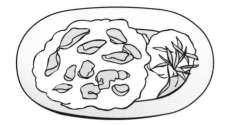

366. Starting to stir-fry

Children tend to be fascinated by the matchstick shapes of colourful vegetables in a stir-fry.

- Brown a few pieces of pork or chicken in a saucepan.
- In the same pan, stir-fry vegetable matchsticks without soy sauce and garlic, throwing in some mung bean sprouts.
- You can use stock and cornflour, perhaps even a little ketchup.
- Set aside the stir-fry and, for the adults, toast some cashews and fry a little garlic with soy sauce. Toss into your portion.
- Serve the toddler portion in a Chinese bowl, perhaps with a 'Chinese spoon' for atmosphere (a soup spoon works here because the pieces are small enough to spoon up, but don't be surprised if the matchsticks are treated as finger food!)

365. Very Continental!

Yes, you can even adapt beef bourguignon to a tot's tastes!

- Hold back the wine, garlic and bouquet garni.
- Brown the meat in a saucepan and simmer in some stock and tomato purée with a small sprinkle of dried herbs or the corner of a bay leaf.
- Spoon the children's portion into a separate casserole dish.
- Simmer the adult portion with the wine and adult-only seasonings.
- Bake both sets until meltingly tender, adding shallots and mushrooms to the adult portion.
- Serve with shredded steamed cabbage and mashed potatoes.

367. Casseroles on a roll

Even with little children, casseroles remain the most fuss-free one-pot meals for friends and family.

- Seasoned lightly, most casseroles can be puréed directly into baby food, adding whatever vegetables you would have served on the side (as long as they are well cooked).
- For toddlers, you need to cut up only the larger pieces. They should be fine with the standard side dishes – a little salad, some peas, broccoli, carrots and new potatoes.
- If you think it might be too bland for adults, make a little roux and stir in extra spices and perhaps a fruit relish to serve on the side.

368. Too tiny for turmeric

Cooking curry from scratch rather than with a readymade paste or powder?

- Toddlers over 12 months should be fine with turmeric as long as you use a light hand.

370. Salad stuffers

There may well come a time when you are desperate for a lighter meal of salad. But you still need to cook something more nutritious (i.e. calorie-dense) for the children, right? Not necessarily.

- If you're making Caesar salad, salade Niçoise or cold chicken salad, simply use the meat or fish as the basis of your children's.
- To make it more substantial, serve the children's portions in toast cups – bread squares pressed into the cups of a muffin pan to toast so it has a hollowed shape perfect for filling.
- You can open a can of sweetcorn or add some chopped sweet peppers to the children's portion, while keeping the olives to yourself.
- Mix in some mayonnaise and yogurt for the children to make a creamy scoop.
- Add a little of the creamy dressing to your own along with lots of crisp salad vegetables and leaves.
- Decide whether to serve them the hardboiled eggs based on their age (*see Tip 340*).

369. Tandoori tonight

Introduce your toddler to ethnic tastes early with this crowd-pleaser. It's close enough to grilled chicken that most children take to it readily.

- Marinate chicken pieces in yogurt mixed with a pinch of turmeric, a little sweet paprika and some mixed herbs.
- For older family members, add curry paste and chilli to the marinade after reserving the children's portion.
- Grill until the juices run clear.
- Serve with cherry tomatoes, cucumber sticks, onion rings (just a couple soaked in cold water for finger food) and some naan or pitta bread. Add a spinach salad for adults.

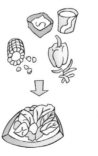

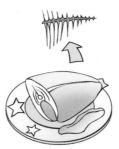

371. Fish foods

Traditional dishes such as paella and kedgeree are great for special occasion meals at home with young children. Their colourful mixed-up appearance holds great charm.

- Stick to plain white fish for small children – no in-shell shellfish or cured products yet.
- Toddlers are old enough to eat a small peeled prawn, however.
- You can add squid rings, mussels, prawns or smoked fish to yours separately, cooked with turmeric and saffron.
- Even fish cakes can be a complete meal with the addition of some grated carrots and chopped greens.

372. Vol-au-vous?

Small individual vol-au-vents are easy for children to pick up and eat.

- Make them more attractive still by using animal shapes (see Tip 377).
- Fill with fish or hard-boiled eggs and vegetables in white sauce, creamed corn and peppers, with a sliced pimiento-stuffed olive, to garnish.

373. Versatile vegetables

Consider serving meatless meals now and then to give vegetables a starring role.

- Grilled cheese on toast is a great start – add vegetable toppings as though making pizza. You can lay on tomatoes, roast peppers, mushrooms and sweetcorn to begin with. Wait a little to introduce courgette and aubergine slices.
- Tomato-based pasta sauce is another great base – you can chop or grate in just about any vegetable with good results.
- Slightly older children will enjoy a vegetable crumble with beans, with a cheesy, seed-speckled topping, in individual ramekins.
- Try bean burgers or falafel in pitta pockets, drizzled with tahini.
- An onion tart may be too much for children, but they'll probably love a tart of leeks in cheese sauce.

374. Sweet stop

Don't make puddings a daily habit. Keep them for weekend treats. Some easy ideas:

- Bread and butter pudding is a nursery favourite!
- Eve's pudding usually goes down well too.
- For a teething tot, baby carrots 'glazed' with jam and rolled in coconut shreds is fun. Older children can use honey for 'glue' instead.
- Everyone likes peaches or strawberries with cream – and shortcake! No strawberries for babies under 12 months, though!
- Fruit brulées are healthier than caramel custard.
- Make individual apple turnovers: place the filling at one end of a strip of filo pastry and fold over the corner, continuing to fold to make a triangular 'pie'.
- Pavlovas are easy to mess with and eat!
- Whole baked apples and poached pears appeal to most children. Tarts are family favourites, but tartlets are easier for toddlers to eat.
- Make mousse by whipping cream, fromage frais (or yogurt) and jelly. Swirl through puréed fruits.
- A parfait of fruits in jelly alternated with a set mousse in a sundae glass will appeal to children.
- Most children like fruit salad – and it's even easier when it's a dried fruit compôte. Or add bananas and oranges to dates and raisins for a warm fruit salad.

■ Big plates, small plates

375. Toddler trays and small plates

By the time they are off to playschool, hand-eye coordination will have improved.

- For toddlers, cut up larger pieces of meat or vegetables into bite-sized chunks or slices.
- A slightly older child will be happy to feel grown-up when you serve him or her the same way you serve yourself (chicken leg with bone in; whole fish steak).
- However, be prepared to help with the cutting up if the going gets tough.

376. Portion control

Children might eat the same foods as you, but certainly not in the same quantities.

- To help a child's plate look more like your own, choose a smaller (salad) plate in the same design. That way, the smaller portions will be perfectly in proportion.
- For 'portioned' foods such as meatballs or hamburgers, thaw and reshape to make smaller patties.
- With foods that won't allow you to do that, halve the portions – 2 fish fingers to your 4; 1 scoop of yogurt to your 2; a single small wedge of pizza, and so on.
- With some foods, you can simply choose a smaller size for the child – a junior-sized baked potato or a smaller whole fish.
- In other cases, just serve half – this works well with most fruits and other symmetrical foods.
- However, half a muffin is less appealing than a miniature. Ditto a burger or pie.

377. Shapely servings

Let the look be lighthearted – under-fives are unlikely to be ecstatic about nouvelle plating! They may well prefer a broccoli 'forest' with pomegranate 'fruit'!

- Make fish cakes in a fish shape – use a biscuit cutter or mould by hand.
- Or support a fishy dish with vegetable slices cut like fins.
- Pepper and carrot 'stars' brighten up most dishes. You can even pillow them on potato clouds or hang them off a broccoli Christmas tree!
- Make baked potato boats with cheese or ham sails.
- However, don't clown around with every meal. Sometimes a bright-rimmed plate provides enough fun to offset a delicious dish.

378. Beef up the bread!

Sometimes, the 'same old' boring slice needs to be brightened up.

- Cut out a toast moon and stars and tuck into scrambled egg clouds.
- Use gingerbread cutters to make bread people and let the child use sandwich toppings of his or her choice to dress the food 'family'.
- Make striped cheese toast by alternating strips of white mozzarella, yellow Cheddar and Red Leicester.
- Or play noughts and crosses in a grid of vegetable strips with ketchup counters.
- How about a clockface pizza? Use biscuit cutters to punch the numbers out from coloured peppers, carrot or cheese slices. Add ham hands!
- If you have a steady hand, spell them a pancake message.

Easy Entertaining

Quantities to feed a few or a frenzy; last-minute, super-quick and no-cook ideas; sure-fire recipes for larger groups; conversation-starting afters; serving suggestions for special diets; and economical entertaining options.

■ Which, how many, how much?

379. How many for dinner?

Don't overestimate the number of people you can comfortably seat or cater for.

- For a sit-down dinner, 6–8 people is a comfortable number.
- You can go up to 10 or 12 provided they are family or close friends, willing to pitch in with serving and clearing, or if you have hired help.
- Any more and you should consider a buffet or barbecue instead.

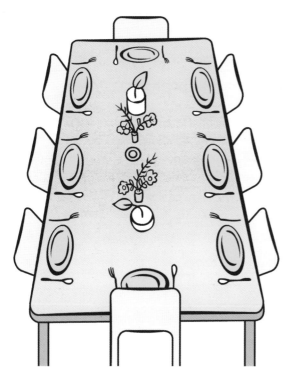

380. Enlist some help!

Whether you're serving a sit-down hot meal, a cold buffet or cocktails and finger food, you can't cook, serve and clear up all by yourself.

- Ask someone else to set the table while you cook, or to top up drinks while you bring out the munchies.
- For a sit-down meal, delegate clearing up and bringing out fresh dishes – if one person has to do both, guests will be waiting a long time between courses!

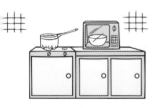

381. A big business

A buffet usually implies a longer guest list. Simplify your prep:

- Should friends offer to do something, accept – and suggest they bring bread (bread, dips or relishes, cheese), cheese, biscuits or salad.
- Roasts, terrines and mince-based pies or curries remove some of the headache of portioning while still looking elegant and eye-catching.
- Avoid steaming hot or frozen cold dishes, especially for dessert – there's no way you can serve 10–12 people at a consistent temperature and it's unfair to make those first served wait until the last serving has been dished out!

382. At the bar

Six people jammed together at the home bar. Too much pressure on the 'bartender'. If you have a larger number of guests, consider setting up more than one bar area.

- For parties of over 12, have two bar stations.
- If the party is in the garden or on the terrace, diagonally opposite corners are a good bet.
- If you open up more than one room, a single bar will mean traffic snarls! Put a bar station in each room.

383. Red or white?

Serving wine? How many different types should you buy?

- If it's just wine and nibbles, stop at two or three. Choose red, white and either a rosé or a sparkling wine (or a sparkling rosé!).
- Alternatively, offer two whites and a red.
- If you're serving a variety of drinks at a summer party, you could skip the red – fewer people will opt for it.
- What to serve with meat if not red? Ask at the wine shop. Some of the bolder New World whites partner gamey flavours well.

384. Hot or cold?

Don't try to cook fresh or reheat everything to piping hot for more than 10–12 guests.

- If you're doing a buffet, offer hot and cold dishes in equal proportions.
- Or have just one or two (one vegetarian) freshly cooked dishes with cold accompaniments.
- Or go for a cold fork buffet.
- You can serve a hot dessert following a cold buffet, although, on a hot day, people will probably be glad to have something cold.
- For canapés, alternate cold and hot. (Send out the first two nibbles almost simultaneously; then appear with each subsequent one at twenty-minute intervals.)

385. How much each?

A rough guide of dinner party portions for a typical adult:

- Main course fish or meat, bone-in cuts or steaks – about 225 g/8 oz.
- Fish or meat as starters, or cut into boneless goujons, or served as pâté or terrine – about 85–115 g/3–4 oz.
- Rice or pasta – 1 cup
- Bread – 2 large slices or 2 small rolls
- Salad – 150 g/5½ oz
- Vegetables – 150 g/5½ oz
- Dips, dressings and sauces – 2–3 teaspoons each
- Fruit or pudding – ½ cup, 1 medium whole fruit (small apple, medium peach or large kiwi) or mini muffin-sized portions of individual puddings.
- Drinks through the evening (pre-dinner and with meals) – 2–3 glasses wine or cocktails, 3–4 whiskeys or glasses of punch, 3–5 shots of spirits or liqueur, plus mixers.

386. Dinner and drinks

If you're serving drinks before dinner:

- Don't offer more than 3–4 types of nibbles. A single crowd-pleaser is fine if dinner will have a few courses.
- Serving just one snack? Keep it vegetarian, and free of common allergens (avoid nuts!).
- Allow about an hour before serving dinner, but never delay more than 2 hours from the start of the party.

387. Noodles for all the neighbours

Adapting pasta recipes is easy.

- Allow 75 g/2¾ oz dried pasta (125 g/4½ oz fresh) per person.
- If you're cooking for a big crowd, test whether the pasta is al dente several minutes *before* the recommended cooking time – and stop when close. A big batch of pasta keeps cooking for a bit, even after draining, because heat is held in.

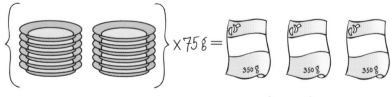

(1050 g)

388. Gobstoppers!

Or 'What Not to Serve' to prevent conversation-halting bad breath! For an even remotely formal lunch or where in-laws, clients or colleagues are involved, *avoid*:

- Pickled onions
- Radish
- Sauerkraut
- Garlicky dips (roasted garlic – *see Tip 267* – is fine, though)
- Hardboiled eggs (except a little as a garnish)
- Stinky tofu or dried prawns (and most other fermented foods and dried fish or seafood)
- Highly scented tropical fruits such as Hawaiian noni and Southeast Asian durian; even pawpaw can be a bit much for some.

If you must serve these, pass around some strong mints after the meal!

389. No-ice impasse

If you are preparing ahead for a large dinner party, you will need your freezer to be as empty as possible for the make-ahead dishes, so you may not have room for ice trays!

- Hire a small freezer, make the ice well ahead and bag it up for transfer, or borrow a neighbour's freezer space!
- Alternatively, buy ice cubes on the day.

390. Picnic packs

Having a picnic? Bring along a couple of hand towels to supplement serviettes.

- They are handier for mopping up.
- You can moisten them with water to clean sticky fingers.
- They're much more eco-friendly than wet wipes.
- On the other hand, baby wipes are better against stains (*see Tip 691*)!

391. Al fresco extras

You've got the food and drinks, but you should also have:

- A large bin liner for disposing of debris
- A bottle of soda water in case of spills (to wash out stains)
- A first-aid kit
- Insect repellent
- Sunscreen
- A large plastic sheet – to sit on if the ground is damp and as protection in case of a sudden shower.

■ The bar's a breeze!

392. Cocktail by the carafe

Unless a professional bartender is present, it's best to dispense with a long drinks list for large parties.

- Serve no more than three kinds of liquor – red, white and sparkling wine; beer, rum and coke; or just a single flavoured vodka.
- Or serve one stellar seasonal drink – sangria or punch in summer, mulled wine or egg nog in winter.
- Provide a non-alcoholic alternative.
- If you're hell-bent on having a signature cocktail, stick to that (plus its teetotaller version).
- When choosing a party cocktail, it's better to opt for a blended rather than a layered drink. You can keep it ready mixed in a jug, then pour and decorate fast.

393. Quick-chill champagne

Haven't time to put your whites and sparkling wines in the refrigerator before company arrives?

- Put the bottles in a plastic bag and tie off before plunging into an ice chest or a bucket of iced water for 10 minutes.

This protects the label and keeps the bottle dry for a non-slip grip as you pop the cork!

394. Flat bubbly?

As you pour out the champagne, half the glasses instantly lose their fizz! The rest are fine. What's wrong?

- If you washed them in the dishwasher, traces of detergent may have attached themselves to your flutes – that's what killed the bubbles!
- Rinse glasses well by hand and wipe dry with a clean tea towel to avoid this.

395. Punch with no punch

For underage guests and designated drivers amongst your guests, make up a non-alcoholic fruit punch.

- Spike a 1-litre/1¾-pint jug of ginger ale with the juice of 4 lemons, a couple of oranges, a couple of grapefruit and a can of pineapple. Serve chilled, with an ice ring (set in a ring cake tin or aspic mould).

■ Nifty nibbles

396. Swift sticky sausages

It's the humble sausage to the rescue for trouble-free entertaining:

- Roll cocktail-sized sausages in Thai sweet chilli sauce and grill until well browned. Make lots – about 6–8 each per guest – and don't bother about other bites for an hour-long party!
- For a longer do, wrap very thinly-sliced bread around each sausage before grilling to add substance!

397. Under wraps

These clever cocktail snacks are easily wrapped up:

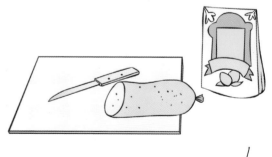

- Strips of Parma ham around breadsticks (grissini) or asparagus.
- Spicy salami slices around a sweet bite – prunes, perhaps?
- Cheese wrapped in bacon slices and zapped in a medium oven for 5 minutes.

398. Salmon on the hoof

Smoked salmon is a lovely starter for a sit-down meal – with just a dollop of crème fraîche, a grind of pepper, some dill and a few capers. This can be translated into a manageable snack for serving with drinks.

- Roll slices of salmon around a dollop of peppered cream cheese with mustard.
- Pop a caper inside.

399. Cheesy cucumber boats

These cheese and chutney canoes make a refreshing and unusual bite!

- Get thin-skinned baby cucumbers, bite-sized, if possible.
- Split lengthways and hollow out in the middle.
- Add a few cubes of diced cheese and a fruit preserve or jelly. Quince goes with most cheese; try a hot mango chutney with a blue cheese.

401. Enoki in obi

An easy and impressive snack that's halfway between sushi and a bacon roll!

- Warm some strips of bacon in the microwave oven.
- Wrap a small bundle of enoki mushrooms in each bacon strip.
- Cut the bundles in two, splitting the bacon strips.
- You now have one set of enoki heads with a bacon ribbon around the end, and another slimline bacon roll 'stuffed' with the ends of the mushrooms.
- Serve with wasabi mayonnaise or a honey-mustard dip.

400. Not pineapple with cheese on sticks

Sticks of cheese with pineapple too retro? Try a twist on an old theme.

- Start with a mature hard cheese.
- Make up on cocktail sticks with quartered fresh figs, diced mangoes, dried apricots or prunes.
- Add a dribble of honey or sweet chilli sauce.

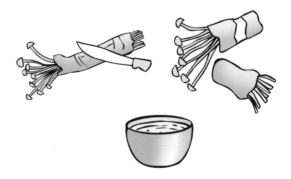

403. 'You're the life of the party'

Got a mixed group of friends not mutually acquainted over for coffee?

- Pass around a box of fortune cookies to liven things up and break the ice.

402. Help party animals 'jell'

Pass around an 'adult' version of jelly shots for a barbecue or poolside do.

- Dissolve jelly crystals in a solution of 2 parts water and 1 part vodka, white wine or white rum.
- Use small ramekins or tumblers to set individual portions.
- When partly set, add some grapes, berries or sliced fruit – kiwi, starfruit or kumquats; avoid pineapple as it interferes with setting.
- Leave them a little jiggly for bar-style shots.

■ Superior sides

404. On the side

Choose side dishes for ease and speed.

- Mix together a green salad to go with a hearty main course such as roast vegetables or a casserole. If it's summer, crisp leaves dressed with vinaigrette is sufficient. For winter, try bacon lardons or slices of salami with wilted spinach; for vegetarians, exchange the meat for bits of onion and roasted almonds.
- With fish, sausages, burgers or a ham, consider a side of mixed roasted vegetables (*see Tip 269*) so you won't have to do potatoes, rice or pasta separately.
- Need a lighter vegetable? Try leeks, fennel or escarole in chicken stock and cream gratinéed with Parmesan cheese and breadcrumbs.
- Crisp greens such as Brussels sprouts, broccoli or green beans can be quickly blanched to seal the colour, then warmed through before serving with fried garlic slices, pancetta or toasted nuts and a pinch of cumin seeds.
- When you have a rich meaty main course, consider serving a fruit compôte or pan-fried apples or pears instead of a dish of vegetables plus gravy or cream sauces.

405. Posh jackets

Yes, you can tart up the humble jacket potato!

- Halve the potatoes – they'll cook faster too.
- Cut a cross in the flesh of the cut side and bake skin side down.
- Scoop out some of the centre and mash it with your filling. Pile it all back in.
- Update the fillings too. Instead of tuna salad, try salmon or smoked haddock. Instead of baked beans, use Puy lentils and celery. Substitute grilled Mediterranean vegetables for coleslaw.
- Drizzle with a few classy condiments – salsa with sweetcorn, capers and soured cream with the fish, pesto on the vegetables…

406. Peas or potatoes?

You might think you're adding a 'vegetable' when you serve a dish of peas along with the potatoes. Blame it on their colour!

- Peas – like beans – are high enough in carbohydrates to substitute for the potatoes!
- Choose another vegetable instead.
- Serve either peas *or* potatoes as the carb-rich staple.
- If you can't give up either with the traditional Sunday roast, pass on the bread basket.

407. Layered fans

Make a basic dish of baked Mediterranean vegetables special by interleaving the vegetables in a 'fan'.

- Line the base of your baking tin with sliced onions and crushed garlic seasoned with crushed coriander and herbes de Provence.
- Slice aubergines or a large plump courgette lengthways, with the stem end left intact, so that they resemble folded Japanese fans.
- Tuck slices of tomatoes or strips of red pepper between the 'blades' and lay on the bed of onions.
- Fill any gaps with bay leaves and mushrooms, olives, fennel, artichoke or other succulent vegetables.
- Add another layer of onions and garlic before drizzling with olive oil.
- Cover and bake at 190°C/375°F/Gas Mark 5 until the vegetables are tender.

408. Hot and hearty

This fantastic vegetable dish looks impressive and doesn't demand much from the cook.

- Dice any winter vegetables to hand – potatoes, sweet potatoes, pumpkin, carrots, parsnips – into 1-cm/½-inch pieces.
- Add diced onions and whole cloves of garlic.
- A couple of red peppers or a bunch of tomatoes will add a succulent texture as well as colour, but don't worry if you don't have any.
- Pile into a large roasting tin and mix in a handful of rosemary, salt, a little balsamic vinegar and olive oil.
- Bake for about 30 minutes at 190°C/375°F/ Gas Mark 5.
- Stir in a can of beans or chickpeas and bake another 20 minutes.
- To make this a posh vegetarian alternative to the standard roast main course, add a grating of good Parmesan cheese or pecorino cheese, mixed with 2 spoonfuls of soured cream, at the end.
- For vegans, top with toasted pine kernels and other seeds instead of cheese.

409. Full head

This makes a lovely vegetable-rich centrepiece for a special dinner.

- Remove any blemished outer leaves from a whole head of cabbage and trim the stem so it 'sits' stable.
- Simmer the whole head in salted water for 10–15 minutes, or until the outer leaves have become supple enough to bend without breaking off.
- When cool enough to handle, place on a large piece of muslin before pulling back the outer leaves to expose the heart.
- Cut out the heart and finely chop. Sauté with cooked rice, bits of ham and peas, seasoning to taste.
- Press this mixture back into the cabbage and fold the outer leaves back into place.
- Bard the cabbage with bacon strips and tie up the muslin.
- Bake in the oven till a skewer passes readily through the toughest area, at the base.
- Lift into a bowl or pudding basin, untie the muslin, place a soup plate over it and upend to transfer to the plate.

■ Elegant extras

410. Better butter

Whether for topping a barbecued steak or garnishing the mashed potatoes, herb butter looks deceptively posh. It's hardly any trouble at all, though.

- Just whiz about 2 bunches of fresh herbs – chives, parsley, coriander or mint – with 75 g/ 2¾ oz butter in a food processor for a couple of minutes. When you see the herbs floating around in bits, it's ready.
- Now place pats of it in the middle of rectangles of greaseproof paper or freezer-safe foil.
- Roll up sausage fashion, twisting the ends like a bonbon to seal.
- Chill until needed – or freeze several rolls for long-term use.
- Slice or dice into a cold dish to serve.

411. Stars for your steak, posies for your toast

No butter stamper to personalize your pats?

- Use little petit four cookie cutters or Playdoh stamps to shape and chill butter on a flat tray or baking sheet. Tumble into a chilled dish just before serving. A galaxy with your bread basket – impressive!

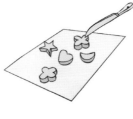

412. A drizzle to garnish

Weight-watchers and those avoiding saturated fats won't be too pleased with the flavoured butters (*see Tip 410*). Try this fresher, more modern take on garnish-with-extra-flavour.

- Mix powdered spices or chopped herbs (you can thaw the ones from *Tip 298*) into a good extra virgin olive oil – cumin and chilli make a lovely pep-up, as do mint or coriander leaves.
- Drizzle over pasta, cooked fish or chicken, even float a little on soups or smear on croûtons. It's nice on pizzas too.
- Consider a hint of fruity olive oil over puddings and fruit salad instead of a thick creamy sauce or custard. Flavour with scraped vanilla pods, a pinch of cinnamon or some lemon zest (*see Tip 162*).

413. Bitter sweets

Decoration for fresh fruit and desserts needn't always be fruity or sweet! Sharp spices and herbs can be an unexpectedly deep counterpoint.

- Sprinkle chilli powder on chocolate mousse.
- Serve melons or citrus fruit with a grinding of fresh pepper.
- Dredge churros and waffles with paprika and sugar rather than cinnamon-sugar!
- Offer celery salt with intensely sweet fruits such as mango or pawpaw.
- Consider a little roasted and powdered cumin on poached or stewed fruits.

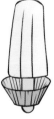

414. Sweeten for savour

A judicious hint of sweetness can uplift savoury classics to fresh heights.

- Scatter lavender instead of mint on roasting lamb.
- Tuck dried rose buds under the skin of a roasting chicken and baste with honey and yogurt.
- Add half a teaspoon of ground cinnamon and/or a grating of nutmeg to lentil soups.
- Pumpkin pie spice is good in creamy winter soups too, even cauliflower!
- Add a spoonful of sugar to pumpkin risotto.
- Extra sugar enhances the natural sweetness of carrots and peas.
- Honey, like chutney, is good with anything involving cheese!
- Add melon chunks and strawberries to summer salads.
- A few squares of plain chocolate can do wonders for a root-vegetable casserole as well as for spicy meat curries.
- Mix some aniseed paste with the potatoes!
- Complement coconut milk in curries with raisins.
- Marmalade is fantastic on fish!

■ Sweet (or savoury!) endings

415. Drip-free lollies

Ice lollies are easy favourites. But they do get messy as they melt…

- Push the stick through a foil muffin cup, paper doily or coffee filter to catch the drips!

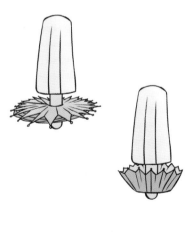

416. Three pretty meringues

Ready-made meringues double as coffee companions and dessert starters – always have some on hand. For a quick sweet treat:

- Sandwich meringues together with a filling of 2 parts whipped cream and 1 part each of mascarpone cheese and lemon curd.
- Roll sideways in flaked almonds so they stick to the filling.
- Serve with some juicy soft fruit – berries or mangoes, or perhaps a few chocolate-dipped cherries.
- Chill liqueur-laced cream in individual cocktail glasses and float a meringue on top.
- Cave in the peak of individual meringues with a quick, light knock from the wrong end of a spoon.
- Add a teaspoon of chopped fresh fruit in the hollows.
- Pipe a swirl of sweetened whipped cream on top and drizzle some puréed berries (fresh or frozen), strained persimmons or crushed pineapple bits on top.

417. Supermarket special!

When you've no time for a homemade pudding and store-bought will look too tacky, buy:

- A rich chocolate loaf cake
- 250 ml/9 fl oz double cream
- A jar of dulce du leche or toffee sauce
- A can of sweetened chestnut purée
- A small bottle of coffee or chocolate liqueur or syrup
- Split the cake into 3 layers and sprinkle each with a tablespoon of liqueur.
- Whisk the cream to get soft peaks.
- Mix together the can of chestnut purée, 125 ml/ 4 fl oz dulce du leche and a spoon of liqueur.
- Fold in the cream.
- Sandwich the cake layers with this mixture and top with some grated chocolate or chocolate flakes.

Pipe a pattern in toffee sauce on top – or just drizzle over. Serve in thin slices.

418. Panettone perfection

A high-domed loaf of panettone makes an impressive sculptural gâteau.

- Slice the panettone into three horizontal layers.
- Spread the bottom and middle layers with some whipped mascarpone cheese flavoured with fruit liqueur or grated plain chocolate.
- Add chopped fruit and sandwich together.
- Sprinkle icing sugar and decorate with a sprig of herbs (mint or rosemary go beautifully) or a few edible flowers (nasturtiums, roses or violets).

Voilà! A stunning centrepiece that you can eat after dinner!

419. It's a snip

The quickest cake covering ever, whatever the shape.

- Cover the top and sides with whipped cream – don't bother smoothing.
- Press chocolate curls along the edges to make a ruffled trim. (You can make the curls by pulling a swivel-bladed peeler along the smooth back of a chocolate bar at room temperature.)
- Fill the centre with a pile of fresh berries and serve.

420. Lighten up the fruitcake

Unless it's Christmas, a dense fruitcake covered in fondant icing is too much.

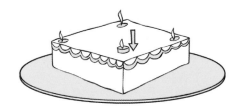

- Lighten up on the icing or forgo it altogether.
- Decorate by pressing in blanched almonds – you can write a message with the nuts, or pattern a swirly design instead.
- Or wreath it in light alone. For candles, try tea lights set in little tins. An appropriate number on the cake's surface will double up as decoration.
- Big-number birthday? An age cake is perfect for more mature years. Pass up the candle-blowing, and stick in the appropriate number of sparklers instead!

421. Candle savers

Dripping wax from the birthday candles can mess up those sugar roses. Save the day by using little props for your candles.

- Slices of marshmallow, Turkish delight or liquorice allsorts make good taper stands, if you're happy to sacrifice some.
- So do ring-shaped sweets.
- You can also make little foil flowers to collect the drips – cut out 4-cm / 1½-inch flower shapes; place on the cake and press candles into the centres. When done, lift off the candles, let the wax congeal, then peel away the foil and discard.

422. Stained-glass shards

Here's an artistic garnish for puddings or ice cream.

- Line a baking sheet with foil and grease.
- Line up several identical greased biscuit cutters on the tray.
- Drop 2–3 small boiled sweets into each cutter.
- Put them in a low oven for about 5 minutes, or until the sweets melt into puddles.
- Leave to cool and peel off foil.
- You can use a tart tin with a removable base for a large sheet. Break into shards to stick upright into a sundae or soufflé – at the last minute or it'll melt away!
- Or use assorted colours melted together to make a 'tabletop' cake topper, piping royal icing around the circumference to anchor in place.
- Consider decorative shapes too, using metal biscuit cutters as moulds.

423. Fruitier toppers

Whether you're serving a ready-made cake or want a quick dress-up for your homemade one, some ideas:

- Use a potato peeler to take the peel off a large orange or lemon in one continuous strip. Loop the curls in a clump on a honey-glazed tea loaf.
- Cut the thinnest slices you can from the centres of whole apples and whole pears, peel and stem still in place. The cross-sections should be vertically down (along the core) for pears and horizontally through the apples. Lay alternate slices, overlapped, along the rim of a cake. Drizzle with melted preserves or ice cream topping.
- Cut slim wedges from unpeeled pears or pineapple rings. Cut inch-deep slits on the surface of an un-iced cake. Push the wedges in carefully so that the narrow end sticks up sail fashion.

424. Sugarcrust surprise

Here's a cheat to making that lovely crunch on top of a crème brûlée.

- Lay a sheet of foil on a baking sheet and brush oil on it in ramekin-sized circles.
- Sprinkle an even layer of brown sugar inside the circle – don't worry, it doesn't have to be very regular in shape.
- Place under a hot grill for 2–3 minutes or until caramelized.
- Leave to cool before peeling up carefully.
- Top a custard pudding in a ramekin – just before serving, or the disc might melt!

425. Citrus fluff

This refreshing dessert makes a cloud-light impression on your guests.

- Loosen some good quality lemon curd with passion fruit pulp.
- Mix together equal parts sweetened whipped cream and Greek-style yogurt.
- Layer the two in a shot glass, add some toasted shredded coconut on top, and serve at once.

426. Pears in ponchos

For something stunningly posh yet effortless, wrap peeled and cored pears (stem on) in puff pastry.

- Cut small squares of puff pastry for the pears to sit on.
- Glaze with some jam and place on a lightly greased baking sheet, then sit the pears on them. You can even add a chopped chocolate, cream cheese or chestnut purée core.
- Roll out as many larger squares – the length of the sides should be about the height of the pears.
- Cut a little diamond out of the centre of each and slip over the stem of each pear to drape like a poncho.
- With a sharp pastry knife or scissors, snip the edges for a tasselled 'fringe'.
- Bake till the pastry crisps up.

427. Custard with crunch

Make a plain custard tart special by adding your own secret topping!

- Line the rim with a ring of dried apple or pineapple slices.
- Or use crystallized flowers – violets, pansies or rose petals brushed with egg white and pressed gently into fine sugar.
- Or scatter with little lozenge shapes cut out of angelica or citrus peel.
- How about a simple scattering of orangettes – those chocolate-covered strips of tangerine peel?
- Elegant enough for a party: a line of after dinner chocolate mints, each topped by a maraschino cherry.

428. Tart transfer

Individual tartlets are chic and easy – but can be messy to cart around if the filling is oozy or crumbly. So what to do when friends request your signature mushroom tart for their barbecue?

Turn them into pielets!

- Start with double the amount of pastry specified in the recipe.
- Instead of tart cases, use baking sheets.
- Pretend you're going to make mini calzones – cut out rounds of dough, fill and fold into crescents.
- Or cut squares to fold into 'fingers'.
- Otherwise, sandwich the filling between two circles. Brush the edges with water and crimp the edges with a fork to seal.
- Or stamp out the dough with biscuit cutters in an apt shape – from gingerbread people for a reunion to a cottage to welcome a new neighbour, to stars for a summer dance…

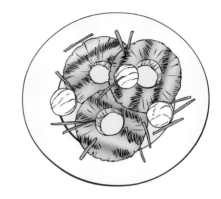

429. Cheese course… or fruit?

Why not both? Serve a two-in-one dessert/savoury course of fruit with cheese, plus a herb or spice. Try:

- Juicy pears with a Stilton and walnut ball filling in for the core.
- Cubed watermelon topped with crumbled feta cheese and fresh mint.
- Sliced apple and Cheddar cheese, with a sprinkling of cinnamon sugar and raisins.
- Fresh figs stuffed with goat's cheese and thyme or lavender honey.
- Pulped mangoes with a grinding of pepper and Parmesan tuiles.
- Grilled pineapple garnished with preserved ginger slices and dolloped with ricotta cheese.
- Lychees hiding a small blob of chilli- and cumin-marinated mozzarella cheese balls in the centre.

430. Pizza finish

Stun your guests by following a grilled main course with a pizza!

- Top the pizza with torn up pieces of a ripe Brie or Camembert and halved green and red grapes.
- Brush with olive oil and bake.
- Serve with a glaze of melted bitter marmalade.
- Alternatively, try Roquefort or Stilton with pears and walnuts, garnished with rosemary dipped in honey.
- Or shredded Gruyère, Cheddar cheese or provolone with prosciutto and figs, served with port.

431. Lite-est libations

Anyone watching their weight? Offer a choice of lower-calorie drinks that won't starve their sweet tooth.

- For those happy to drink alcohol, but looking for a healthier mixer than cola or canned juices, offer one of the many fruit-flavoured waters now available.
- As a non-alcoholic alternative to champagne, try a flavoured sparkling water.

432. Gluten-free canapés

A finger-food base other than the predictable rice cakes if your guest is allergic to gluten?

- 5-cm/2-inch chunks of cucumber from which a hollow has been scooped out with a melon baller.
- A thin ½-inch slice of cucumber or courgette is a good alternative to toast.
- Crisp endive leaves.
- Asparagus spears, celery sticks or roasted spears of parsnip.

Make sure you dry the vegetables well before assembling and serve soon, lest they go limp.

433. Meat-free menaces!

Anyone on a red meat-free diet for medical reasons? When providing a meatless menu for them, be careful that you don't add a lot of dairy instead – although cheese may seem to be a logical swap, it's full of saturated fat.

- Substitute with lean meat or nuts, or simply with lots of vegetables and beans.
- Or see if using a low-fat cheese or yogurt will allow you to tweak a meat recipe.

434. Sugar-free sweetness

For those avoiding sugar for health reasons, offer a sweet beverage free of synthetic chemical additives.

- Brew coffee and tea with a small cinnamon stick or a vanilla pod, or offer one as a stirrer – most people find they don't miss the sugar with these added 'dessert' flavourings.
- A crushed cardamom pod or a grating of nutmeg can have the same effect.
- Sometimes, spice can reduce the need for sweetness! Chilli with cinnamon in hot cocoa, a pinch of pepper on fresh fruit, or a little fresh ginger in tea...
- Use fruit purées to sweeten puddings (apple sauce can also substitute for fats in many cakes and baked confectionery).
- Instead of fizzy drinks, offer water (plain or sparkling) with just a splash of natural fruit juice.
- Instead of flavoured, pre-sweetened fruit yogurts, offer natural Greek-style yogurt with honey and fresh fruit on the side that guests can help themselves to.

435. Spare the salt cellar

For those on a low-sodium diet, stock up on:

- Low-sodium salt, as long as it's approved by your doctor.
- Highly flavoured herbs and pungent spices – including garlic, turmeric, chilli or paprika, pepper, ginger, oregano, parsley, coriander, tamarind.
- Lime juice.
- Sodium-reduced or salt-free meat stocks.

■ All about afters

436. Coffee companions

There's nothing wrong with offering a basic chocolate treat with an after-dinner espresso.

- Make a tiny extra effort, though – remove the wrappers and perch one on each saucer rather than passing the box around.
- Slip in a cinnamon stick for stirring the coffee.

Now that's elegant.

437. Water-free chocolate

Why not serve a cup of luxury hot chocolate instead of pudding, then coffee?

- Melt together 200 g/7 oz dark chocolate in 250 ml/8½ fl oz cream in the microwave oven , at just under full power.
- Add a spoonful of the chocolate cream to each cup and top up with steaming milk.
- Sprinkle with cinnamon or coffee, or have a shaker of vanilla sugar to hand.
- Offer shortbread or strawberries with this.

438. Hot milk spiced up

Another decadent after-dinner drink. This one's a great liquid lullaby for guests who will be staying overnight. It's also the perfect palate soother after a spicy meal.

- Heat 1 litre/1¾ pints milk with a couple of cinnamon sticks, and 3–4 (each) cloves and cardamom pods.
- Leave to stand for a couple of minutes to infuse, discard the spices (*see Tip 192*) and serve.
- Decorate with flaked pistachio nuts and stem ginger, or sprinkle just 2–3 strands of saffron on each frothing cup.
- Ginger nuts are perfect with this.

■ Quickest courses

439. Dinner in a dash

Unannounced dinner guests? No time to shop?

- Some pasta or potatoes, or even a more exotic grain like couscous or basmati rice, is easy to cook on the side.
- The fastest dinner-plate anchor is a piece of grilled meat or fish.
- For vegetarians who are happy to eat eggs, an omelette is the perfect option.
- For strict vegans, consider a stew of canned lentils or beans and quick-cooking vegetables simmered in coconut milk and curry paste.
- Steam some green vegetables or mix up a green salad or easy salsa of chopped tomatoes, chillies, coriander and peppers.
- Garnish the meat or fish with a special homemade sauce – *see Tip 440*.
- For dessert, crumble some biscuits or cake into vanilla ice cream, or drop scoops of ice cream into espresso for an indulgent *affogato*.

440. Salsa-fy!

A dish of boiled macaroni, a slice of bought pizza or hamburger patty can all be 'fancified' with a really good sauce.

- Make your own pesto – food processors, mortar and pestle or even chopping ingredients finely by hand will do. You'll want 55 g/2 oz nuts to every 2 handfuls of herbs and a good olive oil to loosen, plus a proper Parmesan cheese to grate over.
- Roasted peppers and/or tomatoes, peeled and mashed with garlic, perhaps a chilli and a couple of herbs are even easier to throw together.
- If you've got a tropical fruit or some avocado, chop it up and mix with some sliced red onions or chillies, some cucumbers and either lemon juice or crème fraiche for a quick salsa. You can even purée this and serve as a dip.
- Jazz up some plain butter by folding in chopped capers or green peppercorns in brine, a little sharp English mustard, and a few sprigs of any fresh herb you've got.
- Chopped fruit, fresh or canned, can be simmered with any pan juices and a splash of wine to make a fruity relish.

441. Cheese first?

Super-short on time? Bring the cheese course up front and skip the soup!

- Pare down the courses to nibbles, one main dish and a pudding.
- Cook just the main course yourself – roasted balsamic vegetables (*see Tip 269*) mixed with beans or grilled farm-style sausages is just fine.
- For the rest, buy good quality basics that won't need dressing up.
- Get a good artisan cheese and a couple of different kinds of bread – one fancy (such as foccacia or similar), one plain (ciabatta or baguette).
- Serve the plainer bread with cheese and wine by way of a starter.
- If you still think it needs bolstering, a cheese such as feta or mozzarella can be marinated in warm olive oil with a few herbs, spices and flavourings (chilli, fennel, garlic, shredded basil and citrus peel are just some options).
- Serve some olives (you can marinate them like the cheese, but warm through together with the oil) and roasted nuts sprinkled with chilli pepper.
- Serve the flavoured bread with your main course.
- For simple, satisfying pudding ideas, *see Tip 442.*

442. Pudding? Done!

- For a summer dessert, opt for peaches (or another soft fruit, such as mango) and ice cream, with a bit of toffee or fruit sauce, or a sprinkling of pistachio nuts.
- In winter, serve pan-fried fruits. You can sprinkle over some wine or liqueur, or serve with custard if you have some.
- Don't ignore the possibility of biscuits for a grown-up sweet! Instead of milk, though, serve with citrus curd and fudge or chocolate ganache (melt chocolate and whip in cream).
- A compôte of fruits garnished with toasted coconut or edible flowers may be all you need.
- Or just serve berries with cream.
- A crumble is quick to make, bakes while you sit down to dinner (*see Tip 274*), and is hugely satisfying.

■ Off-peak party hours!

443. Affordable entertaining

Rather than counting the costs of every dish when you're entertaining on a budget, look to adjust the basic plan.

- When resources are limited, veer away from dinner or elaborate luncheons.
- Alcohol is a money-guzzler. If a toast to the occasion seems a must, restrict it to a cocktail evening rather than doing dinner *and* drinks. With a mid-grade champagne or a sparkling wine or prosecco you wouldn't need other options.
- Revive the old-fashioned afternoon tea. Keep it light – don't turn it into high tea!
- For close friends, family or business associates, meet for breakfast.
- Get together with friends for coffee after a night at the theatre or an art show – chances are they will have eaten before or nibbled during. Serve a few pastries, a sweet wine, brandy or liqueur, and of course coffee, tea and a choice of biscuits.
- For a smaller number, a picnic is always fun.

445. Chill-out picnic

You start out with chilled drinks and cold food, but by the time you sit down to it, the food's at room temperature. On a hot summer's day, this is an invitation for bacteria to thrive.

- If you're packing any liquids, freeze them in small watertight containers.
- Distribute these throughout your hamper to keep other foods cold, making sure everything is in water-resistant packaging (so they don't get soggy as the frozen foods 'sweat').
- Alternatively, put a Thermos flask of ice cubes in the middle and pack food around it.
- Bunches of grapes that start out frozen will be just nicely chilled for lunchtime.
- Oh, and carry that hamper with you in the car – it's too hot in the boot!

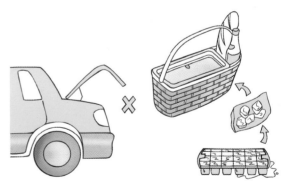

444. Breakfast fruit for a queen

Pawpaws aren't just good, they're great – chockful of vitamins and other antioxidants, fragrant and sweet, plus easy to prepare. And filling enough for a breakfast 'main'. Add a zingy syrup for special-occasion garnish.

- Boil up some syrup with lime juice and zest. Add a sprinkling of orange flower water or rosewater.
- Drizzle over pawpaw slices, add a grind of pepper and garnish with some edible flowers – white or blue look stunning on their sunset hue.

446. Sushi tonight?

To minimize your prep, why not get together for sushi?

- Put together individual bento boxes from your local sushi bar. Let that be the star of the menu.
- For appetizers, avoid tempura; try steamed edamame or spiced nuts (*or see Tip 401*).

- Offer miso soup on the side – made from a mix, garnished with chopped spring onions and tofu.
- Cold soba noodles tossed with toasted sesame seeds, light soy sauce and honey will satisfy anyone still hungry.
- For afters, serve fresh fruit, tea or sorbet.

Setting the Table

A place for every family member and guest, appropriate to every meal – from casual family dinners to formal luncheons; conversation-stopping table décor: centrepieces, flowers and candles given a fresh slant too

■ *Lively linens!*

447. Cute cutters!

Taking a little trouble over the table linen will add a sense of occasion.

- Roll up serviettes and thread through biscuit cutters.
- Add savoury biscuits in the same shape to the cheeseboard or serve sweet ones as petits fours.
- Give each guest a little bagful. Dangle one out of the bag on ribbon – pipe on the guest's name; they double up as gift tag and place card!

449. Old lace updates

Put crochet doilies and vintage lace to a new use.

- Sandwich a doily between dinner plate and charger or the decorative underplate.
- Add pearl or jet beads to weight the 'rim' and use atop carafes and jugs.
- Link them into a long chain or a floral round – no need to match – for a special table dressing.

448. Soft landing

Thick tablemats will prevent china scratching the table and add tactile pleasure.

- Make your own with plain felt rectangles.
- Paper punches can make a patterned perforated border. Pinch up folds at random points near the margins and punch through with the punch, just edging out beyond the crease to get two interlocked shapes out!

These are particularly handy if you like to stack plates and bowls together at each place setting.

■ A place (setting) for everything

450. To match or mis-match?

When in doubt, resort to bone white – use plain chunky china or stoneware every day. Classic and stylish shapes are good for entertaining too. If you don't have enough of the same type of crockery, resort to a mix. To make it look considered rather than cobbled-together include:

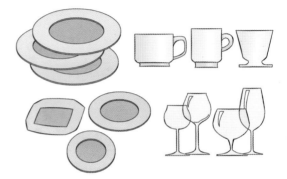

- Several colours in the same shape or several shapes in exactly the same hue.
- Mix no more than two or three shapes and colours for plates, bowls, glasses and cutlery.
- For wine glasses, coffee and teacups, you can go for a wider variety – in which case, each piece can be different! Tell your guests it's to help them remember their glasses.

451. Tots' table

With tots just learning to eat, a mess is inevitable.

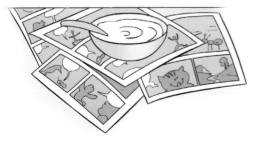

- To protect your best table linen, supply sheets of Sunday comics.
- If you can't do without a tablecloth, choose chocolate brown (hides most stains while suggesting cocoa!)
- Or, use plain white (which will withstand the toughest bleaches).

452. Your glass, or mine?

ID-ing your glass can be quite a challenge at a cocktail do.

- For an informal evening, borrow your daughter's hair bobbles. Make sure they're all different, then slip one onto the stem of each glass.
- For a more formal do, use glass beads on a twist of wire.

453. Buffet in order

Most people put the cutlery at the front, alongside the plates and napkins – and the polished silverware slides about on fine china, getting in the way of food.

- Start with plates and napkins.
- Then offer the main dishes – salads and sides; accompaniments such as bread or pasta or rice come later.
- Put the condiments at the end.
- Have the forks, knives and spoons last.
- Let guests know that the sweet course will be served separately – on a different table or sideboard, or in individual portions along with coffee.
- The cheeseboard should sit on the sweet table.
- Soup gets a table to itself (clear it away and put the pudding there later). Set the bowls out first, then the soup tureen, then spoons.

454. Shakers to the centre

Where does one place the salt, pepper, pickles and relishes?

- For an informal get-together, have just a small set on the sideboard, in the centre on the table or near the hostess. Pass around as needed.
- For anything less casual, the condiments should be clustered in the centre of the table for a party of up to 10. Any more, and you'll need two of everything near the ends of the table.
- Put all the condiments together in a small basket if there are more than two.
- If serving sauces and gravies in boats, dot them around the table, between and close to the main dishes they support.

455. A forest of fir (cones)

For an almost imperishable, yet always remarkable table decoration:

- Fill small tealight holders, larger candlesticks, ramekins and dip bowls with sand.
- Try to choose a single type of material – white china, silvery metal or even foil muffin cups.
- Sit a fir cone in each and line up the container 'forest' in an undulating row down the table.
- You could add a track of gravel or sand beneath to pull it together.

456. Eggs-otic centrepiece?

Asking friends over for brunch? It may be too early to nip down to the flower shop.

- Why not pile some fresh eggs into a wide, squat vase or pretty bowl instead?
- Or put them in an old fashioned basket.
- Don't pile them too deep (prevents messy cracks).
- If you think that looks sparse, add a few fresh herbs or baby vegetables. Or mix brown and speckled shells!
- Baby carrots make a nice counterpoint to the eggs in terms of colour and shape; broccoli florets are sweet too.
- Or have a separate basket or two of mushrooms and/or whole nuts – just make sure you're cooking the mushrooms the same day.
- Or just use some well-washed twigs from the garden.

457. Garden fresh, from the market

Sometimes you want to make a really special impression:

- Scrub some plain terracotta flowerpots and sterilize.
- Dab an appetizing home fragrance or diluted essential oil – apricot, orange, cinnamon, herbs, lavender, vanilla, almond…
- Pile some fruits and nuts into the container with a few spices and herbs that coordinate. Select just one kind or a theme that includes no more than 3–4 ingredients. Your theme may be colour-based or inspired by a favourite dish, or even seasonal – green apples and bay leaves with a few blueberries; peaches and apricots with cinnamon; oranges stuck with cloves.
- Line them along the centre of a long table. Or cluster together in the centre at different heights – stand one on an upturned saucer, another on a small upturned pot, and so on.

458. Frosted fruit

Pressed for time?

- A bowl or platter of mixed fruits can make a fine centrepiece. Add a dusting of icing sugar to make it look special.
- Or you could just tuck in bundles of cinnamon (tie together with kitchen twine or ribbon), some star anise, the odd pine or fir cone, maybe acorns and nuts.
- If you do have a few moments, a bowl of like fruits – pears, say – can be given an identical dab of edible gold or silver leaf each. Brush the spot with egg white, lay on foil to stick!

459. Seating plan, all lit up

For a simple casserole or roast, with a fruit or ice cream dessert, prepare a special table setting – with oranges:

- Use the tip of a vegetable peeler to scrape the peel away in thin curly strips, letting the white show, to 'etch' your guests' initials. Or simply poke in cloves to print their nicknames!
- Sit them in small ramekins (to prevent them rolling over!) and stick a candle in each to have it serve as candleholder. Let the guests light their own. The warm wax will bring out the aroma from the peel. Neat!

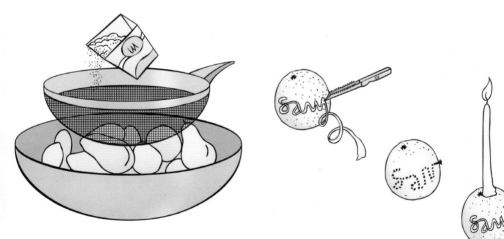

■ Flames and flowers

460. Peppers burning bright

A delicious bit of table décor combines plain tea lights with vegetables.

- Cut the tops off peppers and slip in the tea lights.
- Sit them in small saucers or dip dishes for safety.
- Line up the peppers – all one colour or a regular series.
- Or cluster them together to make a many-petalled flickering flower.

461. Canned flowers!

Use empty food cans for this delightful arrangement.

- Cut vegetable sticks, preferably green, to match the height of the can – unpeeled cucumber, celery, leek leaves, chard stems, stalks of courgette flowers or even the woody ends of asparagus.
- Slip a rubber band around the tin and start tucking in the vegetable sticks until the tin is covered.
- Tie with florists' twine or raffia and remove the rubber band (left on, it might crush the 'stems' as it tightens).
- Fill the tin with water and arrange the flowers.
- Place on a saucer with a splash of water to 'feed' the stalks.
- Colourful flowers look best with green; but if you chose white or blue flowers, a shot of rhubarb red, pepper yellow or carroty orange might yield riveting results.

462. ...Or bottled blooms?

A variant of the idea in *Tip 461* that lets you use fewer flowers over a larger area.

- Select narrow-necked bottles of roughly similar proportions.
- As in *Tip 461*, line the outside of the bottle with slender stems –wild garlic, woody stems of herbs such as thyme or rosemary.
- Secure them to the tapering shape of the bottle with two ties, near the base and beneath the neck.
- Add water and a single delicate flower in each.

463. Teacup full of posies

Another lovely arrangement to complement a summer garden party.

- Use co-ordinating sets of teacups and saucers as 'vases'.
- Nestle some florists' foam into the base of each cup.
- Add flowers and foliage in a tight burst.
- Put a teaspoon on each saucer with a sugar cube on it, or just balance a fragrant teabag against the cup.

Party Planner

Themed ideas for invitations, menu ideas and serving suggestions, occasional dishes, party favours and/or small gifts, and even a cake to match!

■ Organized entertaining

464. Party prep

Good planning means your party will go with a swing!

- Send invites a fortnight to four weeks ahead, depending on numbers and formality.
- State the date, time, venue and dress code.
- Set an RSVP date and provide both email address and telephone number.
- Finish major repairs or cleaning jobs before you tackle food and decorations.
- Check if linen and dishes are clean and cutlery is ship-shape.
- Use place cards to stick to a seating plan.
- For a buffet, dance or cocktail event, figure out the traffic paths and organize furniture accordingly.
- Keep the music ready.

466. Teens? Be seen and not heard

Let teenagers' parties provide practice for adult responsibilities.

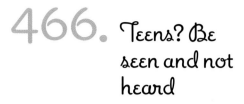

- Lay down the ground rules and help with preparations only if asked; let your child plan it his or her way.
- Discuss arrangements beforehand, though.
- At the party, be seen only occasionally and heard only if sought.
- If you feel things may be getting out of hand, talk to your child quietly. Let him or her try to get things back on track, and intervene only when they give up.
- For food, suggest lots of DIYs for guests – sundaes; customized sandwiches and pizzas; baked potatoes with a variety of fillings; waffles with a dozen toppings; build-your-own canapés.

465. Child-sized choices

Children love choices. And changing their mind! Pay attention to your child's input but remember:

- The younger the child, the fewer the guests.
- Let your child make his or her own invites (with some help).
- For younger children, restrict DIY to garnishing – ice cream toppers, biscuit decorations, relishes for burgers or hot dogs, and dips for crisps.
- Plan the activities yourself. For under-10s, set time limits on each game.
- Unlike with teens, constant adult (or responsible teen sibling) supervision is necessary.

467. Remember my party last summer?

For special occasions and children's parties, mementoes are crucial.

- Take lots of photographs! Arm several people with Polaroid cameras or those disposable cameras you can pick up in the supermarket.
- Try to have one of each guest to take home or send a print later with the 'thank you' note.
- Take time over the party bags. Yes, sweets are a treat, but something that'll last longer will keep memories fresher. Attention span depends on age: balloons for three-year-olds, personalized jack o' lanterns for seven-year-olds, potted pansies for 11-year-olds.

■ Please come to my party!

468. Message in a bottle

Invite friends to a cocktail party with a wine bottle!

- You'll need clean glass bottles (smoky green is mysterious!).
- Write your invitation in a large, bold hand.
- Screw it up, writing outwards, and slip it into the bottle.
- Use glass paints to decorate the bottle.

469. A sparkling do

For a special birthday or pre-wedding party invite, let the cake inspire you!

- Match plain cards to the bride's chosen theme (or the birthday person's favourite colour).
- Make a little stencil of a cake – two tiers for a birthday; three for a bridal shower.
- Cut out paper cake 'appliqués' in white, yellow, brown or pink.
- Pipe glitter glue 'icing' along the tops of the cake tiers.
- Now switch to metallic ink and black pens.
- For a birthday, draw the correct number of candles.
- For a wedding, stick the bride and groom in! Add intertwined hearts on top and write their names within them.

470. Sweet cards!

Great invites to an infant's or toddler's birthday bash, and for birth announcements, baby showers and christenings or naming ceremonies!

- Print or pen a simple message on visiting cards – occasion, date, time, and the appropriate name/s underneath.
- Punch a pair of eyelets at the edge and attach a lollipop with ribbon threaded through.
- Co-ordinate a pastel to a baby's gender or make it colourful for the under-fives.
- Make matching place cards and party bags – centre a sweet on the card or label and write the recipient's name around it.

■ Show a fine theme

471. Spelling wizards to tea

Host a 'School Begins!' or back-to-school party for preschoolers and nursery newbies.

Serve a cold assortment meal:

- Pinwheel sandwiches made by cutting wraps in slices
- Cherry tomatoes and baby carrots
- A carton of frozen yogurt or chilled juice
- A bite-sized biscuit, mini muffin or slice of carrot cake. Pack each portion in a lunchbox and pop it into a small satchel.

The fun bit:

- Spell the child's name on the handle with letter beads on string – scrambled!
- Add some maths? 'Seal' each satchel or lunchbox with luggage locks – coded to open on solving a sum!

472. Barbecue Sunday

A barbecue can liven up a family gathering; no need for a separate children's meal either!

- Make the lunch a sit-down, calm affair.
- Pipe each child's name on a plate in ketchup; use mustard for the grown-ups.
- Serve potato smileys with the meal.
- Have fruit sorbets in cones to round off the meal.

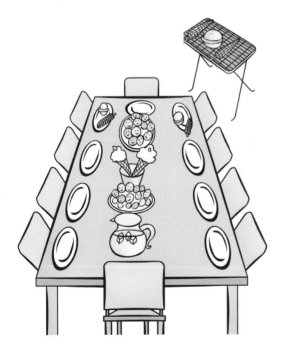

473. Skip to my tune

Outdoors means less wreckage indoors, especially with excited young guests around. Little girls should be thrilled with skipping on the lawn.

You'll need:

- A skipping rope each – look for fun handles; send these with the invite or give as early party favours.
- Sugar-free lemonade.
- Music on a portable CD player or radio.
- A stopwatch and timer for long skips.
- Cold spaghetti and meatballs for lunch.
- Fairy cakes for tea: place loops or coils of liquorice or strawberry lace on each to resemble a skipping rope; add bits of jelly worms for handles.

474. Hula-hooping jamboree

Another active outdoor theme – with hula-hoops!

Serve:

- An assortment of pretzels and bread rings with dips for snacks
- Loopy straws for drinks
- Bagels or spaghetti hoops for lunch
- Grilled pineapple and coconut ice cream for afters.

When they get tired, have flowers – real or silk – to hand to make garlands with. Then some slow music for hula dancing!

475. Bead workshop

Just what little fingers need to stay occupied indoors (Warning: not suitable for under-fives).

- Arrange a 6-cup muffin tray or ice tray for each child.
- Fill each cup (or cube) with a variety of beads, charms, string, wool, ribbon and elastic bands, old buttons and dried pasta shapes (wheels, hollow twists, tubes).
- Let them share alphabet beads.
- Put a tray of supplies where everyone can reach it – fabric glue, fabric scissors (for over-12s), clasps.

Each guest takes home the bracelets or necklaces she made; or the children can do a swap.

476. Dip-your-own sleepover

Pyjama parties mean midnight munchies.

- Keep a big bowl of popcorn with the stack of (parent-policed) DVDs.
- Before leaving the kitchen, lay out muffin trays with age-appropriate nibbles.
- Fill the cups with pretzels, mini biscuits, flavoured yogurt, toffee sauce or dulce de leche, shredded coconut, cereal or rice crispies, crushed nuts, jams or preserves.
- Leave one cup empty and cover each tray with clingfilm, adding the guest's name on a sticky note.
- Add an ice cream scoop with a note to your child permitting <u>one</u> ice cream tub! That's for the empty cup…
- Gift each child a funky little torch – practical and pleasing!

477. Pod-swap party

Teens and tweenies can get together with their favourite tunes and knitting needles! Making cases for each other's MP3 players is super-easy – a rectangle that needs doubling up and sewing along the edges!

You'll need:

- The contents of your old workbasket
- Sequins, jewels, felt patches, braid and trimmings
- A pair of knitting needles apiece; a couple of crochet hooks for the seams and lanyards
- No-drip, no-crumbs snacks: baby carrots and slices of peppers; breadsticks, pitta wedges or pretzels (no messy coatings!); pieces of fruit (not too juicy!), chorizo and cheese on cocktail forks or toothpicks; drumsticks with the ends wrapped in foil; meatballs on cocktail sticks; rice paper parcels (well-sealed!) of dried fruit; fortune cookies…
- Drinks in swig bottles or sippers.
- Music

478. Literary larks

How about a reading session for the budding writers?

- Have your child send each guest a pocket-sized journal and a pen (get different colours of ink for each) – the invitation on page one asks the recipient to compose a small piece to share at the soirée.
- Provide letter-shaped biscuits, ginger beer or hot chocolate.
- To warm up nervous speakers, add fortune-and-fun notes (jokes, challenges, compliments) written on rice paper with edible ink. Fold them small and print names on them (or leave in a lucky-dip bowl), or put out a stack of paper and stand the pens in a beer mug.

479. Spa luncheons

These are great for any gang of girls, young or adult!

- Invite: Gel eye masks or a scented candle with the date and time scribbled on with a marker.
- Dress code: Robes, slippers and a towel – guests can change at your place.
- Goodie bags: Transparent plastic or terry towelling (tip: make from old shower curtains or towels!); fill with hand towels, face mask*, nail polish, nail files, scented oils, rose water, shampoo and lotions.
- Supplies: Cotton wool balls and pads; soothing music CDs; scented candles; hair dryer; curlers and irons.
- Menu: Fruit juices and smoothies; crudités, fingers of rye bread and dips; salads; dried fruits and nuts; fresh fruit and dips.

*Note: Unless you know your friends' individual skin types, stick to basic, hypoallergenic gels or peel-offs.

480. Popcorn and a movie

Gone too long without seeing your best pals?

Organize a Saturday night at your home theatre – with the children asleep!

- Serve popcorn in cartons.
- Serve fruit juice or sparkling water in bright plastic tumblers with a twirly straw.

■ Pat-a-perfect-cake

481. Alien celebration

The easiest 'shape cake' must be the spaceship!

- Bake the cake – a sturdy Madeira – in a pudding basin.
- Upend it to serve.
- Cover with ready-roll icing.
- Decorate with sweet shapes in different colours.
- For tentacles and antennae, stick in liquorice, fruit laces or lollipop.
- Sprinkle on some fizzing sugar candy or paint with food glitter for the 'metallic' effect.
- Cover the cakeboard in dark blue icing and cut out stars, moons and a few clouds.
- Or fashion it as a landing site with almond rocks, chocolate-chip gravel and brown-sugar 'sand'.

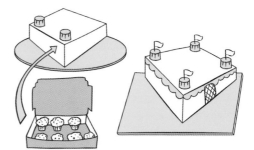

482. Crowning castle

Another super-easy cake is a castle.
- No need to bake specially – buy a square chocolate cake and a box of muffins.
- Cover each cake separately in ready-roll icing (upending the muffins) and assemble the smaller ones on top of the square to make towers.
- Line up mini marshmallows to crenellate the battlements!
- Use a large chocolate wafer for a drawbridge – cut out the entry. Stick on with jam or melted chocolate.
- Add chocolate stick flagpoles and make flags from icing or fruit leather pieces.
- Make the turrets from sliced Swiss rolls.

483. Fairy cakes? No, a princess party!

Another straight-from-the-supermarket idea.

- Get enough fairy cakes, a little frosting or butter cream and some pastel-coloured ready-roll icing. Buy some red or purple sugar (or liquid food colouring) and assorted hundreds-and-thousands or sugar sprinkles.
- Peel off the paper cases, turn over the cakes and cover in frosting.
- Colour the sugar and sprinkle on top.
- Roll out the icing and cut into strips twice as wide as the width of your cakes.
- Using a biscuit cutter or the back of a large piping nozzle, scallop one edge of each strip.
- With dabs of melted chocolate on a cocktail stick and tweezers to pick up the sugar sprinkles, decorate the straight edge of the strips.
- If you have stamps for decorative shapes, use the nozzle to cut out those shapes from the middle of the icing strip.
- Let dry before cutting the strips into lengths to match the circumference of the cakes. Press in place gently. Leave to dry.
- You can paint over the crowns with metallic food colouring.

484. Sweet flowerpot

Make a garden-proud pal a container-garden cake.

- Sterilize a well-fired ceramic flower pot.
- Bake your cake in it.
- Cover the top with heaped brown sugars. Add some instant coffee granules and a couple of nutty white-chocolate rocks.
- Put about a dozen fairy cakes – preferably the pale golden kind – in metallic green cases for 'flowers'.
- Smear some melted chocolate in the centre of each cake. Press in a large flat chocolate button or some chocolate chips to make the flower centres.
- Cut ready-roll icing or sugar paste into petal shapes – triangles, teardrops or hearts.
- With a dab of melted chocolate or some frosting coloured to match, anchor the petals in overlapping circles around the centres.
- When dry, stick each flower on a strand of straight green ribbon pasta and push it into the flowerpot cake.
- Add leaves cut out of green leather or sprinkle some green hundreds and thousands beneath!

485. Balloons for baby

Babies aren't impressed by cake shop offerings.

- Make a bunch of balloons – speckled, sparkly or animal shapes – the birthday centrepiece. Tie each to a short strand of spaghetti and stick in the cake – making sure it won't float away!
- Each little friend could take one away after the party.

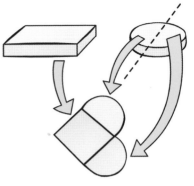

486. With all our hearts

Versatile and easy – to buy or bake – is the heart-shaped cake.

- No cake mould? Bake a cake in a round and a square cake tin – the round should have the same diameter as the side of the square. Halve the former and fit the semicircles against two adjacent squares –a heart!
- For a romantic or feminine feel, cover in pink or peach ready-roll icing. Sprinkle the top and plate with heart or flower-shaped candy. Use sugar paste flowers as candle holders.
- For a grown-up feel, use red icing and chocolate hearts.
- For a younger theme, stripe multi-coloured icing across the top or polka dot with colourful buttons or mini macaroons.
- Or just cover the top with chocolates.
- Whatever the theme, tie a ribbon round the cake – use a dab of royal icing or melted chocolate to anchor it in the crease on top, let dry, then make the bow.

487. Cake chocolate boxes

This is an impressive, individually portioned cake.

- Stamp out 2½-inch rounds from a pair of sandwich cakes. Lightly smear some jam along the sides. Line up on a baking sheet or platter.
- Cut strips of baking paper or buttered greaseproof paper into strips 3½ inches long and about 2½ times as high as the cake pieces.
- Melt chocolate. Working quickly, use a palette knife to spread it on the strips, completely covering one half lengthways.
- Extend some horizontally into the other half, creating a wavy top edge to the chocolate strip.
- Still working quickly, wrap each strip, as soon as it's done, around one round of cake. Take care not to overlap the paper at the end; let any excess stick out.
- Chill to set.
- To serve, pipe whipped cream in the hollow and fill up with strawberries. Tie a ribbon around the chocolate case or encircle the base with rosemary.

488. Chocolate wings!

With white or dark melted chocolate, a paper icing cone and a little practice, you can make pretty butterflies flit around.

- Fill a greaseproof paper cone with melted chocolate.
- On a sheet of greased paper or baking paper, pipe the letter 'B'.
- Next to it, pipe a mirror image! (For practice, use a runny paste of flour and water.)
- You can fill in the wings with squiggles.
- Pipe as many pairs of wings as you want.
- Make as many bodies – a small dot joined by a long oval and then a longer leaf shape.
- Leave in the refrigerator for 45 minutes.
- When ready to use, peel off the paper and assemble on your dessert plate on a piped cream swirl or a flower squiggled with berry-flavoured ice cream topping in a squeeze bottle. Or prop it directly in a soufflé, sundae, mousse or other creamy pudding.

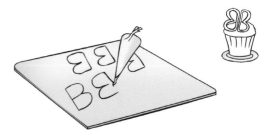

489. Cupcake sundae

Ridiculously easy but novel for a summer party.

- Have a small muffin or fairy cake for each guest.
- Divide a large quantity of thick yogurt and tint with food colouring – think of ice cream flavours. Chill until firm enough to whip stiff.
- If you like, mix in crushed pralines, nuts, chocolate wafers and chopped fruits into some of the yogurt.
- Thread each muffin on a skewer to allow you to hold it up while you cover it with the chilled yogurt.
- Pile the muffins into a large deep glass dish, preferably a long boat shape, and garnish with wafers, chopped fruit and drizzled toppings.
- Chill until ready to serve, with dollops of sorbet or frozen yogurt.

490. Party chickens

Eggs and chicks are good for a birthday bash too.

- A simple theme for a larger party uses marshmallow chicks. Or you can use candy or sugar-coated almond 'eggs' instead.
- Line up a pie dish of butter cream and a plate of desiccated coconut shreds coloured green.
- Holding a muffin by its case, first dip its 'face' into the butter cream and then the green coconut 'grass'.
- Refrigerate to set while you make chocolate flakes by running a peeler along the thin edge of a chocolate bar.
- Wearing disposable plastic gloves, make 'O'-shaped chocolate nests on top of each cupcake. A basic round will do – the hollow isn't necessary but is nice for adding depth.
- Sit a yellow marshmallow chick on the nest, or add a clutch of three eggs each.

491. Animal craters

For a zoo or circus-themed party, children will love filled pastry shells.

- Use animal-shaped cutters to cut puff pastry. You'll need three of each to make one animal.
- Keep one of each shape whole and cut a circle out of the other two.
- On a baking sheet, stack carefully with the intact shape as base and the cut shapes overlaid.
- Brush with egg and bake till well risen. You will get a case similar to a vol-au-vent.
- Fill the animals' bellies with cooked vegetables or a salad.

492. Caterpillar-ed cakes!

For a quick kiddie party, get a box of assorted fairy cakes with:

- Liquorice laces or strawberry string
- Some desiccated coconut
- An assortment of small sweets
- A set of round chocolate 'beads'
- Ready icing.

Now

- Make a green lawn for Mr Caterpillar. Colour the coconut with green food colouring and spread in a large plate.
- Place the cupcakes on it in a large curl, leaning them against each other – stick together with extra buttercream if need be.
- Prop the last cupcake sideways on top of the one before it.
- Pipe on his face with icing in a piping bag, or stick on sweets for his features.
- Add liquorice legs to each segment and pop the end into a chocolate bead 'foot'. Give him antennae too.

■ Exciting extras!

493. Stop/Go! Sundae

A fun idea for a children's party to go with the automobile cake – traffic light parfait!

- Set jelly in green, yellow (or orange) and red colours. Chop up small.
- In clear tumblers, layer slices of kiwi and green jelly first.
- Follow with orange segments or melon or mango pieces and amber jelly.
- Finish with rosy-skinned apple pieces, cherries or berries in the red jelly.
- Add a whipped cream or custard hat.

494. Fruit split

A healthier traffic light dessert.

- In oval ice-cream dishes, lay a spliced banana as if for a banana split.
- Use fruit scoops shaped with a melon baller.
- Try kiwi for green, cantaloupe melon for amber and watermelon for red.
- Top with toasted sunflower seeds and pomegranate seeds.

495. Bubbly for all!

While the grown-ups pop the cork, give the children their own bubbles.

- Give them a party phial – wide-mouthed mini wine bottles are perfect – filled with soap solution and a bent wire loop each.

Cleaner than confetti!

496. Serve a sweet spoon

A luscious surprise – a chocolate-coated coffee spoon!

- Melt couverture chocolate (or run your fondue fountain) and dip the spoons in to cover – it may take 2–3 dips to get a really rich robe on them.
- Dry them bowl-down on a tray or baking sheet lined with waxed paper.
- Store in a cool place.
- For an extra-special touch, dip the spoons in a bowl of sugar right after the chocolate – choose vanilla-infused, cinnamon-flavoured, golden or mix in some dried lavender.
- Or bake some biscotti swizzle sticks and coat the ends the same way.

In cool weather, use these to decorate party bags. Tie to a bag of sugared almonds or give each guest a boxful.

497. Crackers with your coffee?

Sometimes it would be nice to take a party bag away from a grown-up party!

- For a 'grown-ups only' dinner party, serve your own crackling cantuccini in transparent paper. Tie with red or gold ribbons. Guests can dip them into coffee or port, or take them away.

498. Sweets for the sweet

Fudge is easier to make and as sweet as hand-dipped chocolates.

Use biscuit cutters to punch out:
- Flower shapes for Mother's Day (dot the centres with a chocolate kiss)
- Valentine hearts to lay in pink paper cups
- Stars for Christmas
- Chick shapes for Easter
- Fudge faces
- Plain squares tied up with shoestring liquorice.

499. Boat race

For a tiny tots' pool or tub party.

- Make paper boats from different colours and add ring-shaped sweets along the inside 'decks'.
- Fly a different flag on each, supported by a cocktail stick and tucked into the central peaked fold.
- After the sweets have been munched, launch a boat race!

Warning: Adult supervision is needed throughout.

500. Bacchus' wreath

For a really mythical touch for a spring garden party:

- Drape ivy around the wine bottles and/or the ice bucket!

501. Balloon crackers

Take a cue from Christmas crackers for a fun party bag:

- Keep your chosen gifts small but sturdy.
- Put each into a balloon and blow up using a bicycle pump.
- Write the recipient's name on the balloon in indelible marker and tie to their chair.

- Pop with cocktail sticks or bamboo skewers, slipped into the napkin ring, after dinner.
- Use confetti-filled balloons for more excitement (if you don't mind the mess).

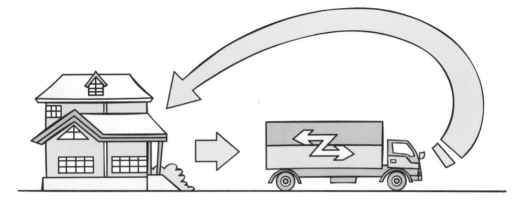

AROUND THE HOUSE

The Organized Home
Scheduling and systems

Time management is key to running an organized household – having your own systems and drills in place minimizes scheduling conflicts (and family rows!)

■ Keeping time

502. Chalk it up to breakfast

Notice-board notwithstanding, the family keep missing messages!

- Buy dark stoneware mugs and tumblers with a matte surface. Chalk urgent reminders on their first cuppa!
- Include good wishes, loving notes and compliments in your morning scrawls too!

503. Water retention

Water-retaining granules don't just save you time and effort, they mean you can go away for the weekend without organizing a house-sitter.

- Mix some into your garden compost and potting compost so that your plants will hold more moisture for longer.

504. Make that call!

You may be tempted to shoot off an email asking for immediate action. However:

- The best way to get something done is to make a call.
- For what can wait, an email forestalls telephone tag games!

505. Picture plan

Ask your child to paint seven themed pictures (or make collages) to hang in the hall, one for each day.

- Use these to remind the family that Wednesdays are football nights, Fridays mean food shopping trips, etc.

Children will take pride in their art while strangers won't be privy to your weekly plans! The children will remember their chores better too, having lavished care on them!

■ Handy helpmates

506. End the pen hunt

Hunting through your deep bag for your pen is frustrating. To keep it close to your notebook:

- Choose a diary with its own bookmark, or use sturdy fabric glue to attach a ribbon or braid to a plain one – put it in the middle of the book so putting the pen in won't strain the spine.
- Tie or sew a lightweight plastic pen to the end of the braid, and then clip it to the diary – on the outside cover or in the middle.
- A soft-covered notebook allows flex; in an organizer with a roomy binder cover, tie the ribbon to a binder ring.

507. Shop by the centimetre

No point buying pull-out baskets deeper than your shelves!

- Always carry a carpenter's, or tailor's, tape measure with you.
- Devote a page in your organizer to the measurements of all your rooms, the depth of all your fitted storage.
- Jot down the measurements of all holding spaces like alcoves and room above shelves.
- Carry the shoe sizes and measurements of all your family – saves waiting in dressing room queues or dragging unwilling kids along.

508. Mix and match bedlinen

Never run out of clean sheets or matching pillowcases. Buy multiples in *coordinating* colours and patterns.

- Except for whites – it's best to buy three identical sets of those.
- Don't match the colour and pattern of pillowcases and sheets exactly.
- Pick coordinating patterns and colours. For pale blue striped sheets, choose pillowcases in toning blues, solid or a different stripe; or choose a darker solid colour (say, plum) that will go with blue stripes, pink ginghams and cream damasks; or get different patterns in the same colours!

What's best about mix-and-match is zero boredom!

509. Writing on the wall

Many families use notes to schedule and coordinate activities, or maintain a diary of birthdays and anniversaries on a notice-board (whiteboard, blackboard or cork).

Make your board work harder:

- If you use pens, attach different coloured ones to easily locate where each person might be on, say, Friday night.
- Errands for each person could also be left in 'his' or 'her' colour.
- Attach a cord to the cap of each pen and pin it to the board – it won't get misplaced or carried away. Do a quick check before shopping for any refills needed.
- If you use chalk, keep a box of each colour on a narrow shelf just below the blackboard.
- Add an extra colour for all-family events.
- Also handy: a separate colour for must-remember occasions and doctor's appointments.

■ In and out of the closet

510. The everything box

No, you don't have time to sort the laundry *and* the post *and* lunchboxes each night. Even if you did, there's still more! Get an 'everything box' for each room:

- It should be large, yet compact enough to keep coins and keys safe. It should be low enough to hide under the bed and small enough to carry around.
- Put all clutter in it each day – get everyone to collect their own belongings.
- Set a sorting time each weekend – 20 minutes should do.
- Get everyone together for quicker resolution of what belongs to whom or goes where.
- Anything you can't decide on stays in the box. But if no one claims (or uses) it in a month, give it away or discard it.

511. Before the big shop...

A change of seasons, a landmark birthday, a new school year – anything can trigger a buying spree.

Tidy the cupboards before you shop:

- Don't just aim to 'declutter' – tell yourself (and the children) that you need space for new buys.
- However, don't actually assign cubbyholes for additions – that will be an irresistible pressure to buy.
- Take everything out and put it back neatly – chances are your cupboards need a tidy.
- When you see what you have, you'll realize what you need.
- If you find an item you're sick of, that's dated or tired, or a never-worn, perhaps you know someone who will love it.
- Now you can go shopping with better perspective – and a list!

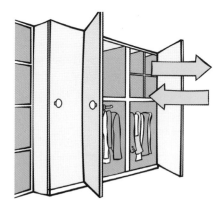

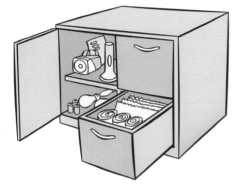

512. Utility cupboard must-haves

These are the fix-its you need:

- Light bulbs, an assortment.
- Fuses, various.
- Batteries, half a dozen in all the usual sizes.
- A couple of torches.
- A good supply of bin liners.
- Extra bags for the vacuum cleaner.

■ *Primping planner*

513. Handy hand cream

When is the best time to use hand cream? Just after your hands have been in sudsy water.

- Keep a heavy-duty hand cream near all soap-and-water areas – kitchen sink, bathroom basin, potting shed and laundry room.
- For longer-lasting benefits choose a brand that resists a couple of washes.
- Buy cream in pump dispensers or decant cream into pumps – they're easier to use with damp hands (which is better for your skin).

515. Old ball and chain

Tethered to the desk with no prospect of getting active outdoors?

- Swap your chair for a Swiss ball. Choose between sitting upright or rolling off!
- With even the tiniest movement, your abdominal core muscles will need to flex to maintain your balance. A working workout!

514. Order of dress

When getting dressed, follow this sequence to minimize stains, discoloration and damage to clothes and accessories:

- Perfume and make-up first – that includes hair products!
- Give it time. Some cosmetics can smudge onto clothes; alcohol (in perfumes, hairspray, deodorants) can affect fabric dyes, especially on silk, which doesn't take dye in too deeply anyway.
- When sure you won't 'wipe off', get dressed.
- Put jewellery on last for maximum protection. Pearls are particularly vulnerable to damage from the alcohol in perfume.

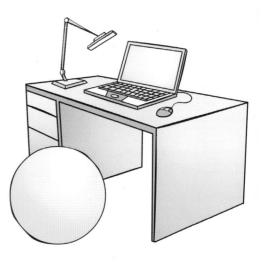

516. Home work for more playtime

Working from home can mean more 'play'!

- Multitask and refresh yourself by alternating household duties with bread-earning!
- Take a 10-minute break every hour – you need to move around for your health's sake. Stretch, run up and down the stairs, do ab crunches or curl weights.
- Set a kitchen timer to prompt you to rest your eyes every 15 minutes – look away from the screen, into the distance. Roll your eyes up at the ceiling, down at the floor, from side to side. Now turn your head to do it again!
- On breaks soon after breakfast or lunch, substitute a quick errand for exercise – put the washing on, feed the cat.
- Advertise your work hours far and wide – because you're working from home doesn't mean you're 'at-home' to work all the time.

517. Slow down the information highway

Instant information and continuous connectivity can put you under pressure to be a super-speed superhero! But you don't have to respond to technology 'instantly'.

- Answer emails immediately only if it's an emergency; otherwise don't reply until it's 'mail hour'.
- Better still, turn off the alert and check no more than twice or three times a day.
- If it's urgent, an intelligent colleague will say so in the subject line. Use your discretion regarding the 'high priority' button!
- If it's an emergency, people will call if you don't respond to emails.
- Avoid non-urgent calls in the middle of a deadline crunch. Put the answering machine on and ignore chat requests till you have the time.
- Keep your mobile phone on a silent or discreet setting – check who's calling and decide whether they can wait.

518. Pocket those papers

Household papers need filing. Then again, it's laborious sorting mail into 'mortgage', 'school', 'household', etc. daily.

Have a single-file system for daily mail – it'll be less intimidating and faster and it's efficient enough:

- Get an accordion file with 12 pockets and label them for each month.
- Get 48 clear-plastic envelopes – 12 each in four colours — to fit the pockets. Use an indelible marker to label these 'Week 1', 'Week 2', etc.; colour-code simultaneously.
- Put one 4-week set of envelopes in each filing pocket.
- When a bill, notice or letter arrives, aim to deal with it early and file accordingly. If a payment's due on the 15th, aim to pay by the end of week 1 – and place in the correct envelope.
- At the beginning of each week, fish out the relevant envelope and deal with everything in one go. Set aside time for this every weekend.

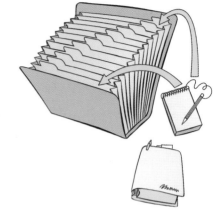

519. Piggyback those pockets!

Now make the single-file system (*see Tip 518*) more efficient!

- Treat your file as an extension of your organizer. When sorting mail, get your organizer too.
- Keep a little notepad and pencil in the file – the first or last section is easiest to find.
- Transfer all appointments to individual slips of paper and put them in the relevant envelope.
- When you settle the bills, bring out the family calendar and transfer your schedule to it!

Best bit? It recycles every year!

520. Stamped!

You've pocketed the lot (*see Tip 518*) but are still unsure whether the chore was completed.

- Get a rolling 'professional' rubber stamp made stating 'Paid!', 'Returned!', 'Replied!', 'Wishes Sent!', 'Gift bought:_____', 'Checked' and 'Done!'.
- Buy an inkpad and refill. Store both in a box beside the file. Add a stapler, some stamps, a nice notepad and a box of pins.
- As you finish tasks, stamp them out!
- For gifts, pen the details.
- Answer the mail.

You're finished!

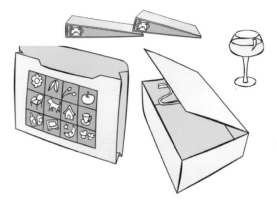

521. File away!

Make a date – yourself, coffee and those pesky ring binders!

- Schedule filing for every second Saturday, say, or quarterly. If there's not much paperwork, you could get away with yearly (a month ahead of filing your tax return!).
- If your file bulges, you need to clear it out more often. To a dozen (one for every month) identical ring binders, add labels 'Electricity', 'Mortgage', 'School', 'Receipts', etc. Or choose a really deep, sturdy one with divider cards.
- Get another tabbed pocket file for 'annuals' and long-term records. Label tabs 'Medical', 'Bank', 'Insurance', 'Car', 'House', 'ID', etc. Add loose pockets as needed.
- A third bunch – manuals, instruction booklets, guarantee cards – goes in an expanding accordion or big box file plus plastic envelopes. Once in five years, armed with a glass of good wine, weed out dated documents.

522. Coupon bank

Keep cutting out those money-off coupons and then forgetting to use them?

- Get a large version of a money bank with a transparent window for the coupons you cut out.
- When you've finished the weekly payments (*see Tip 518*), put the coupons you've to use up soon in your wallet. Discard any you're unsure about.

No bulging wallet and you get time to think about the 'Buy 1, Get 1 Free' vouchers.

523. Net pay!

Set up direct debits for all monthly bills:

- utilities such as water and gas
- mortgage and insurance
- recurring deposits
- school fees
- loan instalments

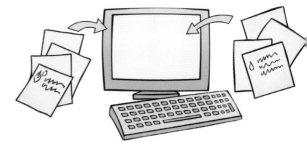

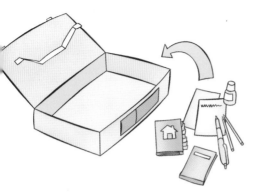

525. Emergency rescue!

Make your address box (*see Tip 524*) your emergency rescue service:

- List emergency numbers at the front or back of each – most address books offer 'Notes' pages.
- Add a trusted family member's number – with their consent.
- For the 'Work' diary, add the numbers of your most reliable colleagues and contacts. Duplicate those alphabetically too.
- In the 'Service Directory', add your favourite takeaways, the plumber and electrician, and the closest pharmacy.
- Have the best babysitter options and best friend's mother's number in the front of the children's diaries.
- Carry a copy of all frequently called and emergency numbers in your wallet.
- Add photocopies of the list to your partner's and children's wallets.
- Give a copy of that same list to your 'emergency family member'.

524. Don't juggle, multiply

Do you know your daughter's best friend's number? Does she know your best friend's, for emergencies?

- Put them all together in a box file with a pen, refills and correcting fluid.
- Get several address books, with space for anniversaries, birthdays and email addresses.
- Label 'Family & Friends', 'Children' (or one per child), 'Work', 'Services & Supplies'.
- Update the children's diaries every major school holiday, or even monthly if you can.

■ Penny pinchers

526. Switch for savings!

With service providers, play kangaroo – if they aren't offering the best rates, hop to another.

- Shop around before a new financial year begins; agents hoping to improve their bottom line may offer bargains.

Check service providers for:

- Telephones
- Cable TV
- Internet connection
- Electricity and gas

Check financial outgoings and income for:

- Bank savings accounts, fixed deposits and mutual funds
- Credit, debit and ATM cards – note reward points and interest charged
- Loan and mortgage payment rates – check for pre-payment penalties, rollover policies, and flexibility

527. Saved from work

If you're working from home, cutting a few corners where it doesn't hurt will help pinch those hard-earned pennies.

- Print documents for reference (rather than for sending out to someone) on both sides of the paper.
- Print on the draft quality setting of your printer rather than letter quality.
- Save the coloured ink for when you really need it; print regular documents in black.
- Avoid printing white space (waste of paper) and elaborate visuals, especially large photos (waste of ink). Most websites offer information in a text-only or printer-friendly format. (Hint: try the site map or choose the HTML version of a website.)
- Recycle envelopes – they can be handy 'folders' for short projects of 'work in progress'.
- Use energy-saving practices (*see Tip 645*).

528. Tiny tasks

If you have growing children, review the roster of chores frequently and delegate more. Here are some jobs even toddlers can help with:

- Putting rubbish into the wastepaper basket.
- Emptying all the wastepaper baskets into the main bin once a week.
- Keeping the family pet's water bowl filled (a squirt bottle is least messy for a child still acquiring motor co-ordination skills).
- Feeding smaller mammals, birds and fish – just keep an eye on how they are doing. It's wonderful training for the responsibilities of a more demanding pet like a dog.
- Watch and advise; communicate your standards; offer praise for a job done well – but never 'do it better' or redo what has been done.

529. Lock up when leaving

Moving house?

- Prime furniture for transport by locking all drawers and doors to prevent accidental opening (and consequent splintering/shattering).
- If you can't lock a movable portion, see if you can remove it; pack separately.
- Pad all corners; protect jutting parts (knobs, hooks) with bubble wrap.

530. While you were out

Going on holiday? Make some arrangements to ease your homecoming.

- Stop post delivery up to a day after your return date (ask the post office to hold it for you).
- Stop the newspaper. If you are a direct subscriber, try to arrange delivery to your doctor's clinic, library or community centre. It won't pile up announcing that no one's home!
- Stop the milk. Shop for cartons of UHT to keep in the larder till you return (check expiry dates so it's good to use even beyond then).
- In summer, pay someone to mow your lawn. In winter, hire someone to shovel any snow off your driveway. The house won't look 'abandoned'.
- Installing timers? Make sure there are separate switches for each room set to different hours. The shifting on-and-off cycle appears more natural.
- Don't forget the sprinkler timers. Ask a friend to take an occasional walk around your garden if you'll be gone for more than a fortnight – for maintenance and the appearance of occupation.

The Organized Home
Storage

Innovative and dedicated solutions for every room: from
your wardrobe to your workstation, from utility rooms to
nurseries, from larder to family living zones.

■ Hard(er)-working
   hideaways

531. Drawers versus shelves

Fed up with stacks of stuff toppling when
you need to pull out that large pot from the
bottom of the pile? Drawers can be more
practical than shelves, but unless you're
planning your home storage from scratch,
you may end up with not enough drawers.

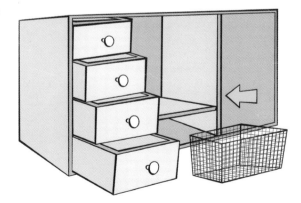

- If you have cupboards rather than drawers,
  fit some sliding wire baskets under the
  shelves – you'll be able to see what's in
  them at a glance.
- If you have enough drawers and are still
  short of storage, add trays and inserts to
  maximize the use of horizontal space.

532. Enlarge your cupboard capacity

For the same reason that a drawer can hold more stuff, certain additions to your storage can help you stock more without stacking.

- Tiered racks that divide shelves into horizontal layers
- Tiered carousels
- Ultra-slim shelves in the door
- Hanging rods and hooks on the backs of doors

533. Storage with a view

Window seats make a great dual-purpose addition to any room with recessed windows.

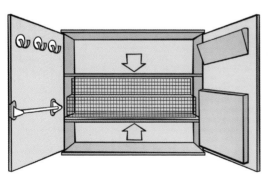

- A lift-up seat hides seasonal or occasional items; place cushions on top.
- For readier access, fit lightweight baskets or drawers to hold paperback books, distracting cushions and pillows, toys, cleaning equipment or extra bathroom supplies.
- Open shelving's good for larger or frequently used items: towels in the bathroom; childhood toys in a young adult's room; large ceramic bowls or copper utensils in the kitchen; heavy stone sculptures; or a basket of candles or seashells.

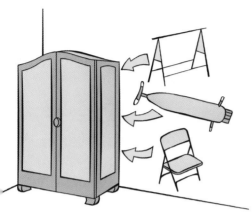

534. Standalone stowaways

Use space behind standalone furniture as 'slim storage space':

- Stand cupboards, dressers and chests of drawers a couple of inches away from the wall; you might not miss that extra space – especially as standalone furniture on legs frees up floor space visually.
- Slide in an extra folding table, a couple of trestles, folding chairs or the ironing board.
- Make sure you can reach it easily when you want it – the stowaway item shouldn't be pushed too far back, with other objects preventing you sliding it out easily.

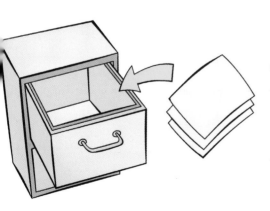

535. Paper liners

Paper liners are great for protecting drawers and shelves, as well as their contents.

- If you've got breakables sliding around and knocking into each other, however, switch to felt sheets – it should minimize shifting and prevent those chips.
- If you have a problem with moths, look out for lining paper that's been impregnated with lavender or cedar essence.

■ Kitchen (and larder) buddies

536. Top up your shelves

Deep shelves or uneven stacks of dishes on smaller shelves waste vertical space. Stacking high makes removal difficult. Some solutions:

- Screw or superglue the lids of spice jars to the underside of a slim shelf – screw the jar in. Simply unscrew to use.
- On sturdy eye-level shelves, screw some cup hooks into the cabinet 'ceiling' or under the shelf.
- Add a slim wire drawer or a woven basket on rails under the shelf – for lids, baking paper, baking sheets and occasional cutlery.

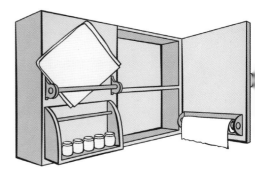

537. Stack in the door

The insides of kitchen-cabinet doors are perfect for slimline storage, and almost every shelf has a few empty inches in front where you can slide something in.

- Slim wire racks or short towel bars can hold pot lids and lightweight chopping boards.
- Slim shelves house spices neatly and allow an at-a-glance view.
- Hanging rails can hold flat utensils and extra tea towels.
- Attach foil and paper dispensers to the insides of doors – neater than having the caddy in the open where fumes and pests get all over them.

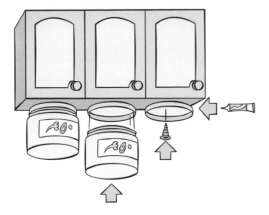

538. Cubbyholes for cutlery

There's no need for cutlery to take up an entire kitchen drawer.

- All but the tiniest table should have room underneath to have a couple of inches of drawer space added flush beneath the surface. That's enough to store your everyday cutlery.
- It's also a handy place for napkins and tablemats – just where you need them.

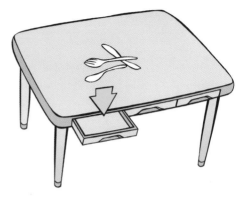

539. Guard your goblets

A good way to keep your special crystal safe from chips and cracks.

- Line a sturdy cardboard box with a layer of felt. Place your glasses so they don't touch – leave an inch between – with every alternate goblet placed upside down.
- Shake packing pellets (styrofoam beads available at stationery and DIY shops) over the lot to fill the gaps and the empty cups.
- Add a layer of felt and a sheet of corrugated cardboard on top; fill with packing pellets to the top and seal with masking or parcel tape.

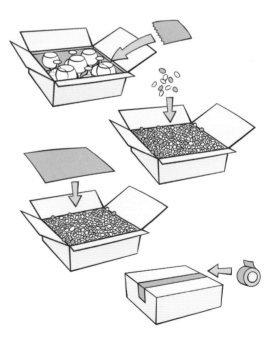

540. Frills and filters

Ever wonder what to do with that pack of paper doilies at the back of the cupboard?

- Those frilly doilies may no longer be in fashion, but they're great for interweaving with your fine china to prevent scratches.
- For smaller saucers and for cups, try using coffee filters.

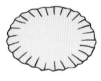
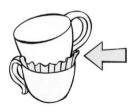

■ Clutterfree clothes storage

541. One season at a time

Store only this season's stuff in your wardrobe.

- Decide how many seasons (not retail, climatic!) you really have where you live.
- Put this season's things into the wardrobe.
- Break up all-season garments (T-shirts, shirts, blouses) into seasonal collections by colour, pattern or material.
- Store the rest by season.
- Use vacuum storage bags; or plain large zipped or re-sealable bags (get the extra air out using a vacuum cleaner, unzipping just enough to fit the nozzle).

This will be better for your clothes – they won't get squashed in the wardrobe.

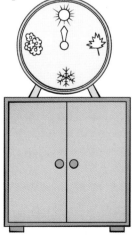

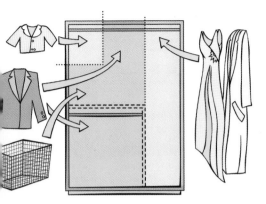

542. Halve your hanging space...

...to store twice the number of garments!

- Divide full-length hanging areas into a two-tier one.
- Leave just enough full-depth hanging space to fit in about half a dozen more long garments than you have – about 2 inches for long dresses, 3 for coats is plenty.
- Organize clothes by length. Use the space under mid-length dresses by adding storage boxes, baskets or removable shelves. That's a handy nook for handbags and shoes too.

543. A few of my foldable things

Not all garments *need* to be on a hanger.

- It's better spacewise to fold or roll up garments that hold their shape without hanging (knitwear, T-shirts, etc).
- Fold and stack stretch fabrics only if you have shallow drawers and shelves.
- Jeans and casual trousers can be folded too, as can dresses and long skirts in stretch fabrics.
- Fold socks in half and interleave to keep the pair together.
- Knickers can be rolled up; but bras need to lie flat.

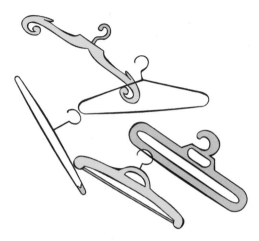

544. Hang-ups

Some garments *do* need hanging.

- For skirts, use hangers with rubberized clips, or hang by the loops on the waistband or side seams.
- For formal trousers, use dedicated trouser hangers or smooth wooden hangers (snags and splinters will damage the fabric). When folding, align the inseams.
- Use curved, sturdy coat hangers for outerwear and suit jackets.
- For tops and dresses in delicate, textured or slippery fabrics, use padded hangers.
- Choose straight-shouldered hangers for strappy garments, or pass a ribbon through the straps and tie loosely to hold them together.

545. Shoe-in space

Dusty shoe boxes and odd shoes squashed at the bottom of the wardrobe?

- Store your shoes in clear plastic drawers or hanging pockets. Not only can you see what you have at a glance, your shoes will be better protected from dust, humidity, mildew and pets than they would be in the original cardboard box.

546. Leather on wood, silk in paper

To keep your best pair of shoes in good shape, a little post-wear consideration is needed.

- Avoid wearing the same pair on two consecutive days. Give shoes, leather especially, at least 24 hours to dry out and return to their original shape.
- Use wooden shoe trees to help leather shoes keep their contour.
- If you don't have boot stretchers, roll up two magazines and pop one down each leg.
- Wrap strappy evening sandals and satin slippers individually in acid-free tissue paper and place each pair inside a sturdy box.

547. Tubed tops?

For delicate and decorated garments, minimize friction with tubing!

- Clear plastic tubes (such as those tennis balls come in) are perfect for protecting delicates.
- Tumblers can also be used for garments and accessories that scrunch up small.
- Try to stick to the same type of tube.

Note: This method will not prevent crushing. It is best for knits and garments that can be ironed, or that won't show creases (e.g. a fully beaded scarf).

548. Set and match

Perfectly matched sets of bedlinen are not very versatile in terms of changing your decor. In addition, losing, staining or tearing any one item means a full-set replacement – not very budget-friendly. Go with co-ordinates instead *(see Tip 508)*.

• If you *must* match, store sheets and second pillowcases (folded) inside one pillowcase to hold the set together. Easy to find, easier to carry.
• Use all white – even if your linen isn't all from the same set, nobody will notice.

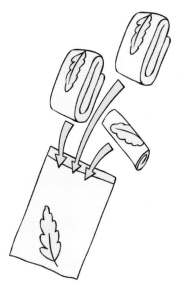

549. Umbrella stand

These seem to have fallen out of fashion, although it hasn't stopped raining! An old metal pot caddy makes the ideal umbrella tidy.

• Drips won't pool inside your container.
• If you live in a seriously wet climate or have carpeting or wooden flooring in the hall, you could put a large plant saucer under the caddy.
• The pot-holder is probably moisture-resistant – after all, it was designed to withstand watering – so a mildew-treatment is all you need to render it brolly-proof.

550. Remote hook-up

Sick of hunting for the remotes? You have two choices:

- Have a dedicated remote-control box in each room.
- Alternatively, glue a bit of Velcro to each remote and attach its counterpart either to the side of the TV or to the shelf or wall behind. Let them stick together now!

The real key to success, though, is remembering to put the remotes back after every use.

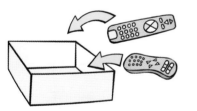

■ Better bathrooms

551. Rail against the door

For large families, the average length of towel rail can be a tight fit on busy mornings.

- Consider a ladder-style radiator rail instead.
- Choose a pedestal basin with a built-in rail under the rim.
- Add a rail at waist height behind the door.

■ Child-sized clutter busters

552. Children's hideaway in plain sight

Choose at least one large and stylish piece of storage furniture for the living room.

- A storage cube that doubles as ottoman
- A rattan chest
- A closed picnic basket
- An old-fashioned trunk

Keep it empty for emergency storage of household clutter and children's things that you need to clear away in a hurry when you have company at short notice. It's especially useful if you work from home and clients might drop in to your 'office'.

553. Child-high shelving

High shelves keep things out of the reach of little fingers. But shelves in the children's room should be low enough for them to access safely.

Run a narrow line of shelving around the room at picture-rail height with a row of pegs beneath wherever larger furniture doesn't interrupt them. They can use the space for favourite toys and books, even a small radio or CD player, as well as for hanging bags, jackets, scarves, etc.

When they're older, that space can house their model aeroplanes, CDs, jars of seashells or beads…

554. Sticky blackboard buddies

For the children's room, it's worth investing in magnetic blackboard paint. It's handy for them and saves space too.

- Paint the cupboard doors or half a wall (behind the desk, perhaps) with it.
- Drawings, timetables, photographs, pin-ups and other keepsakes can go on the same surface they scribble on.
- It's versatile enough to stay useful for toddlers to teens.
- If you're worried that all the dark matte paint will darken the room, paint the *inside* of the cupboard doors instead! Visual clutter vanishes too!

■ Ship-shape workspace

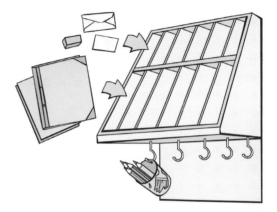

555. Dish up the paperwork

You don't need expensive filing systems for household paperwork.

- Sort papers into folders and expanding/accordion files that are colour-coded by subject – household bills, children's school papers, identification documents, etc.
- Reclaim an old wall-mounted dish rack with a lick of paint. The slots for the plates are perfect for sorting your files!
- Shelves are an added bonus – perfect for a box of stamps, a set of envelopes and note cards.
- Hooks for hanging cups can be used to dangle some cleaned-up paint cans for pens and pencils!

■ Oddments and ornaments

556. Stuck sharp

A magnetic board mounted on the inside of a cupboard door will safely store an assortment of small, sharp metal objects.

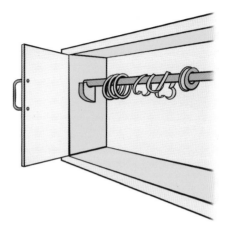

- In your sewing and craft cupboard you can use it for hanging scissors, stray pieces of hardware, knitting needles, even coils of wire.
- For the DIY cupboard, you can line up all your tap washers, different gauges of fuse wire and other electrical wiring.
- In your bathroom cabinet, it can hold tweezers and hair grips.
- In your laundry cupboard, it's ideal for safety pins.

557. Don't spare the rod

Biscuit cutters, napkin rings, bangles, scrunchies, rolls of ribbon and spools of thread – more than a dozen of these become a pain to store.

- Fit some wooden dowels or curtain rods inside your closet. Instead of screwing the ends into the walls, rest them in cupped brackets to lift out easily.
- Run the objects along the dowels, by type.

This way you can see everything at a glance – and find what you want without rifling through the lot.

558. Tangle-free trinkets

Necklaces forever in a tangle?

- Place them in individual zipped or re-sealable bags – allow the clasp to protrude beyond the slider track when you seal! Easy to find.
- Store earrings with hooks the same way, with the ends of the hooks protruding outside the bag.
- Makes it easier to open the bag without tugging!

559. Mesh your accessories

Costume jewellery spilling out of the jumble basket?

- Frame a rectangle of fine wire mesh or window-screen netting.
- Mount it on the inside of your wardrobe door with hinges along one side so you can open it out like a book.
- Thread earrings and brooch pins through the mesh.
- Add small S-hooks, and your necklaces and belts (hang by the buckle) can join them.

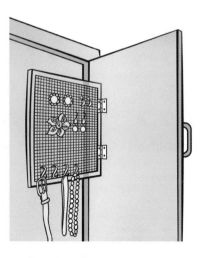

560. Hanging bangles

Bangles spilling out of a drawer? Hang them.

- Put on your work gloves and, with a wire cutter, snip through a wire hanger just where the horizontal turns up towards the hook on top.
- Using pliers, bend the curling corner into an open loop (U-shaped).
- File the free edges of wire smooth.
- Press the sides downwards a little, and the horizontal should sit neatly in the loop – the hanger is now rather like a giant safety-pin.
- Thread your bangles through – watch the weight or the wire will bend and bow!

■ Maintain your memories

561. Keeping keepsakes

Precious stuff clutters our cupboards and shelves, reducing immediate-access storage space.

- Special mementoes deserve their own treasure box.
- Choose a pretty, sturdy trunk for the collection.
- Get smaller cardboard and metal boxes that fit easily into it to house the little things.
- Get tiny decorated keepsake boxes for individual precious bits.
- Pack delicate items in acid-free paper.
- Use special fabric sleeves, envelopes or drawstring bags for expensive and vintage fabric or leather items.
- Replicate for each family member.

Unpack and enjoy those memories from time to time.

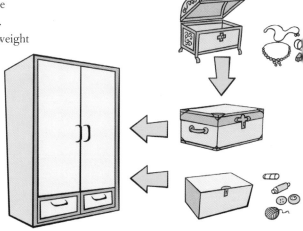

562. Once in a lifetime

For all those life-defining documents, you need to get a fire-resistant and water-resistant box. This is what you grab in an emergency evacuation, so keep it within easy reach (but in a safe place).

A heavy-gauge metal box or sturdy wooden box treated with fire-retardant material on the outside and lined with metal sheeting inside is best. Put in:

- Birth certificates
- School and college certificates/diplomas
- Passport and other state-recognized IDs
- Duplicate of driver's licence
- House deeds
- Marriage certificate
- Copy of your will/living will

563. Memory keeper

You can choose a very few defining memories from your memory box (*see Tip 561*) to put in your evacuation kit (*see Tip 562*):

- Your wedding ring – if not on your finger
- The heirloom pendant (though it should really be in a safe deposit)
- Your baby's first photo
- Your parents' wedding photo

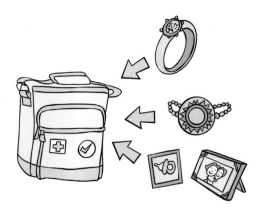

■ Keep it manageable

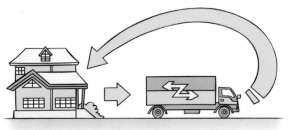

566. Keep things dry with gel

Problems with mould and damp when storing those precious items?

- For expensive equipment and accessories – camera lenses, fine leather bags – silica gel is the dehumidifier of choice.

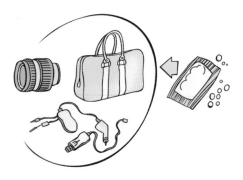

564. Practice moves

If your household seems clutter-prone, have a make-believe moving session every year. There's probably a lot you wouldn't bother to bring if you moved.

- Try scheduling the make-believe around New Year – call it 'moving into a new year' and children will readily make a tradition of the game.
- Get young children to draw their ideal room every year and make changes to their existing room accordingly.

565. Chalk it up

In humid climates, moisture can be difficult to keep at bay.

- Add bundles of blackboard chalk to drawers and shelves!
- Use them in the kitchen, bathroom, utility room and drawing room, as well as your wardrobe.

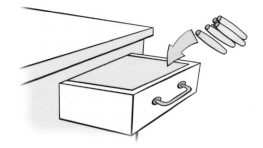

The Organized Home
Safety, first aid and home remedies*

Here's what you should keep to hand for safety and security at home; what precautions to take; and what to do when accidents do happen.

*All content on health is provided for general information only, and should not be treated as a substitute for the medical advice of your own doctor or any other healthcare professional.

■ Store up safety

567. The Essential Medicine Cabinet

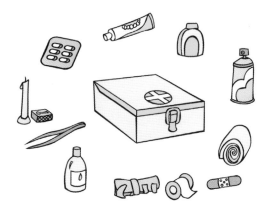

Collect the listed items in a sturdy metal box. Top up monthly.

- Toothpaste (basic white) – relieves the itch of minor insect bites.
- Borax – mix a mild solution in warm water for cleaning out minor injuries, sores and boils.
- Anaesthetic sports spray – for painful rashes and stings.
- Sterile gauze, a roll of sterilized cotton and cotton pads for bandages.

- An assortment of medicated adhesive bandages; sticking plaster.
- Splints.
- Antiseptic liquid.
- Pointed tweezers, a candle and a matchbox.
- Antipyretics, painkillers – clearly labelled with dosage and date.
- Emergency numbers (*see Tip 524*).

568. Peas for the pain?

A packet of frozen peas makes a versatile ice pack – the peas roll around like pellets, nicely shaping the bag around awkward spots like knees and elbows. What's more, it's a great freezer standby, so you don't need a separate space for your supply!

- Remember to put a thick folded towel against your skin before applying an ice pack to protect your skin from serious freezer burn! (Do the same for a hot pack.)

569. Pull on your gloves

Keep colour-coded sets of rubber gloves. They'll protect your hands from cuts and burns (chemical and electrical), and may even save your life.

- The yellow ones are for working with toxics.
- Keep thick and sturdy blue or green ones for DIY and gardening.
- Pink gloves are for general clean-ups.

Skin-deep — trouble on the surface

570. Sunburn!

It's not just unsightly or painful, it can even call for medical intervention.

- Cover the area at once with a clean cloth or towel, until you can get some cold water to sponge the area as well as to sip and rehydrate yourself.
- A light application of calamine lotion is soothing and helps healing.
- However, if that doesn't soothe the discomfort, you should see a doctor.
- Do not break any blisters that form!

571. Stung by a plant!

Summer brings with it a few plant pitfalls . . .

- Should you fall foul of poison ivy or nettles, a cool layer of calamine lotion should help.
- If it doesn't subside, you should see a doctor.

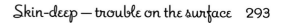

■ In the flesh – broken skin

573. Know your enemy

If you can tell a doctor what bit you, you may not need to go to casualty.

- If it's a spider (if there are poisonous varieties in the vicinity), get to the doctor *at once*.
- For mammalian or non-poisonous reptile bites, wash with soap and water, apply a clean dressing, then call your doctor.
- For a severe bite with profuse bleeding or an unidentified insect bite, get yourself to the hospital fast!
- You may need a tetanus shot within 24 hours – your doctor will advise.

572. Itching insects!

If you're bitten by an insect that's left your skin stinging or itching:

- Check that the area is clean.
- If there's no debris, a paste of equal parts vinegar and baking soda should disinfect the wound and neutralize any mild venom.

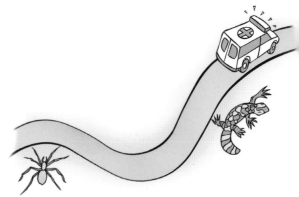

575. Splinter in my thumb

Don't tug it out!

- Clean with soapy water.
- Disinfect tweezers in a candle flame for several seconds.
- Wait until cool – do not touch or wipe! (Ignore soot deposits.)
- Try to avoid touching the skin – grasp the splinter close to its base and pull out.
- Lightly press the sides of the wound – an absence of blood might indicate that a bit of the splinter is still in. On the other hand, any small fibres left should be dislodged as the wound bleeds.
- Clean the wound again and dress.
- Check it with your doctor.

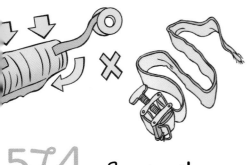

574. I got cut!

If it's deep enough to bleed profusely:

- Press a clean cloth or dressing pad against the wound to stem the flow.
- Elevate the cut area above the level of your heart, if possible.
- Holding the cloth pad firmly in place, bandage the wound.
- Do not lower the cut area until bleeding subsides.
- If the bandage gets soaked, quickly remove it and dress afresh, still applying firm pressure. Then seek medical attention.
- Do NOT use a tourniquet. Cutting off circulation is likely to do more harm than good.

■ Down in the mouth – and throat

576. My tooth hurts!

One of the worst non life-threatening pains, toothache!

- Soak a small piece of cotton wool or the head of a cotton bud in clove oil; dab on the painful area.
- If it doesn't subside at once, leave in place for 2–3 minutes.
- However, don't lodge the cotton wool in your cheek and forget about it – clove oil can irritate the delicate membranes in your mouth and cause sores!
- See your dentist as soon as possible.

577. My throat is sore

This is an old-fashioned remedy but makes an effective palliative for the sore throat.

- Mix a little warm honey with lemon juice.
- Add a few drops of fresh ginger juice and some crushed basil leaves if you have any handy.
- Take a spoonful every 20 minutes to 1 hour.

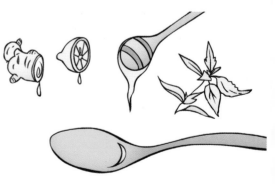

■ Fire burns!

579. Lavender and vitamin E for burn scars

Skin often stretches drum-taut as even a minor burn heals up.

- Lavender oil has long been a traditional remedy against the inevitable scars.
- A little Vitamin E oil will ease the tightness, enabling skin to stretch back to normal.
- To get both benefits in one, dilute the lavender oil with the oil from a Vitamin E capsule. Both are available from herbalists and natural pharmacists.

578. I got burnt!

It can be difficult to tell how bad a burn is at once, so you need to act immediately to minimize damage.

- Plunge the affected area into cold water for at least 10 minutes. A running tap, filled bowl or even bottled water will do.
- When the pain subsides a little, apply a sterile gauze pad and bandage.
- Do NOT use cotton wool or other lint-shedding material, or any ointment.
- Secure the bandage with a knot; do NOT use tape or sticking plaster.
- Get to a doctor.
- Do not puncture any blisters that form.

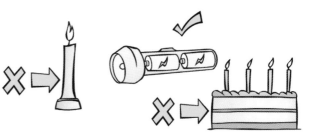

580. Wash the ashtrays

Ashtrays can be easily overlooked sources of fires.

- Always add a little water or sand to them to help extinguish butts.
- Never empty an ashtray into the wastepaper basket.
- Sprinkle water into the ashtray before emptying or wash it out in running water.

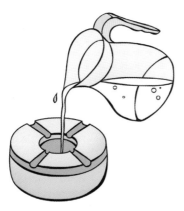

581. Contain the flame

Yes, our ancestors did it all the time; but we have safer means.

- Avoid moving oil lamps, stoves or candles while lit.
- Use battery-powered torches for emergency lighting.
- Keep a couple of torches in each room where you can reach for them in the dark.
- Don't carry a lit taper to the fireplace, bonfire or candle – light it where it is going to be used.
- Be careful carrying a cake with lit candles or a Christmas pudding flambé.
- If possible, flambé using a flambé ladle, not on the stove.

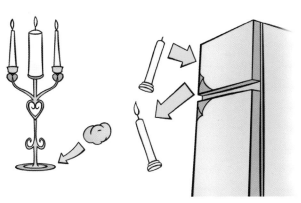

582. Candles standing against the wind

Tall candles in silver sticks or a mass of church candles bunched together on a platter – such an elegant, warm look for your table. But what if you topple one? Accidents happen.

- To minimize the chances of a hot wax disaster, add a spot of non-permanent adhesive at the base to hold them firm.
- Before lighting candles, place them in the freezer for 10 minutes. This will reduce dripping, helping them to stay in shape – and burn – longer.

583. Tumbling hot

Never ever switch off your tumble dryer or unload it before the entire cycle – including the cool-down phase – is complete!

- Unless it's helped to cool down, your piping hot laundry will be difficult to handle.

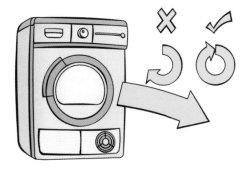

584. Not so hot!

Electric blankets can be brilliant – or, improperly used, a catastrophe.

- Never fold or tuck in an electric blanket.
- Unless it's specifically designed for use as an underblanket, never allow anything else to rest on it – a person, a pet, the jacket you just shrugged off or even a light coverlet or throw.
- Electric blankets are not safe for children or pets!

585. Fire alarm

Make sure your fire alarm is ready to alert you!

- Check smoke detectors during your weekly cleaning of each room and space.
- If your detector isn't wired to the mains electricity, replace the batteries regularly; set a reminder on your phone or an alert on your computer.
- Check fire extinguishers every year – New Year's Day is a good choice.
- Make sure there's a fire extinguisher in easy reach of hotspots: stove, oven, microwave, fireplaces, and outdoors if you have bonfires or barbecues in the garden.

586. Smother that fire!

It's a great idea to keep a few fire blankets in the house.

- If you can't buy any, get some large, thick canvas sheets with a tight weave and good drape.
- Keep one near the kitchen, one by the fire extinguisher for the back yard, one just outside the children's room (but out of a very young child's reach because it can smother), one in the hall downstairs and one upstairs (preferably near the stairs).

587. Sand blanket

Rather than relying on buckets of water or snow as fire safety back-up, have some buckets of sand to hand.

- Water (liquid or frozen) can increase the danger of an electrical fire and is likely to make a fat-fed flame (such as cooking oil) worse. The blanketing action of sand is more likely to work in either case.
- Sand is also good for putting out fireworks. Have some to hand before you light up the sky.

■ Safety in motion

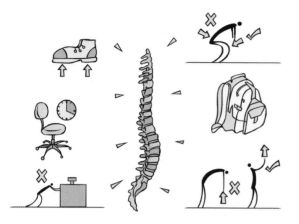

588. Ergonomics for safety

You don't realize how important your back is until you put it out. Put the mechanics of motion to work:

- Bend at the knees when lifting. Don't hinge from the waist.
- A shoulder bag is better than a handbag; a rucksack is safer than both.
- Divide loads evenly into two, one per hand.
- Don't 'pull up'; 'push up' instead – cradle heavy objects close to your body, arms underneath; don't let them drag your arms downwards.
- Wear well-cushioned shoes – even for household chores.
- Don't sit still too long. Pace or stretch every 20 minutes.
- Don't drag or shove heavy furniture; get help to lift and shift.

■ Unsafes away!

589. Hunt down the hardware

Stray screws, washers, sprockets, staples – sharp, small, rusty metal can kill!
Do a daily sweep – you can use them again!

- Put a large magnet in a discarded shower cap or small polythene bag.
- Slip the open end over the vacuum nozzle.
- Hold in place with a rubber band, scrunchie or torn stocking.
- Pass over all hidden corners and under furniture. There's no need to plug in the vacuum – all iron will jump to it! Afterwards, remove the tie, invert the cap or bag and safely stow away your hardware (*see Tip 614*).

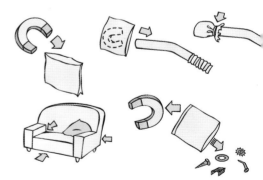

590. Safe storage

Many daily essentials are hazardous substances. Safety lies in careful storage.

- Keep corrosives away from metal.
- Volatile substances need a cool, ventilated home.
- Store flammables away from sparks.
- Keep hazardous substances away from children and pets.
- Place a copy of emergency numbers (*see Tip 524*) near such substances.
- Dry rags used with flammables (paints or solvents) outdoors – away from smokers! Store in tightly sealed metal containers.
- Protect hazardous substances against moisture – it corrodes containers.
- Never keep flammables and corrosives in breakable containers.

591. I smell gas...

At the very first whiff:

- Open all the windows.
- If it's a strong smell, evacuate the family and pets to the garden.
- Do not switch anything on or off – don't even try to turn off the mains. The smallest spark could set off an inferno!
- Do not use the phone – once you get outside, call your supplier from a mobile phone or neighbour's phone.

592. Household hazards

Treat these as hazardous and store accordingly (*see Tip 593*).

- Garage – motor oil, anti-freeze, batteries, brake and transmission fluids, fuel, kerosene, car wax.
- Workshop – paint, primer, varnish, stains, thinner, stripper, adhesives, mineral spirits, tar, anti-rust solutions, fixatives, solvents.
- Utility room – toilet cleaners, tile cleaners, drain unblockers, oven cleaners, stain removers, furniture polish, window spray, bleach, dyes.
- Garden and pets – pesticides, insect repellents, weed killer, pet products, pool cleaners, sealants.
- Indoors – mothballs, batteries, fluorescent bulbs, electronics, aerosols, smoke detectors, lighter fluid, shoe polish, hobby equipment, cosmetics, mercury thermometers, medications.

593. Danger – Plaster ahead!

If you have a young child it's a good idea to flag up the danger points:

- Consider pasting stickers with a child-friendly figure with a bandage on potentially dangerous objects. (Establish early on with the child that this is a 'BIG OUCH' sign!)

■ Safe as houses

594. Lock up the keys

If you leave your keys near the door, they could easily be hooked out.

- Make sure keys can't be reached even with a long-handled tool. If you must have them near the door, hang them inside a key cabinet with a stiff bolt.
- Don't keep your keys in the same place as your money – a pickpocket going for one could get lucky with the other.
- Lock up all ladders and tools, especially if you keep them in outdoor locations such as the garden shed or garage.

595. Vault-worthy valuables

Expensive goodies belong in the bank's safe deposit box. If you must keep them in the house, at least make sure they can't be seen through windows.

- A cupboard that's right opposite or next to a window, let alone a door, is a poor place for valuables.
- Carry your jewels in your handbag and put them on at the party venue (and vice versa on the way back).
- Or at least wrap up so your bling is hidden by your collar or shawl.

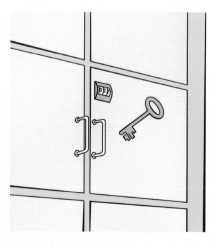

596. Post-free zone

Don't let the post pile up while you go on holiday – it's an open invitation to burglars.

- If possible, get the post office to hold or redirect your mail.
- Otherwise, ask a friend or neighbour to look in daily and collect.

597. Personal is private

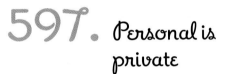

You may be just an internet search away; but the whole world needn't know your personal details.

- Shred documents that display personal data; dispose in batches over 2–3 days (to prevent reconstruction).
- Put surnames only on nameplates and ID tags – not full names.
- Don't state your name on the message on your answering machine. Never record your child's voice.
- Live alone? Get a friend to record your answering machine message; change monthly.
- Talking to a handyman or telecaller? Use the royal plural: '*We* would like…'
- NEVER carry passwords in your wallet!

■ Secure your outdoors

599. Get a grip on the garden

Tidiness in the garden means safety.

- Always carry tools in a trug or gardener's caddy. Put it back as soon as you've finished using it.
- Have individual compartments for all tools, so you know at once if something's missing.
- Check and clean tools before storing.
- Put away pesticides and fertilizers immediately after use.
- Take them out one at a time if you're working with large containers.
- Promptly fill holes and ruts to prevent stumbles.
- Fix loose paving or damaged decking at once.

598. Stay hooked up

- You should switch to cordless phones when you have a baby. However, don't pull the plug on the old handset yet. Should the electricity fail, most cordless phones won't work as the base unit requires power.
- Keep one handset for emergencies.

600. Lawn perils

When working on the lawn, watch out for these common pitfalls.

- If you use a powered mower, make sure you rake away any rocks or gravel – the mower could fling them out and injure someone.
- Don't leave the mower out of sight while you take a break.
- If you stop to go inside for a drink, make sure you can keep an eye on the equipment from the kitchen.

601. Good fences

Those are the ones that keep trouble out and contain the residents safely.

- Check fencing, posts and stakes regularly for splinters, breaks and protruding nails.
- Also look out for peeling paint, which can lead to rot and rust setting in.
- Make sure there isn't a gap under the fence that an animal could slip through – such as your pup burrowing out to explore.
- A gate that swings to and clicks shut on its own is always preferable.

■ The contingency plan

602. Shout for safety

Teach the whole family your emergency drill – and practice it weekly (monthly should do with over-12s). Use a codeword signal as well as an alarm.

- Choose your codeword with care. Try 'Scramble!' or 'Scram!' or 'Scoot!'; not 'Emergency!'.
- Tell children they can use the emergency word to warn you if they feel threatened in public.
- Teach your dog to take his place in the drill.
- Make sure your codeword is short enough to use as a signal to your pet!

603. What's the drill?

Improvise based on your children's age and where you live.

- If there are neighbours within hailing distance, include a warning shout.
- 'Help!' should be among your infant's first words. However, guard against a 'cry wolf' tendency!
- Practise using a multiplicity of exits.
- Keep all emergency exits clear.
- Not all safety equipment is safe for children to handle; have a list of what is accessible to them, and teach them how to survive without the rest.
- Teach children that loud sounds, flashing lights and bright colours attract attention.

The Organized Home
Greener living — recycle, reuse, renew, ration

Do your bit to restore your old stuff to new glory, rather than cart it to the rubbish tip; make your garden greener, and your shopping list too; add some small steps to save.

■ *Ecological rescue*

604. Polonecked warmers

The poloneck pullovers your child outgrows can easily be transformed into covers for hot water bottles.

- Simply detach sleeves at the seams and sew up the sides.
- Raglan sleeves are particularly good as you don't need to take in the side seam — just closing up the armhole gives a nice shoulder to fit the bottle.
- Pop the bottle in and sew up at the base.

Some lovely warm memories to snuggle up to!

606. Intoxicating candlelight

Short stubby candle ends don't do much for your silver candelabra. However:

- They're the perfect height for sticking in the top of old wine bottles for a romantic café ambience – and you won't mind the drips messing up the holder so much, either.
- Place the bottle in an old ramekin to catch the drips before they reach the tablecloth, though.

605. Framed out of the box

Filling up the wall with framed prints is a bit passé. Put those old jam jars to use instead.

- Carefully roll up each of your holiday photos and pop into a jar.
- Add a little pillow of silica gel to each.
- Screw them shut and line them all up on a shelf at eye level.

These *will* get the conversation rolling.

608. Splash of cool

Does your old but serviceable umbrella turn your day greyer than the cloudy skies? Rescue it with a game of paintball.

- Pop the old umbrella in a large cardboard box and turn on its side.
- Cover up everything in the vicinity!
- Now shoot a smack of vivid colour or two with a paint gun. Fluorescent and glow-in-the-dark fabric paints are an especially bright touch.
- Leave it to dry. (If you don't have a paint gun, see if your child will sacrifice an old water pistol.)

607. Bar art

Got more olive oil, wine and vodka bottles than you know what to do with? Fill them up and colour your home bar crazy.

- Pour in some thick plastic emulsion paint into each bottle, swirl around and tip out the excess.
- Leave to dry completely.
- Wipe any dribbles and smudges on the outside with a rag dipped in thinner.
- Display on the shelf.

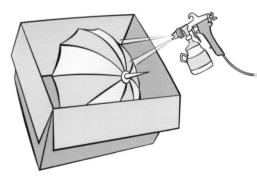

609. Shoe in the door

One half of your favourite pair of shoes is beyond repair, but it breaks your heart to show your old pals the door.

- Disinfect the mangled shoe and offer it to a dog kennel for a chew toy.
- Use the still stylish stiletto as a wedge to stop the door slamming!

610. Ice tub

That old inflatable paddling pool could be just the thing for grown-ups to drink from!

- You can fill it with ice to chill the beer bottles in for a big bash.

Handier than an ice chest, cheaper and not as space-hungry.

611. Gifting jars

Be a domestic goddess and give homemade treats as gifts.

- Save all jars and bottles, steaming off the labels; any leftover glue usually yields to make-up cleanser followed by alcohol-based toner.
- If the lid has a brand name on it, cut out fabric circles a bit larger than the lid and paste down with non-toxic glue.
- Stick on some ribbon or braid to hide the raw edges!
- After filling the jar, place a square of gingham, linen or muslin over the lid, secure with a rubber band and tie a bow around it.

612. Flowerpot caps!

It's difficult to keep small potted plants, especially kitchen herbs, adequately watered.

- Use old shower caps to keep the air humid and counter evaporation, and at the same time protect them from city grime and pet 'accidents' – you don't want a dog to spray your salad, do you?
- Of course, the plants do need to breathe too, so remove the caps every couple of days, or pull them on only when you're away on holiday and can't water or keep constant vigil.

614. Haute hardware

When you find stray metal bits and bobs lying around the house (*see Tip 589*):

- Put the odd shapes and sizes and those you recognize into your tool kit until you identify where they came from.
- For the more generic stuff – standard sizes of screws and sprockets– use your child's bead basket (over-tens only, please!) or your own workbasket.
- You can string them together as bracelets and pendants on a rubber or leather thong.
- For ponytail rings and elastic or leather wristbands or belts, sew or glue them on (use non-toxic fabric glue).

613. Toothbrush tube

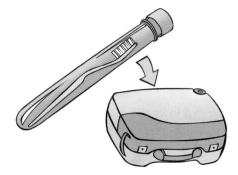

Those old plastic test-tubes that herbs, spices and bath salts come in are good friends to travellers (never use glass tubes for this).

- No more waiting for the toothbrush to dry – and then forgetting to pack it. Pop it into a test tube and pack at once.
- Do replace any natural cork stoppers with rubber or plastic ones – the real thing will crumble.

615. Loofah for the lot!

Buy these natural scrubbing aids by the dozen – the plainest you can find (no handles or fancy shapes to boost the price).

- Use them as an alternative to plastic scrubs in your eco-friendly kitchen. They're good for pots and worktops alike.
- Bring them back to the bathroom to scrub basin and bath, and to clean gardening equipment.

Completely biodegradable, they – literally – don't cost the earth!

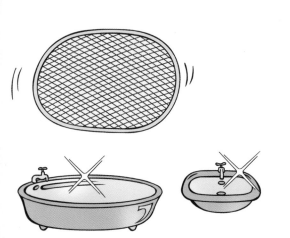

616. Packing peanuts for pots

Adding broken crocks and gravel chips in the bottom of pots keeps the roots of plants well-drained, but the extra weight makes the planters a pain to shift.

- Try re-using the polysterene beads used to cushion goods during transportation. They're lightweight, and it's a good use for a non-biodegradable material that's difficult to recycle.

617. Super sections

Hold on to those old egg trays and use them to store:

- Delicate Christmas baubles
- Spare light bulbs
- Freshly sprouted seedlings waiting for the pot

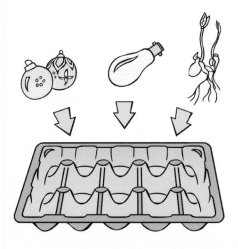

618. Soft stuffing

Stuffing handbags with tissue to help keep their shape is all very well, but the acid used to bleach the paper can damage the leather! And it's another unnecessary use of paper.

- Roll up old T-shirts or tights to pad bags instead.

You can also use the same technique for coat sleeves.

619. Short, stout, spouted – and string-y!

Got an old cracked teapot or kettle that you haven't the heart to throw away? As long as the spout is in place, you can keep your balls of twine in it!

- Pop the ball of string in and thread the free end through the spout.
- Repeat with as many spools as will fit in comfortably with a little room to roll around in. Shut the lid on them.
- When you want some string, just tug it out of the spout.

You can keep ribbon for gift-wrapping this way too.

620. Ramekin lights

Transform old ramekins into stylish LED candle holders.

- Spray-paint if chipped.
- Take a length of non-stick baking paper about 2½ times the circumference of the ramekin and about 5 cm / 2 inches wide.
- Using superglue, fix the strip at a slight diagonal under the rim.
- Continue to overlap the parchment strip so it swirls to a second level.
- Glue tinsel round the rim.
- Tie on some cloves to exude a mild aroma.
- Add your LED candle.

Never leave unattended while lit!

621. Plastic mesh scrubbies — for free!

Save those little mesh bags the oranges or potatoes arrived in.

• Next time you have a greasy pan to clean, don't waste your usual scrubber on it (if used on a really gloopy mess, it will probably be beyond rescue or reuse). Use the clumped up mesh instead!

Now you can throw it away with a clearer conscience...

622. Scissors soapbox

Keep things separate in your dressing-table drawer:

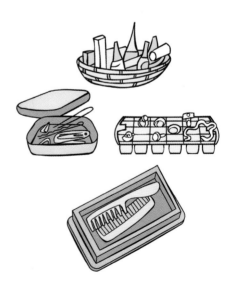

• Recycle biscuit tins, small baskets or a cutlery tray for lip colour and nail varnish.
• Mint or pastille tins could house hairpins and small clips.
• Ice trays can hold rings, brooches, cuff links and flexible bracelets or necklaces.
• Keep your watch in its box.
• Get a covered box for hair accessories.
• An old cigar box is ideal for combs and brushes.
• Cardboard soap boxes are perfect for tweezers, manicure staples, scissors.
• A biscuit tube is perfect for cottonwool pads.

623. Filter again, and again

Paper coffee filters, like any other paper product, require trees to be cut down to make them.

- Switch to the reusable mesh type.
- The golden colour means you can wash them one last time and use them in craft projects like tinsel once they're really done for.

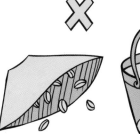

624. Spice rolls

Until the digital revolution really takes hold, you can use the empty plastic canisters from film rolls as spice jars.

- They are the perfect size and shape for small quantities of herbs and spices.
- The opaque material guards against deterioration caused by light.
- They are easy to get hold of for replacements.
- They are easy to label, on the lid or the side.
- They are lightweight and unbreakable.
- If you like, you can even use a drill bit to perforate the lids and make shakers.

■ Environmentally sorted!

626. Don't bin the books!

Many councils offer recycling services for books, or at least paper. But why spend energy pulping them when they can be re-read?

- Giving to a charity is the easiest option.
- Go to the nearest children's hospital or care home, with every paperback, magazine and boardbook you've finished reading.
- If possible, check with your council where the 'recycled' books go. If they are reselling, that's fine too!
- Or, pinch a few pennies: sell them to a second-hand store and treat yourself to a new book with the money!

625. Bin bounty

Decluttering shouldn't just be annual.

- Have standing bins for things to: give to charity; 're-gift'; and take to the collection centre.
- Line each bin with a drawstring sack so it's easy to gather up and take away later.
- Make your own sacks by doubling up and sewing the sides of old sheets or curtains. For the drawstring, either feed in cord through the hem fold (stitches picked out at sides) or simply tie the mouth shut.

■ Green house!

627. Refresh your recycle bin

Got your own compost heap? Good for you!

- However, if you don't tip out the compost bin at least daily, try popping in a charcoal briquet in the bottom to combat festering odours.
- Every month or so, scrub the charcoal out well (use a stiff toothbrush) in hot water to which bleach has been added and dry in the oven or on the barbecue grill to 'recharge' for action.

628. Greener greenery

Plants cancel your home's carbon footprint and reduce energy usage.

- Deciduous trees are better close to your home than evergreens. The leaves will shade you in summer, but after they fall in winter, your home will receive sunlight!
- If you need extra shade in summer, a creeper or vine across the western or southern walls is a good bet. Allow them to trail and shade windows where possible.
- If cold winter winds are more of a bother, plant evergreens as a windbreak to the north and west.

629. Limit the effects of sun

Strong summer sunlight will damage your furniture and carpets.

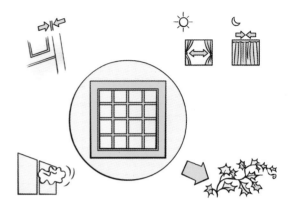

- Consider putting reflective film or other sun-control treatments on south-facing windows, especially if you have large expanses of glass.
- Double glazing also helps.
- Install awnings on the south and west.
- Keep curtains drawn during the day, especially to the south and west.
- Choose fabrics in paler colours and tighter weaves that are more light-reflective.

630. Keep the heat in

In colder weather, your windows can help reduce your heating bill.

- Make sure all gaps are well sealed. Weatherproof your windows.
- If they still feel draughty, consider putting a tight, insulating blind across them.
- Keep curtains drawn at night to minimize heat loss; open in the daytime to maximize solar gain.
- Make sure southern windows in particular are kept clean to let the most sun in.
- Don't allow plants to obstruct the sun coming in through the window or falling on and warming a wall.

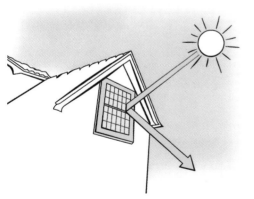

631. A nice cuppa in the garden?

Many plants love an occasional feed of used tea leaves (or leftover cold tea), and several don't mind a shot of spent coffee grounds either!

- Not only are both great fertilizers, they also act as mulch if lightly spread over the soil, holding in moisture.
- As with any concentrated plant food, don't put too much too close to the root. Make it an occasional treat as an excess will kill the plant.
- Follow with a drink of water to dilute the nutrients and help them sink deep.

632. Peat-free peat!

Yes, peat is good for your garden. However, mining it isn't so great for the ecology.

- Switch to peat-free composts instead – a fabulous choice is 'coco-peat', made from coconut coir, which is a by-product of harvesting coconuts. Also, it is much quicker and easier to replenish than peat (which took millennia to develop).

633. Pave the path only

Why spread stone and brick around when there's precious water waiting to soak into the earth?

- Green cover holds on to soil and moisture – paving lets good rainwater run off into the gutter while exposed barren earth runs right away with the water.
- Have just a single driveway or path up to your front door. You don't need a maze of paved strips for the average-sized town property.
- To water, pull on your wellies and go wade in the grass! Or install timed sprinklers, adjustable for the season.

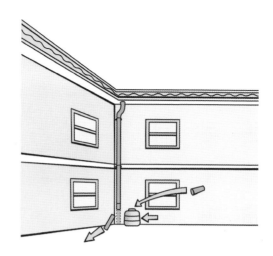

634. Butt before gutter

Don't lose water to the storm drains!

- Cut pipes to about 1 metre/3 feet above ground level.
- Add a water butt under each with a hole in the cover to accommodate the pipe.
- Make sure you can swivel the lid on the pipe!
- A charcoal brick in each butt will keep the water fresh for a week.
- If you have rain spouts, put a flexible garden hose down the mouth of each spout to catch the water without leaving an uncovered barrel beneath (this is dangerous as it can drown pets or small children).

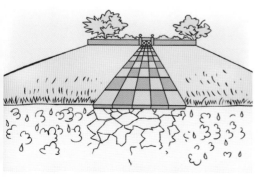

635. Green fingers not required

You don't really need gardening skills to grow the hardy English ivy, golden pothos or peace lilies, yet all three are spectacularly good at filtering out household air pollution from common volatiles such as benzene and formaldehyde (they're everywhere – in your furniture, home-office equipment, filing cabinet, even kitchen and cleaning cabinets, not to mention your dressing table).

- All three have eye-catching sculptural shapes that give your décor an energizing 'lift'.
- Feng shui practitioners consider peace lilies good for absorbing the negative energies from electrical equipment. Put a pot next to the PC!

636. Water-based is best

Those harmful volatile toxins (VOCs, or volatile organic compounds) are most perceptible when you're in the middle of a paint job.

- Try to use water-based latex paints rather than oil-based paints for zero or low volatiles. It's the eco-safe thing to do.

637. Put a lid on fumes

Household volatiles are hazardous to air quality (*see Tip 636*).

- Buy water-based (such as zero-VOC paints) rather than solvent-based products.
- Paint with a brush rather than a spray gun.
- Switch to a propane or liquid gas barbecue rather than one burning solid fuel.
- Upgrade your fireplace too.
- Revert to a push lawnmower. If it has to be powered, electrical is better than gas-powered.
- Avoid using leaf blowers. A rake will take only a little more time and effort.
- Get natural sprays rather than aerosol.
- Ban smoking indoors.

638. Faster wood

Avoid buying hardwood cooking utensils.

- Grasses grow faster than trees and bamboo is one fast-growing grass that yields wood quite similar to a tree's!
- Choose bamboo for utensils in the kitchen, especially those that see heavy use and a relatively short useful life – chopping boards and spoons.
- You can consider coconut wood for cooking utensils, especially the shell – coconut wood is proof against moisture.
- Keep the precious tree timber for furniture that you hope to pass down instead – it's that rare.

639. Look — free water!

Why buy mineral water when every tap in the house yields potable water?

• Tot up your monthly food bills. Check how much you spent on water.

Buy watertight metal flasks that you can sterilize. Fill up from the taps!

640. Glass that's greener from the other side

If you're shopping around for new glassware, consider Spanish.

• These recycled glass products are now widely available (even in supermarkets!) in beautiful designs with a high-quality finish. And the cool green hue gives them a covetable vintage look.

■ Green your gadgets

641. Don't fan too freely!

Ventilator and extractor fans in kitchens, bathrooms, and other work areas certainly are indispensable; but they do have energy implications.

- Heated or cooled air is pulled out very quickly by these fans, resulting in higher energy bills.
- Switch them on for the minimum necessary time and switch off as soon as possible during extremes of weather – whenever you are using an air conditioner or heater that is!

642. In hot water

Avoid heating water unnecessarily. Turn on the boiler just before you need hot water and let it run for no more than 15 minutes.

- For just a little water, don't turn on the hot tap. This heats more water than you will use! Put the kettle on or heat a cup of water in the microwave.
- Insulate the hot water tank to minimize loss and wastage.
- Don't use hot water when cold will do.
- When cooking, use the smallest vessel and cover when bringing liquids to a boil.
- Adjust the dishwasher thermostat to a lower temperature.
- Set your washing machine to a cycle with a lower temperature.

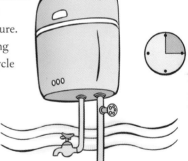

644. Laptop beats desktop

Portability isn't the only reason laptops are preferable to desktop PCs.

- They guzzle less energy.
- Plus, with having to plug it in and work around the wires every time you move – not to mention needing the socket for something else – you're unlikely to leave it on standby for as long!

643. Cool it

Excessive cooling also wastes energy.

- Don't turn your fridge thermostat too low. The freezer should be at about -15°C/5°F and the main compartment 2.8–4.4°C/37–40°F.
- For long-term storage, invest in a separate freezer chest and keep it at -18°C/0°F.
- Defrost regularly. Never let frost build up to a depth of more than 5 mm or $^1/_4$ inch.
- Cover liquids and wrap moist solids in the fridge. Evaporation from foods puts greater pressure on the compressor.
- Vacuum the coils regularly to help the fridge run for shorter periods at a time.

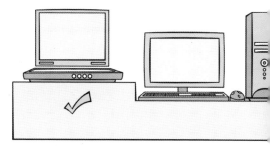

645. Conserve to save

Saving electricity not only helps the environment, it cuts your bills.

- Don't leave the modem connected or the computer on when not needed.
- Use the energy-saving settings of your monitor – let the screen go blank after 5 minutes of inactivity.
- Keep the brightness setting low and the contrast high – it's better for your eyes too.
- Use a dark background whenever you can – on the desktop, in your word-processing window, even on your web search.
- Turn off the screensaver.

■ Green light to power!

646. Light right

Get the lighting right and save on energy.

- Lights fitted with sensor switches, timers and dimmers save energy.
- Concentrate light where you need it. Use good task lighting – under-cabinet lighting for kitchen counters and a bright directional lamp on your desk; leave ambient lighting dim.
- To maximize the light you get from each bulb, use dedicated CFL fluorescent fixtures rather than fitting them inside existing shades.
- For spot lighting, use CFLs backed by reflectors. Good for the garage, workshop, laundry/utility area, basement or attic and task lighting.
- Send CFLs to your local recycling centre (they contain mercury).

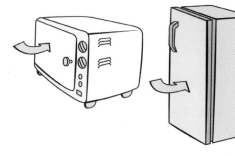

647. Bright LED

For decorative lights, CFLs may not be an option. However, there is a better choice than the traditional incandescent bulbs.

- Switch to LED – they use 80 per cent less energy and are even more environment-friendly than CFL. However, they cost quite a bit more, so you have to factor that in if you are thinking of all your traditional lighting requirements.
- For special occasions, however, the one-time cost of decorative LED is possibly one most families can happily absorb.

648. Keep the door shut

It saves untold kilowatts of energy and prevents pollution.

- Don't open oven doors too often, especially in winter, when cold draughts will make the temperature drop sharply.
- Don't keep refrigerator doors open too long either – for the reverse reason.
- Shut and insulate any gaps in doors between rooms with different sources of heating or cooling.

■ Reduce!

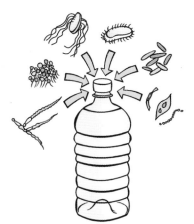

649. Plastic problems

Yes, do reuse those plastic milk and juice bottles – but not for more than two years, and try not to buy plastic in the first place.

- Once bacteria from saliva or sweat (on your hands as you unscrew the top), or even from the air, is introduced, there's no way to sanitize them completely.
- Plastic begins to decompose after a while. That's where the expiry date on packaged water comes from – water can't deteriorate, but its packaging can.

650. Let the car idle

Drive less, drive smarter.

- Shopping via phone or internet saves time, energy and fuel.
- Accelerate gradually rather than revving up.
- Replace your air filters and get the car tuned regularly to minimize emissions.
- Keep tyres well inflated.
- Drive more slowly on unpaved roads to avoid raising dust.
- Use the air conditioner only on the motorway; in slower city traffic, turn it off and roll down the windows.
- Remove the luggage rack when it's not required. It reduces fuel efficiency by adding weight.

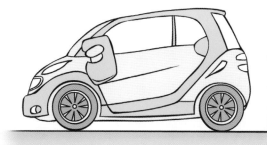

Home Care
The big clean-up

Roll up your sleeves and muck right in for a sparkling clean home! We've got the equipment (and we're stocking some strange but super stuff under the sink); the short-cuts and time savers; the grime busters; and even help for some odd nooks and crannies that you (and time) forgot! Psst – for help with the laundry, look to the next couple of chapters!

■ The supply cabinet(s)

651. Complete clean-up caddy

Multitasking and mild is best for cleanliness. The 15 must-have implements are:

- Feather duster, with static-generating bristles
- Colour-coded lint-free dust cloths
- Mop for wet cleaning
- A dry mop
- Half a dozen pairs of white cotton gloves
- Multi-surface spray
- Anti-mildew tile/grout cleaner
- White vinegar
- Borax
- Pure household soap
- Wax polish
- A sack of plastic bags or bin liners for rubbish
- Mini-vacuum cleaner
- 2 pairs of thick rubber gloves
- Goggles
- Knee pads

653. Bleached clean!

Chlorine bleach is a stain remover and disinfectant.

- A weak solution is great for washing surfaces in the kitchen and bathroom.
- It's the safest bet for almost any surface in the nursery.
- A more concentrated solution (or the neat liquid) tackles most stains.
- It's even handy for plugholes, sinks and loos, as well as for disinfecting wipe-down appliances.

Keep the neat stuff away from plastics, acrylic, wood and marble.

Never use in conjunction with soap (or any detergent containing soap) as this will produce a poisonous green gas!

652. Where it's at

Sometimes, the difference between completing a job and not is whether you'll have to go up and down the stairs again for supplies. Keep specialized or frequently-used supplies in small baskets with carry handles, dotted around your home.

- A toilet brush and disinfectant in every loo.
- The full array of stain busters in the laundry room.
- Shoe polish and leather cream in the utility room.

The only multi-tasker to spread around is chlorine bleach. Keep small bottles in the kitchen, utility room and bathroom. Store away from soap (*see Tip 653*).

654. Better be big on borax

Besides acting as disinfectant (*see Tip 567*), borax is also a fantastic general-purpose cleaner – many 'natural' household products list 'borax' among the active ingredients.

A solution of borax is not as corrosive as the same strength of vinegar or lemon juice.

- Use a solution for almost all surfaces for regular everyday clean-up.
- Keep the tougher stuff for stains and deep dirt-shifting operations on a weekly basis (*see tips 656 to 658; but note 657*).

655. Strange stuff under the kitchen sink!

These unexpected additions to the cupboard under the sink should jazz up your cleaning routine:

- White toothpaste (basic) cleans most porous substances gently (stone and china) and shines metal fixtures.
- Mouthwash – quickly and easily removes garlicky and fishy odours; even curry seems to yield!
- Used lemon wedges and salt – together or with a dab of that toothpaste (for really stubborn stains), these shine up taps and metal sink bowls.
- Baking soda – good for dealing with milder food odours; fantastic for the stainless steel sink when made into a paste with vinegar.

656. Be good to wood

A monthly once-over polish is enough for most furniture and floors. A quick dusting every other day – even weekly – will suffice.

- Wipe down a well-waxed, laminated or varnished surface with a damp duster.
- A damp wipe-down in the kitchen at the end of the day with a very well-squeezed cloth and a solution of either mild detergent or bleach (to disinfect) is in order.
- Once every week or two, rub all wooden furniture with some vegetable oil into which a few drops of lemon oil or juice have been shaken.

657. Citrus is sweet – and strong

Besides leaving your home smelling of sunny Majorca, lemon juice shines all sorts of surfaces – laminates, ceramic tiles, stainless steel. It's great against grease and is a natural disinfectant and deodorizer.

- Reach for those used lemon quarters for stubborn splatters.
- Squeeze a few drops of juice onto a moistened sponge for a daily swipe.

Warning: Keep lemon away from stone worktops or quarry tiles; all stone will be burned through and stained by the acid and the stains are impossible to remove.

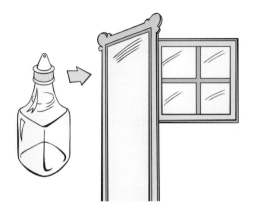

659. Don't mix cleaning agents

In general, mixing cleaning agents is almost always a bad idea. At best, an acidic and an alkaline cleaner will neutralize each other; at worst, the fumes can be lethal.

- Don't ever mix bleach with acid or ammonia. Both combinations generate toxic fumes.
- Always try to use one cleaning product, rinse well and wait to air out the space before trying a different one if the problem persists.

658. Vinegar for vim and vigour

Plain white vinegar will save you lots of elbow grease – and a pretty penny too.

It's invaluable for:

- Cleaning mirrors and windows.
- Removing limescale from vases and tumblers.
- Removing soap scum from tiles and shower panels, baths and basins.
- Removing the odours left by pet accidents, as long as the material can withstand bleaching – avoid using on coloured fabrics or untreated wood for this reason.

660. Happy hands

Dusting and dipping into hot water can really mess up your hands. Yet not every job can be tackled with rubber gloves.

- Smear a little petroleum jelly around your fingertips, working it well under your nails, before you tackle household chores.
- Slip on cotton gloves, pulling on rubber gloves over them when needed.
- Afterwards, just wash clean – no grime under your fingernails, either.

Bonus: You might find your cuticles nicely conditioned too, especially if you've had your hands in warm water!

661. Don't leave... yet!

After every shower – and this goes for every family member – do a quick tidy and wipe.

- Wipe down bath/shower, basin and surfaces with the appropriate implements – squeegee, sponge, tissue/paper towels.
- Dry that misted mirror.
- Bin all refuse – including hair clogging up the drainage.
- Put towels on rails or hooks, or in the laundry basket.
- Close the lid on the loo and flush.
- Make a habit of wiping the basin dry every time you wash your hands.

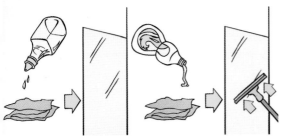

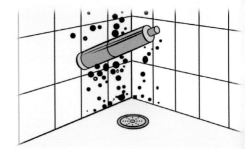

662. Scummy shower doors?

Hard water and soap suds can turn transparent glass into an ugly mess.

- Dip a cloth or plastic scrubber in white vinegar and wipe – this should shift the surface film.
- For a deeper scale, lather on some economy-brand shampoo and leave for a few minutes.
- Use a rubber-bladed squeegee to scrape it away.
- Spray on some vinegar for a squeaky-clean shine.

663. Mildew tactics

Regular wipe-downs after every shower and bath get tedious, even though they're effective for keeping stains at bay.

- Avoid using bleach, baking soda, borax, toothpaste and vinegar to shift scum, as they can compromise the sealant, which means the mildew problem usually keeps recurring.
- Reach for the anti-mildew cleaner at the first whiff of damp or dark smudge in the grouting! This is one specialist product that's worth its price.

664. Mist-free mirrors

It can be such a pain wiping the mirror clean after every hot bath or shower before you can see your face!

- Rub the surface lightly with a dry cake of soap or some neat shampoo each time you clean to keep the surface condensation at bay.

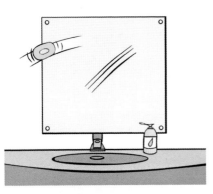

665. Spray the cloth, not the glass

Never spray glass cleaner directly on to glass – you risk damaging the window frame or mirror backing.

- Use the spray to moisten your cleaning cloth and wipe.
- Use a soft dry cloth to shine the glass and remove any excess fluid.

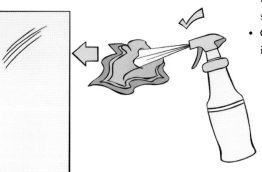

666. Worktops tough granite

Granite worktops are better at taking punishment than wood or marble, and won't show scratches in quite the unforgiving way that brushed stainless steel does.

However:

- Avoid all-purpose cleaners – the harsher ingredients in these cleaners will dull the stone over time.
- Clean with mild dishwashing liquid instead – it's gentler.

667. Sink freshness

Sometimes nasty niffs rise up from the kitchen drain.

- A sprinkle of baking soda down the drain should do the trick.
- Follow with some cider vinegar and cover with an upturned saucer.
- Finally, flush with boiling hot water.

668. Crystal clear

Hard tap water is tough on fine crystal.

- To get your vases sparkling clean in a jiffy, fill them with some vinegar solution and leave overnight, then rinse out in the morning.
- If you're in a hurry, drop a couple of fizzing denture tablets into them and fill with warm water. Sit for a couple of hours, then rinse.

669. Wax off!

Clean wax from a metal candlestick:

- Wrap in a freezer-proof polythene bag and freeze for half an hour until the wax has become brittle.
- Rub briskly (through the bag) to remove the biggest drips.
- Tap lightly with a blunt knife to loosen.
- Those last smears? Lay down some newspaper, wrap the candlestick tightly in brown paper, scrunching it into crevices, and blast with your hairdryer.

Warning: Don't try this if the candlestick is made of glass, crystal or a mixture of two different metals.

670. Wax on glass

So you can freeze a brass candlestick to get the drips off. But glass or pottery?

- When cool, tap the wax gently to crack it.
- Ease and scrape off.
- Now get some kitchen paper, some scrunched up foil and the hairdryer. Direct the hairdryer on to the wax – don't let the glass get too hot! – and keep scrubbing away with foil.
- When a thin layer is left, wrap the glass in the kitchen paper and give it a final blast of hot air.

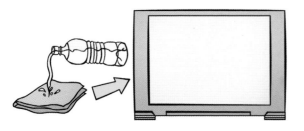

671. Only water for the TV

Never use those spray cleaners and glass-cleaning aerosols on the TV screen (or a computer monitor). The film left behind makes the dirt attracted by static stick!

- Remember to switch off and unplug from the power socket before cleaning.
- Use a soft lint-free cloth moistened with water.

672. Hand-in-glove cleaning

For smooth but fiddly surfaces such as slatted blinds, a dusting cloth or feather duster are not very effective.

- Pull on your white cotton cleaning gloves.
- Spray all-purpose cleaner directly on to the fingertips and swipe.
- To clean and wipe at once, spray cleaner on the right-hand glove and mist the left with water, then swipe with alternate hands.

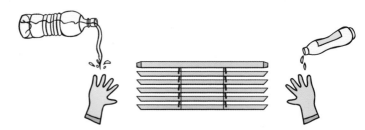

674. Pristine PC

This is especially important if you have a home office.

- Switch off and unplug from the power socket before cleaning.
- Turn over the keyboard, shake out any crumbs and dust, then vacuum with an air spray attachment.
- Clean the tops of the keys and side surfaces with methylated spirits or even a spritz of aftershave!
- Open up and clean the mouse.
- Damp dust the display, CPU and printer.
- Vacuum all vents gently.
- Wipe clean CD drawers.

673. Cleaning nooks and crannies

All those intricately carved wooden frames, pleated lampshades, grooved panels and window sliders collect dust that's tough to shift. Although a thorough weekly vacuum will keep them in acceptable order, you'll need to get out your 'specialist' tools once in a while.

- For metal and stone crevices, an old baby toothbrush works best.
- For wood, glazing or ceramics, try a cottonwool bud.
- Fabrics can be brushed clean with either a toothbrush (sturdier fabrics) or a small fluffy paintbrush (delicates and intricate textures, such as devoré).

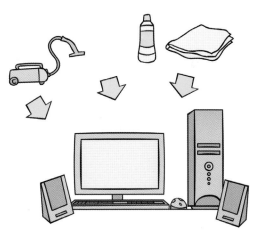

■ Cleaning up the odds and ends

675. Wipe the washing line!

Putting out the washing?

- Wipe dust off the washing line or drying rack first, otherwise you'll end up with ugly streaks on freshly laundered clothes!
- Wash the line or rack once in a while too.

676. Bins for cleaning?

When your kitchen bin is ready for a scrub, make it multitask first.

- Empty the bin.
- Now use the bin as your mopping bucket – fill with whatever disinfectant solution you use to clean the floor, and get to work!
- By the time you're ready to pour the water away, the bin should be quite free of debris and germs! Now all you need to do is rinse and dry.

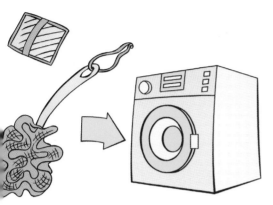

678. Mud-busters

If you live in a muddy area you'll know just how much of the stuff can get tracked into the house.

- Place thick coir doormats inside and a bootscraper outside your front and back doors.
- Get a rectangle of beautiful window/railing fretwork for outside the door. You can spray-paint it every other season for upkeep and rust prevention.
- Or just use a length of sturdy fencing mesh laid into a thick, solid frame. It's cheap and easy to replace when worn.
- Every week, let it dry and clean it outside with a coir-bristled brush to dislodge the mud.

677. Rinse and machine

You probably rinse your sponges and bath mitts after a shower, and hang them up to dry. However, warm and moist fabric is a favourite breeding ground.

- Pop them in the washing machine with the towels once a week.
- Don't do that to a natural sponge, though, or it'll come apart mid-cycle! Swill in a basin of soapy water, rinse, squeeze and leave on a sunny window-sill to dry.

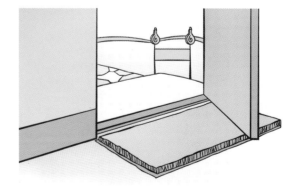

680. On the way up or on the way down?

Should you clean the staircase on your way up or on the way down?

- Work from top to bottom if you're mopping or sweeping debris down a hard surface.
- If you have a runner or carpeting on the stairs, it's better to get the vacuum cleaner and start on the bottom step. You won't damage the pile by literally scouring it away with dirt and grit!

679. Banish grimy banisters

Can't get the grime out of those mouldings and crevices with the vacuum nozzle?

- Tie an old towel, lightly moistened, over a soft bristle broom or dry mop.
- Brush the banisters from top to bottom.
- Switch the towel inside out when dusty.
- Spritz the railings with water and go over them again, this time with a dry towel. (Spray lightly though, or you'll have to clean dirty drips off the wall below!)

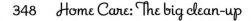

■ Sparkling windows

682. Side-to-side, top-to-bottom

Fed up with streaky, smeared windows?

- When washing windows, use side-to-side motions with your cloth on the inside. But on the outside, go up and down.
- That way, should you spot a stray streak, its direction will tell you whether it's on the outside or inside of the pane.

681. Good for cars, great for windows

If you have the modern aluminium-framed windows, the best protection for this soft metal may be in your garage!

- A couple of times a year, wash down the frames with warm soapy water.
- Open the windows wide and let the sun dry them out.
- Now give them a coat of car wax, and they'll be easy to look after all the rest of the year!

■ Clean-up by the clock

684. Emergency tidy!

Unannounced visitors at the gate! For a jiffy shine-up:

- Don those cotton gloves and dampen one hand with the multi-surface spray.
- Do a quick swipe of dusty and grimy spots, using the appropriate glove for each surface.
- Give metal fixtures a quick once-over too.
- Chuck the soiled gloves in the washing machine and answer that doorbell.

683. Super-fast spruce up

Guests at short notice? Pay attention to places they'll see.

- Close doors to bedrooms, playroom, home office, utility room and garage.
- Give the TV screen a wipe.
- Straighten rugs, plump up cushions.
- Open-plan kitchen? Put clutter in or under the sink.
- Wipe down the work surface and hob.
- Put cleaner in the downstairs loo.
- Get all unnecessary items off the surfaces and wipe down.
- Put out a nice soap and add fresh towels.

685. In the basket

If you live in an untidy household a stair basket is a fabulous idea.

- Place a wicker basket or small plastic crate at the bottom of the stairs, and another one at the top. Stuff that must go upstairs can be plonked in the downstairs basket throughout the day, and vice versa.
- It's the owners' responsibility to retrieve their possessions, upstairs and downstairs, before the basket fills or is emptied at the end of the week. Anything left is dumped in a (clean!) bin in the garage, loft or basement.

686. Living room straightener

Do a 5-minute straighten-up and collection before bedtime.

- Put away whatever you can.
- Plump up cushions.
- Remove things that don't belong (take stray coffee mugs and bowls to the kitchen, your handbag to the bedroom).
- Other people's clutter goes into the stair basket or collection box (*see Tip 685*).

Stains

Stubborn stains don't stand a chance – we're swapping smart attack strategies for elbow grease! Check off your rescue team and get down to the business of dissolving, fading and guarding against mishaps before they happen. For general clothes care, look to Garments and Accessories, page 362.

■ Spill first-aid

687. Lift off!

On spotting a spill, get the excess away from the fabric – as much as you can, as fast as possible.

- For solids and semi-solids, don't rub – it'll drive the mess deeper into the fibres.
- Scrape off with a blunt knife or spoon.
- If it's already dried on, use some masking tape to get the surface layer off without applying pressure.
- For liquids, move fast while it's fresh. Dab with a clean white towel or serviette.
- For grease, dust on some talcum powder or cornflour and gently brush away (soft bristles, please!).

688. *Float it away!*

Once you've got any excess mess out of the way, it's time to lift the soaked-in stuff free of the fabric.

- Use cool running water on all except oil-based stains.
- For oil-based stains, at home, do a spot test clean with white methylated spirit. If it doesn't work, get the stained item to the dry cleaners.

Warning: Warm water will set the stain!

689. Saved by the soda

Baking soda – also a good deodorizer – is brilliant for attacking stains, since it's a mild abrasive and cuts through grease and mineral deposits. Not just your clothes, either – everything from vacuum flasks and casserole dishes to wallpaper and carpets respond well to its stain-busting properties.

- Make into a stiff paste, apply, let dry and brush away.

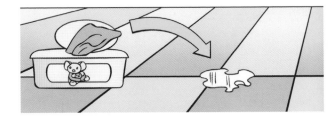

690. Biological warfare

For most protein-based stains – such as egg, milk, blood, gravy – take the biological approach:

• Make a thick paste with a biological (enzyme action) detergent and apply to 'digest' the stain.

Warning: While this works beautifully on cotton, don't subject wool or silk to it – both are protein fibres themselves, and the enzyme might chew into the fabric!

691. Baby wipes for grown-up spills

Even if you no longer have a toddler or infant about the house, an emergency pack of baby wipes is a good idea.

• Use them to mop up spills and stains. Any slight residues should be gone when you do get round to vacuuming.

■ Warning!

692. Wine spills

Upending the salt cellar over the red wine spill will only make matters worse, contrary to the old wives' tale! That goes for cola, coffee and tea too – the salt will drive the pigments in and set them in the fabric.

- Sprinkle cornflour over the spill.
- Get table cloths, etc. into the washing machine as soon as possible.

693. Out with oxidation

Not all oxidation (*see Tip 700*) is helpful! Some fruits such as banana and avocado blacken if cut and exposed to air and will do the same if applied to fabric.

- Jump to it with a little washing-up detergent and tepid water as a preliminary treatment.
- Wash at the highest temperature your fabric will stand, using a detergent for delicates.

■ Rescue efforts against tough 'uns

694. Meltaway mess

Candle drips on your tablecloth?

- Gently scrape off what you can with the blunt side of a palette knife.
- Bundle the cloth into a freezer-safe bag and chill for a couple of hours – the remaining wax will become brittle, so it'll come off more readily.
- For what's left over, lay an old absorbent towel on the ironing board. Place a brown paper bag on it, place your tablecloth on top and another towel on top of that. Run a medium-hot iron constantly over the top towel. The wax should transfer to the paper.

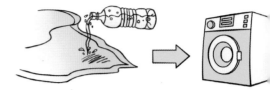

695. Bubbles to the rescue

Always keep an extra bottle of soda water in the fridge for emergency action on spills.

Red wine, greasy gravy, curry… all fizz up to the surface, letting you perform major rescue operations on most fabrics, from wool carpets to silk shirts.

- Use to dilute the stain and prevent setting when you can't get it properly cleaned at once; launder or otherwise treat as appropriate as soon as you can, however.

696. Food stained foodsavers?

Not all plastic storage containers respond well to the dishwasher or even to running water. Sometimes, heat worsens food stains! Try these fixes:

- Rub with a little baking soda paste.
- Scrub with a lemon half dipped in salt.
- Fill with water, add a spoonful of vinegar and leave overnight.
- Use an enzyme-based detergent. Afterwards, rinse thoroughly with a squeeze of lemon juice.
- If nothing else works, put the container in full sun – some edible pigments, such as turmeric, are light sensitive (*see Tip 701*). Wash well.

697. Gum freeze

It may be disgusting, but you must get rid of chewing gum stuck to your hard surfaces.

- Freeze with an icepack until brittle, then scrape off gently and carefully with the blunt side of a knife.

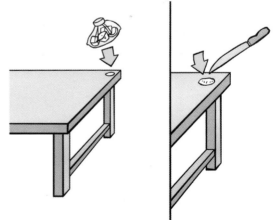

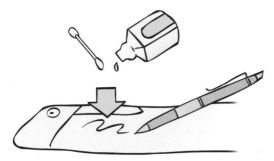

698. Biro buster

A quick-fix for ballpoint ink on fabric:

- First test for colour fastness on a discreet area.
- Lay the garment flat on an old towel or teacloth.
- Spot-treat the stain with repeated applications of eau de cologne – either with a cotton bud or a natural pump spray bottle – working from the outside to the inside of the mark.
- Wash immediately after removing the ink.

699. Tea in bed

Ah, the joys of breakfast in bed! But they quickly fade when you end up with a spilt cuppa that ruins your snowy duvet.

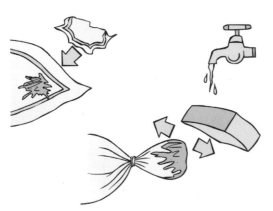

- Working quickly, mop up any excess and remove the outer cover of the duvet.
- Now pinch and lift the stitched casing away from the filling, and try to tie off the stained area with a rubber band to isolate it.
- Sponge with cold water, taking care to keep the filling away from the water.
- If necessary, rub away any remaining faint marks with mild detergent.

■ Last resorts

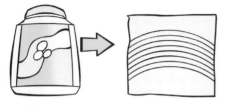

700. Fade away...

If stain removal hasn't worked for cottons with a non-protein stain – try some bleach as a last resort.

- Use an oxidizing bleach if there's any colour in the fabric at all; chlorine bleach is only for pure white cotton fabric.

701. Sun power

Many chutneys and spicy Asian pickles are preserved by turmeric, which is a difficult stain to shift. However, it is photo-sensitive, so it should fade in the sun.

- After you've washed and dry-cleaned (the solvent will help shift most of the pigment), hang on the line for several days.

Warning: This won't work so well on synthetics or animal fibres – in fact, hot sun may not be a great idea for those in the first place.

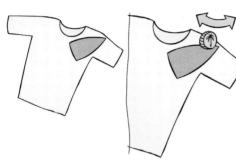

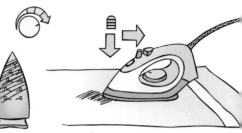

702. Scorched!

If you've managed to scorch a cotton garment, help is at hand.

- Gently rub the mark with the edge of a coin with a 'ribbed' texture along its 'rim'. This will often brush out the scorched fibres and expose the undamaged thread.
- Rinse well, and perhaps use a scented linen spray to counter the smell.

It's difficult, often impossible, to rescue scorched silks and synthetics as the fibres are easily damaged – even if you get the mark off, the fabric is unlikely to retain its strength.

703. Smeared soleplate

A too-hot iron has melted your blouse beyond rescue – and smeared it on the soleplate!

- Heat the iron to its highest setting, gliding it over an old cotton towel.
- Press hard to 'wipe' off the smears.
- Unplug the iron, let it cool slightly and use a scrunched-up wad of tissue paper to rub away any remaining marks.
- For an uncoated soleplate (not non-stick), a small ball of foil can usually shift stubborn debris.
- Clean with water to remove lint or foil residues.

■ Prevention is half the battle

704. Light white on white

White tablecloths?

• Don't even think of burning a coloured candle without placing something under it to catch the drips.

Most of the wax may be possible to take off with an iron (*see Tip 694*), but the dye that gave it colour is going to be rather more stubborn!

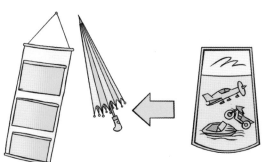

705. Clear plastic

Ordinary household cleaners can cloud transparent flexible plastic – the kind used for hanging pockets and see-through umbrellas.

• Use the polish used on the plastic windshields of convertibles – available from motor factories.

Garments and Accessories

Take the load off! From selecting the washload to fixing a runaway dye and washing up the machine, we're making washday a breeze! The folding, ironing and mending too. And also spruce up the rest of your wardrobe – coddle your accessories (we've got special tips for leather too).

■ A load of laundry

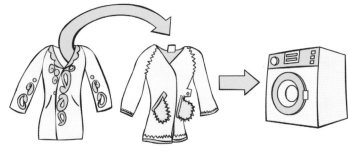

706. In reverse for washing

Some garments are best turned inside out before washing.

- Corduroy, velvet, devoré and other textured fabrics should be washed smooth side out.

- Anything with a raised or rubber print, or surface glitter, should also be washed inside out.
- This also holds for tufted knits – you don't want the loops to snag on a button or hook in the wash.
- For the same reason, turn embroidery inside out – provided the back is neat, of course. (If it isn't, try a gentle handwash or dry clean.)

707. Softest woollies

To keep your fine woollens really soft and shapely:

- Always handwash with pure soap solution (the kind intended for woollens and delicates) in cool water.
- Do *not* soak! Just swish around to loosen dirt, then knead gently.
- Rinse thoroughly till the water runs clear.
- Add a few drops of glycerine to the last rinse as a softener.
- Never squeeze or wring – roll up in a towel to get rid of excess water, then dry flat in shade.

708. Do not soften!

You may be tempted to maintain the softness of your precious cashmere garments.

- Never add fabric softeners, or you'll end up with a freshly felted garment!

709. Shades of silk

Printed silk fabric – as opposed to yarn-dyed silk – is particularly prone to fading and losing dye. That's because silk isn't very porous, and doesn't hold dye too deeply even when immersed.

- Always reverse printed silk garments before washing them.
- Ideally, dry-clean rather than wash.
- Always cool iron on the reverse, after making sure the dye doesn't transfer; test an unobtrusive corner on white fabric to check.

710. Salt and vinegar fix

Those beautiful vegetable-dyed garments are works of art. Treat them with care.

- Before the first wash – ideally, before your first wear – soak them in half a bucket of water to which 2 tablespoons of salt or white vinegar has been added.
- Rinse and drip-dry, inside out, in the shade.
- Turn the garment inside out for all subsequent washing, drying and ironing as well.

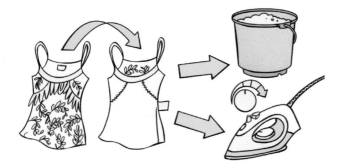

711. Sink for smalls

Underwear, especially anything with lace panels or underwiring, is best hand washed.

- Soak overnight in cool to lukewarm water, with a mild detergent.
- Hand wash in the morning, rinsing thoroughly and rubbing folds together gently to get the dirt out.
- Be careful not to twist underwired elements.
- Wring by scrunching in your hand; do not wring moulded or underwired garments.
- Hang bras upside-down by the baseband rather than the straps; if very lightweight, you could hang over a rod, supported by the centre-front panel.

712. Washing the machine

Once a month, clean out the washing machine:

- Remove and clean the filters.
- Replace mesh if need be – just sew on the same size of fine nylon mesh.
- Run the machine on a short wash with some vinegar to neutralize any detergent or mineral deposits.

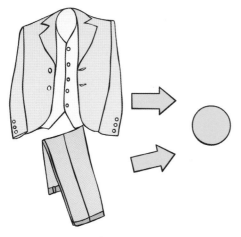

713. Do not split

Dry-clean all the parts of a suit – skirt, jacket and trousers, or jacket, waistcoat and trousers – together.

- The solvents can affect the dye a little, and it usually isn't noticeable – until held up against the same fabric. Cleaning them all together means they'll match and will wear evenly, too.
- If you have a blouse or shirt that tones in, a favourite scarf or tie that matches, consider cleaning it at the same time.

■ Pressed to please

714. Pull, then press

Smaller items made in absorbent fabrics can get pulled out of shape along the hem bindings when washed.

- Before ironing, ideally while they are still damp, tug them back into shape.
- First take hold of diagonally opposite corners and pull taut, gently, especially with lace or silk!
- Gently stretch from top to bottom: starting at the hem, hold along the sides (hands opposite each other) and pull gently.
- Keep walking your hands up the opposite sides until you reach the top.
- Stretch lengthways the same way.

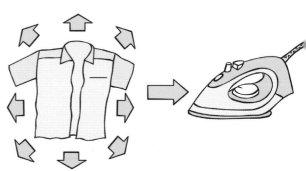

715. Trousers pressed

Not easy to iron, a pair of trousers.

- Straighten out (for in-seam pockets, turn out) and iron pockets.
- For a lightweight fabric, do up the fly and button down the waistband and pockets.
- Pull trousers over the board's narrow end. Iron the waistband, front pleats and yoke (back and front).
- Then iron the hems.
- Lay the trousers down the centre, with in-seams together and centred between front and back creases.
- Fold back the top trouser leg and iron the inside of the lower one, then the outside.
- Repeat with the other leg.

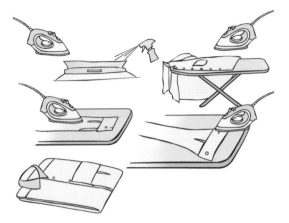

716. Crisp shirts

Make swift work of shirts.

- Iron damp cotton and linen, or spritz to dampen.
- Do the collar first – inside, then outside. Work inwards from the points.
- Draw the shirt over the ironing board one side at a time to iron the front, back, shoulders and yoke.
- Iron the sleeves. Do the cuffs opened out flat first, avoiding the buttons; button up and press from cuff to shoulder, with the opening upwards.
- Flip over and iron, cuff opening downwards.
- Press the fronts, then the back.
- Button up the front and neaten creases.

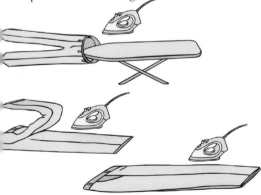

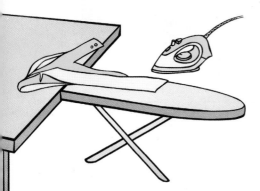

717. Perpendicular pressing

Avoid having one end of a garment trailing in the dust while you tackle the other side!

- Place an ironing board at right angles to your folding table or worktop.
- Let any surplus lap onto the table rather than dangle off.
- This will also prevent garments pulling out of shape or sliding off when, say, the heavy yoked waistband pulls on trousers while you iron the leg hems.
- It also prevents you accidentally standing on longer garments that trail off!

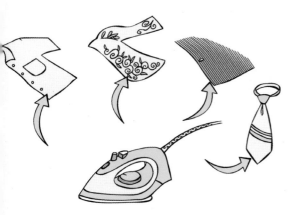

718. Iron inside!

Some garments should be ironed only on the reverse:

- Dark-dyed cottons – ironing on the right side can leave shiny marks!
- Embroidery – it will stand proud if ironed on the wrong side over a towel.
- Corduroy and velvet – otherwise the pile will flatten.
- Ties – otherwise the forked hem and seams will show up.

719. Don't press it!

Never be tempted to iron clothes in need of washing or dry cleaning to get 'just one more wear' out of them! Heat will set the dirt.

- Clothes could, in an emergency, be steamed with a handheld steamer or hung behind the bathroom door while you take a hot shower.

720. Do not iron!

Yes, the garment care label says you can iron that shirt – but you need to avoid the fiddly bits (or at least treat them with caution).

- Never iron over buttons or piping inserts – you'll leave a shine on the fabric on the other side!
- Avoid the velvet bits – those need to be steamed with the handheld device instead.
- Iron only on the reverse of embroidery and appliquéd or printed motifs.
- Iron on the wrong side first for collars, cuffs and pockets to prevent unsightly wrinkles.

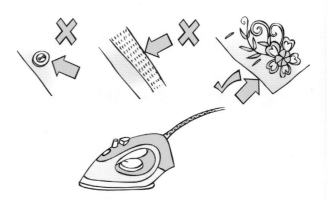

721. Look at the lining!

Always check the lining before you start pressing a jacket. The fabric may require a hot iron (cotton or linen); but if the lining is silk or a synthetic, you'll need to switch to a cool setting.

- Hang the garment outside a hot shower to steam out any wrinkles first, since those are difficult to shift, particularly from linen.
- Don't be tempted to steam iron the garment, though! It's too hot for the lining fabric. At most, use a cool water spray to dampen the fabric as you press.

722. Press and release

Gliding the iron over well-tailored formal wear could ruin the lapels and sleeves, and make suiting material shiny.

- Start with a slightly damp garment, or moisten a clean folded sheet.
- Add an extra layer of padding if needed.
- Lay the damp sheet (dry if the garment is damp) over the garment.
- Now use a 'press-and-release' action to iron the garment. Don't glide – just press down long enough to raise a puff of steam, then lift and move to the next area.
- Don't worry about covering every last inch.

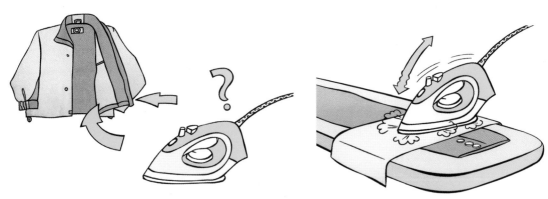

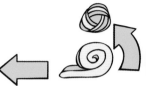

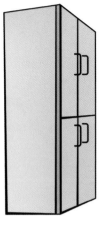

723. Button protection

The smallest graze from an iron heated for cotton or linen will melt those plastic buttons out of shape.

- Protect them by placing a thimble over them one at a time as you work on pressing the placket.

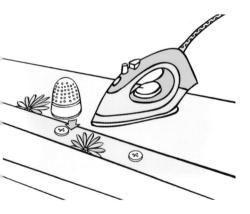

724. No-wrinkle woollies!

Natural wool fabrics bring yet another advantage to your winter wardrobe (besides warmth) – of the natural fibres, they are the least prone to wrinkling!

- Just roll up and put away for the summer.
- Air on unpacking next year and any creases should vanish!

Warning: If you have a problem with moths, take the usual moth-protection precautions before packing away woollies (*see Tips 815 and 816*).

■ Mending and altering

725. Hemline help

Shortening a garment?

- Measure the depth of the existing hem.
- Leave the same amount of fabric to fold over. Duplicating the old hem means the garment should still drape and hang the same way.
- Press flat.

Lengthening?

- Try to duplicate the original hem depth.
- Press out the old hem fold after you've finished and press the new hem flat.
- If the old crease refuses to disappear, one option may be to add a small line of machine embroidery or a bit of trim to hide it.

726. Un-sew a fine seam

Need to take apart a garment seam that's sewn tight?

- A very fine crochet hook helps take out the finest stitches without gouging the fabric. And it's safer than a needle held backwards or scissors that may rip the cloth!

T27. Cord for cords

Sewing buttons onto denim, corduroy or velvet can be a bit of a pain with an ordinary needle and thread.

- Try using a carpet needle threaded with dental floss instead.
- Add a drop of clear nail varnish to anchor threads more securely.

As a bonus, clear floss matches most buttons!

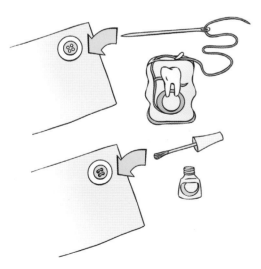

T28. Shanks for smoothness

Tight closures can distort the fabric around button attachment points. You can add a shank to flat sew-on buttons.

- Take a couple of loose stitches to position the button.
- Slide a cocktail stick under the button and through the stitches.
- Make tight stitches to secure the button, 6 up-and-down stitches per hole.
- Remove the cocktail stick.
- Wind the thread repeatedly around the loose threads between the fabric and the button, taking a half-knot at each winding.
- Secure the thread to the fabric with a couple of backstitches, knot and snip.

Note: A button shank is a loop of metal, plastic or fabric on the underside of some buttons. A shank will stop stress occuring to fabrics between the button and the garment.

729. 'Old lace'

Lace fabrics are too delicate for some stain treatments. It might be best to think laterally if you find a spot.

- Dye it! Don't worry – it needn't be as drastic as that sounds. Just steep in cold, strained tea for 10–15 minutes and wash to get that creamy 'old lace' colour throughout – that should camouflage all but the darkest marks.

And it still looks like the heirloom it probably is, only more so!

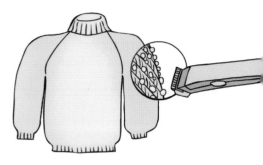

730. Proof against pilling

You can't completely protect clothes against pilling as they're subjected to friction – fold against fold, surface against skin, against each other in the machine.

- Minimize pilling by choosing clothing that's not too tight and by turning inside out for the wash.
- If not heavily soiled, opt for a gentle 'delicates' cycle to minimize agitation.

Already got the bobbles? An electric shaver or trimmer applied gently against fabric held taut should get rid of most of it. Be careful though – you don't want to take off surface fibre and thin the fabric!

731. The garment manicure

Got fraying threads around a zipper seam that constantly get caught in the teeth?

- Coat them with clear nail varnish to help them lie flat.

This also works for loose threads poking out of a textured weave or embroidered fabric.

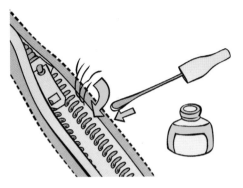

732. Clean, smooth zip-up

With a little care, zippers will stay rust- and snag-free.

- Free zippers of tufts of yarn or thread as well as dirt and sticky debris that can clog teeth regularly. A quick scrub with an old toothbrush dipped in detergent should do it.
- Rinse well and dry unzipped. (Normally, you should always zip up before washing.)
- After drying, slide a white candle along the zipper teeth to coat lightly with wax.
- Zip up and unzip a couple of times to distribute the wax evenly and loosen any clumps.

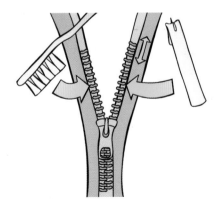

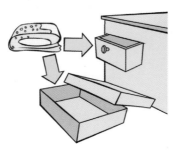

T33. Keep your beads off the hangers

Keep your fine beaded eveningwear in good shape. Hanging can distort the fabric and it will no longer drape well.

- Fold flat in drawers or boxes as appropriate.

T34. Acid-free wrapping

White cottons and linens as well as vintage fabrics and leather deserve an acid-free stuffing and protective layer. Acid-free tissue and boxes can be specially bought for the purpose, or:

- Cut up your old washed-out sheets for stuffing and use your old pillowcases for protective casing.
- Use any unbleached natural fibre.

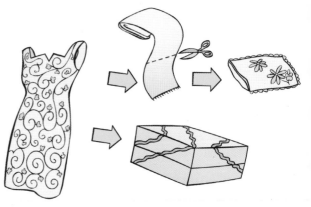

735. Fold-free heirlooms

Crease lines aren't the only problem; finer aged fabrics could wear and weaken at the creases.

- Don't fold antique brocade, heirloom lace or fine silk.
- Roll them up instead and place in a pillowcase (*see Tip 734*).
- If you must fold, refold every few weeks so crease lines don't set in.

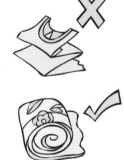

■ Love your leathers

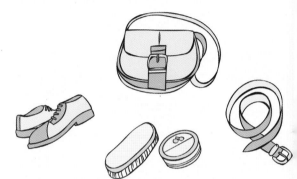

736. Polish is not just for shoes!

You look after your shoes, but what about your leather bags and belts?

- Use cream conditioner or neutral polish on your leather bags and belts to give them extra protection against cracks, scuffs and rain spots.

737. Kid glove treatment

For unlined leather gloves, the easiest and quickest clean-up is to put them on and then wash your hands:

- Wash up quickly with cool water and mild soap, using soap to rub away any little spots and stains.
- Rinse clear, remove the gloves and wrap in a towel to blot excess water.
- Smooth away any creases and dry flat on a fresh towel.

Warning: Lined gloves need a professional drycleaner's help.

738. Collar that leather coat

A good leather coat, with regular conditioning (using leather cream) and professional cleaning, could last you a lifetime.

However, the collars tend to get grubby long before the rest of the garment needs attention – and it's expensive to send it for full-on care that often!

- Try a detachable (button-on) washable collar in a fun or fancy fabric – faux fur or a paisley weave (machine-washable) never fail to look festive.
- Or drape a chic scarf along the neckline to shield the collar from skin oils and perspiration.

739. Rescue for scuffed leather

A small scrape need not spell the end of your favourite knee-highs.

- Try camouflaging the scratched spot with a matching shoe polish or a little indelible ink (check on an inner seam, such as on the back of a collar, to see that solvents in it don't make the leather dye bleed!).

740. Salt off!

Salt stains can retire leather boots and shoes long before they're old.

- Use a solution of equal parts white vinegar and water to clean as soon as you possibly can.
- Let dry before reconditioning with leather cream.

741. Second soles for special shoes

Get a thin rubber sole and heel cover attached to those high heels and expensive evening shoes.

- They are kinder to your feet.
- They'll save you wearing through the thin soles of a sandal.
- They'll help you avoid skids and falls by providing better traction than smooth leather or synthetic soles.

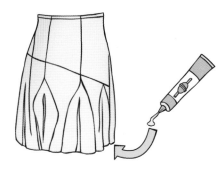

742. Hem raw hide

If your not-too-precious leather skirt is looking a bit tatty around the edges:

- Refinish or tidy up the hem with a dab of shoe glue.

Warning: Do not use on synthetic leather substitute, though – the solvents in one could release harmful gases from the other!

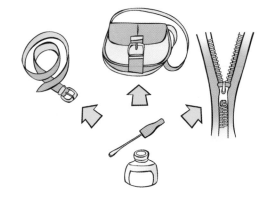

743. Metal enamel

Rivets, buckles, zipper tabs and other metal hardware on bags and belts can rust and tarnish quite quickly.

- Apply a coat of clear nail polish before using or wearing.

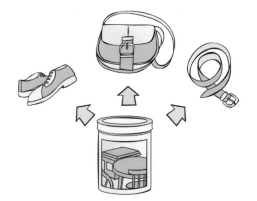

744. Wood wax for leather?

You don't have to invest in several tins of matching shoe polish for your entire footwear wardrobe.

- Use neutral furniture polish instead.

745. Feed your footwear

Similarly, don't despair if the supermarket shelves run out of leather cream.

- A few drops of unscented bath oil or baby oil will be a fine substitute.
- Use kitchen paper to absorb any excess before buffing.
- At a pinch, you could use any edible oil. But don't make a habit of it or the shoes will start smelling rancid!

746. Sporty smart

White footwear is an activewear classic. But dirt shows so easily. Try one of these tricks to smarten up between washes:

- Rub on white chalk for light soiling left after brushing away dirt from canvas shoes.
- A little white correction fluid will take care of small stains, even quite dark ones.

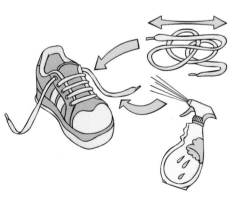

747. Loose laces?

If your shoelaces – or your children's – are forever coming undone, you have two choices:

- Switch to elastic laces – the knots on these tend to tighten with stretching!
- Dampen shoelaces slightly, stretch out and tie – the knot will tighten as the laces dry out.

748. Sweet feet

Banish the smell from those stinky trainers:

- Pour potpourri into socks and pop them in the shoes to absorb moisture while they deodorize.
- Add a few drops of any essential oil.
- Use deodorant on the soles of your feet and in-between the toes.
- Dust your toes with arrowroot powder or cornflour mixed with a good pinch of baking soda and a few drops of essential oil or perfume.
- Rub your feet with an alum crystal.

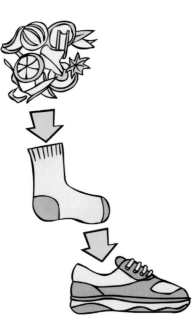

749. Spirit away the tar

Been walking down a melting tarred road?

- Blot the soles of your shoes with a wad of newspaper dipped in methylated spirits to shift the sticky stuff.

750. Soap on a belt

For leather bags and belts that really do need a thorough clean, you have two choices:

- For the really good stuff, you should ideally get it to a professional.
- For hardier, everyday accessories (satchels or cowboy boots, say), use saddle soap. Dab on with a moist cloth to clean the leather, then wipe dry and buff.

This is useful for leather luggage and sofas as well.

751. For seats, for bags

Synthetic bags that can't be washed in the machine need a different care regime from leather.

- Use a specialist product for cleaning car seats.
- Alternatively, remove any marks with a cleansing wipe and dry; then mist with hairspray and buff.
- For non-washable fabric bags, a baby wipe may help clean up stubborn grime. But first try a brush-down with talcum powder or cornflour, unless there is intricate surface embellishment.

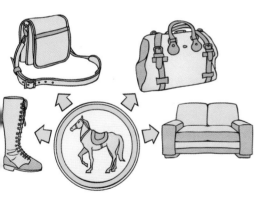

Furniture and Furnishings

Now lavish some TLC on the rest of your possessions!
The furniture comes first; furnishings follow suit. Take care of your
bed and it will take care of you, we say. And get down on the floor too.

■ Tables and chairs, chests of drawers

752. Spread the wear

There's always a favourite seat in the house, and it can end up looking tired and battered long before its mates have succumbed to wear and tear.

- From time to time, switch the chairs and covers of identical chairs around so that they wear evenly.
- Similarly, turn pillows and cushions, carpets and mattresses over and around regularly.
- Do the same with identical curtains hung on windows facing different directions – that way the southern or western sun won't fade one set faster.

753. Grime busters

Like shirt collars, your favourite sofa can attract a lot of grime along the top as people lounge back happily! And that's especially hard on leather. The Victorians invented antimacassars to deal with the problem, and there are a few measures you can take, too.

- Add a decorative throw across the back.
- Make a little fitted cover in a dark velvet or satiny fabric.
- Go Victorian and add a lace-edged white cloth over the headrest.

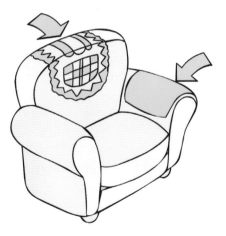

754. Soap for your sofa?

The advantage of cane or rattan furniture is that it doesn't mind a soapy scrub.

- Give cane furniture a bath in warm water and soap in the summer.
- Rinse well with water.
- Leave to dry in the sun.
- Refinish with clear varnish – this will add years to the life of the furniture and make dusting easier.

Warning: Be careful about giving the same treatment to plastic or vinyl — detergents can discolour them!

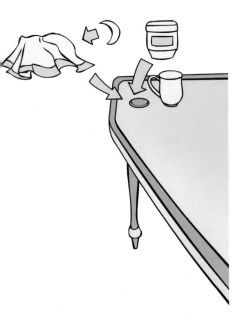

755. Banish those rings

Discoloured rings from coffee mugs or condensation from glasses can ruin a wooden surface.

- Apply a thin layer of petroleum jelly over the ring.
- Leave overnight.
- Next day, wipe off and buff briskly with a cloth.
- If the surface still feels greasy, a quick swipe with a vinegar and water solution can help. Dry well.
- If there are still some leftover marks, try a dot of white toothpaste on a baby toothbrush.
- Then rub beeswax along the grain to condition and season.
- Any residual discolouration could be treated with a matching shoe polish!

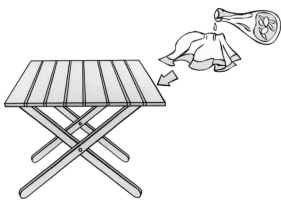

756. Oil – good for wood

If your wooden furniture is treated with a pigmented wood stain rather than varnish or paint, it could do with a little extra TLC.

- Protect it with an oil rub every so often – use a little olive oil on a soft cloth. After wiping away the residue, buff with a damp cloth.
- Use a dry cloth to sponge off any excess oil.
- Repeat every season.

757. Lemon for varnish

Varnished wood can also benefit from a little extra care from time to time.

• Substitute the olive oil in *Tip 756* with a dab of lemon oil diluted in olive oil, and apply every other month to retain the shine.

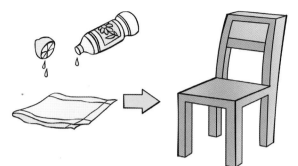

758. Smooth sliding

There's nothing more likely to damage your heirloom furniture than drawers that stick all the time.

Rub a candle stub along the sliders.
• Give the top edge of the drawers a coat of clear varnish (nail varnish is good) in case there are snags in the wooden surface and the drawer fits too tightly in the frame.

■ Household linens, soft furnishing, upholstery

759. White is right

White may seem completely impractical for soft furnishings, but it's actually an extremely sensible choice.

- Just make sure the covers are loose and washable.
- Cotton or canvas is ideal – white becomes even whiter when dried in the sun.
- You can bleach white cotton and linen if stain-busting doesn't work.

760. Separate the towels

Luxurious deep-pile towels are such a bathtime pleasure! However, that same fluff that dries you in a jiffy also gets all over the lint of your washing machine – and all over other clothes.

- Avoid washing towels with other garments.
- If you must, choose colours that are identical.
- Certain fabrics pick up lint more than others – keep corduroy, velvet, plush, velour, fleece and looser knits (such as piqué) clear of the towels!
- Terry towelling itself is lint-loving! Don't even dream about washing dissimilar colours of towels together.

761. Hang curtains while wet

Don't dry washable curtains completely before you return them to the window.

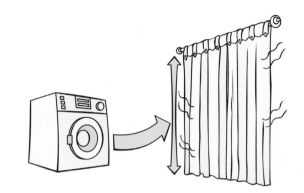

- Spin dry at a low speed rather than tumble drying.
- If drip-drying, wait till there are no more drips but the fabric still feels damp.
- Clean the pelmet, rails and window.
- Hang up the curtains while still damp – the damp weight will pull them down, straightening out any creases and kinks.

762. Freeze those dust mites!

You know all about the amazing durability of dust mites and their debris (*see Tip 822*). But what about the sheets you can't hot-wash?

- Pop them into a plastic bag and put them in the freezer overnight after laundering.

It may not destroy all the mites, perhaps, and certainly won't get rid of the eggs and debris. But it'll at least slow down the population explosion and bring the numbers down!

This is also a good tactic for dealing with moth larvae.

763. Fold before drying

Just washed the sheets? Don't tumble-dry, as this will set the creases, and you'll spend more time ironing!

- Shake out and fold the sheet neatly into a smaller rectangle before you hang it out to dry.
- This will make the sheet quicker to iron – just whip it off the line and lay on the board.
- If you smooth out the hems nicely and give the sheet a sharp snap while folding, you may not even need to iron!

764. Bonus pressing

When ironing garments with buttons, corded details or raised textures, it's a good idea to have some extra padding under the items (*and see Tip 723*).

- Lay folded sheets on your ironing board before ironing the decorated items.

The bonus is pressed sheets that needed no extra work!

765. Dripping duvets!

Drying machine-washable, anti-allergy duvets can be a bit of a job. Here are a few options:

- Roll in a bath sheet or heavy bedspread and drape across a large metal drying rack – over the two topmost bars that are furthest apart – pulling more of the surface flat.
- Dry flat on a large, pale-coloured picnic blanket or bath sheet.
- Drape across the backs of two chairs, placed back to back about 1 m/3 feet apart. Use only plastic or rattan chairs, not wood or metal!

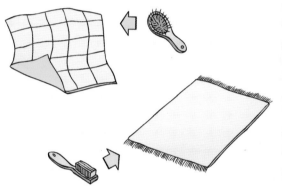

766. Shaggy blankets

Dry-cleaning can flatten the tufts of a shaggy rug, throw or blanket. You can brush them back gently to fluff up again.

- Don't use a brush with nylon bristles, and certainly not wire. Even plastic can damage the pile or tear out fine fibres.
- Get hold of a hairbrush with rubber bristles set in a wooden handle for best results.
- For hardier cotton shag, use a suede brush.

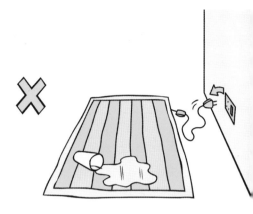

767. Don't fold the (electric) blanket!

You could damage the wires inside and cause a short-circuit.

- Store it under the mattress so it stays flat (only if the bed has a box base – slatted bases are not suitable).
- If you don't have any space in summer, roll up the blanket loosely – do NOT fold! Store in a spacious, uncluttered storage box.
- Check carefully before using it again. Holding it up against strong light or shining a torch through from the wrong side should help you spot any signs of damage.

768. Don't wash the blanket!

Again, it's the electric blanket we mean. It won't like to get wet, and neither will you!

- Should a spill happen, unplug at once.
- Mop up as much liquid as you can and let dry thoroughly.
- Sprinkle a little talcum powder on any stain left behind while it dries.
- Once quite dry, brush away the talcum powder.
- If you still have a visible mark, take it to the servicing agent, who may be able to help. Do NOT try to clean it yourself or have it dry-cleaned!

769. Quilts in the air

A quilt or duvet with a natural filling should be professionally cleaned. However, the thick wadding can retain solvents – you don't want to inhale or have them taint other things in the cupboard.

- After cleaning, unfold and air quilts and duvets to get rid of trapped volatiles.
- Hanging them over the back of a chair by the window will do. Turn once to expose both sides to fresh air and sunshine.
- If you have a deck, spread the quilt on a picnic blanket – take in after an hour.

770. Bed maintenance

Vacuuming the mattress?

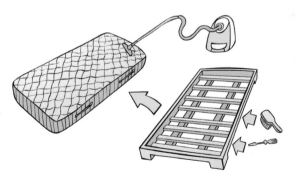

- Take it off the bed to do it on the floor.
- This will give you a chance to clean the bed base.
- While you're at it, check the mesh and screws, if any – get the drill at once if you find the screws need tightening; if the mesh seems warped, see if you can turn it over while you order a replacement.

771. Don't wash, just dry

Washing won't do the natural fillings in your pillows any favours.

- Either have them professionally dry-cleaned (if the manufacturer's label advises it) or just air them frequently in natural light.
- If they can take the heat, it's a good idea to pop them in the tumble-dryer for a few minutes to freshen and fluff them up.
- If the casing seems greasy (it will absorb some skin oils, despite the pillowcase), try sprinkling with talcum powder and brushing it out after a couple of hours.
- Protect the pillow as much as possible by placing a pillow protector under the pillowcase.

772. No foam in the water!

You might think synthetic foam cushions and pillows could do with a nice soapy wash. However, foam is not the most stable material and will soon crumble under the assault of water and detergent.

- Give them a sponge bath with a little soapy water, then with clean water to rinse away the detergent.
- Wrap in a towel and squeeze to get the moisture out.
- Dry in the shade.

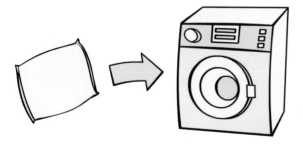

TT3. Roll up the rug

Putting rugs, mats and carpets into storage?

- Roll up with the pile or shag side facing outwards.
- Never fold rugs and carpets.
- Place in a box made of acid-free paper or in a drawstring bag (cut from an old well-washed sheet) placed inside a chest or closet.
- Unless space is truly at a premium, avoid keeping the roll standing up.

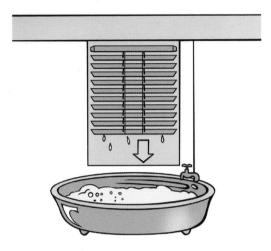

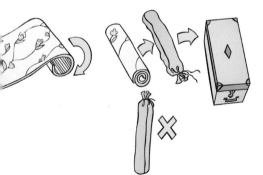

TT4. Give blinds a bath

The easiest way to clean metal and synthetic blinds is in the bath.

- Fill the bath with hand-hot water and a cup of washing-up liquid.
- Dip the blinds in and rinse well – empty the bath and re-fill with clean water as often as necessary.
- Hang them back up to dry, with folded sheets or large beach towels rolled up beneath to catch drips; change the sheets/towels often, wringing them out and drying to replace again.

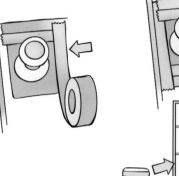

775. *Bread for blinds?*

For the weekly dusting, use a few crusty slices of bread to mop up the dust from blinds if you don't want to get out the vacuum cleaner. You could use a paintbrush too, but that just redistributes the dust.

- Hold the bread with the crust facing into your palm and press the softer edge into the top slats.
- Wipe along from left to right, then move down and repeat.
- If you go gently, this works well for paper blinds and split-cane weaves too.

776. *Knobs, sills, knockers*

The best way to clean door furniture is with a proprietary polish for brass or chrome. However, those aren't kind to wood or paint!

- Before you begin, apply masking tape to the gloss paint around the metal strip up to an inch on each side.
- Now polish away, dry and strip off the masking tape carefully.
- On a matte or distressed finish, masking tape may lift paint, so consider using a coat of petroleum jelly instead.
- Protect window frames in the same way when washing windows.

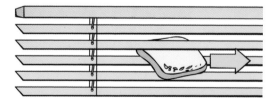

𝒯𝒯𝒯. Bread basket

Once again, it's stale bread to the rescue – of woven baskets.

- Wad up a thick slice of bread, moistening with a spritz of water, if necessary.
- Press into the weave of baskets, changing around often, to lift out dust.

This means you won't have to subject the cane or rattan to moisture too frequently.

𝒯𝒯8. Linseed for unsealed wood

Unsealed and unwaxed floorboards call for the care that only linseed oil can give.

- Moisten a rag with oil and dab onto the floorboards until it sinks in.
- Buff to a shine.
- Damp-mop daily to maintain.
- Repeat the 'oil feed' twice a year – you probably won't need to do much more than swab lightly if the boards were well impregnated the first time.
- If you prefer, add a few drops of lemon oil for a nice aroma.

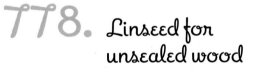

779. Trainers for vinyl stains

Got a stain on your vinyl floor tiles?

- Moondance across it in your slippers (or any soft-rubber soled shoes) to 'erase'!

780. Top up the polish

Varnished wooden floorboards need a daily damp mop to prevent dust from scratching the finish.

- A fortnightly addition of a few drops of furniture polish to the mopping water will renew the surface treatment.

Do It Yourself

Doing It Yourself needn't be a task, nor a minefield. Navigate and stock your workshop or workroom with our bright ideas – from powering up and sorting your hobby stuff, to minor household repairs and easers, to smart projects for your home and garden and wardrobes that call for mere minutes!

■ Workshop basics

781. Power down!

Electricity is potentially life threatening. When working with electricity:

- NEVER work on a live circuit.
- Always test with a voltage tester: it looks like a screwdriver but lights up if the wire is live.
- If the tester lights up although you've turned off the switch, the circuit breaker may be faulty. Switch off the mains power.
- Never pull out a plug by the cord! Always hold the plug firmly and pull gently. Never touch the prongs while doing so, either with your hands or an instrument.

If you ever have any doubt about what to do, get professional advice first!

782. Hang it all!

You don't need a fancy, niche-for-every-last-screw toolbox to keep DIY equipment sorted.

- Fix a large section of grating or length of strong wire fencing along your garage wall, and hang it all off it!
- You can use S-hooks, bulldog clips to hold flat objects (like sandpaper) in place, small metal flowerpots or sand buckets to hold nuts and bolts, and perhaps some strong magnets to attach awkward shapes like hard hats and keep pairs of gloves together (*see Tip 783*).

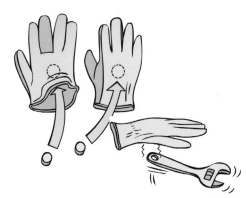

783. Get a firmer grip on gloves

Missing one of a pair of gloves? Prone to having tools flip out of your hands? Here's a stick-together solution for you!

Get a set of small round magnets – like those used on magnetic boards or the fridge door.

- Attach one to the inside of each of your work gloves, in the palm.

So when you put them away, they'll hang together, and when you handle a tool with an iron core, they'll hang on to that too. Plus, has clearing up a spilled box of nails ever been so easy?

Repairs and household maintenance

784. Stop that drip, quick!

Leaking taps waste gallons of water yet are usually easy to fix – especially the old-fashioned sort. They usually just need to have their washers replaced.

• Keep an assortment of washers in different sizes and thicknesses in your repair kit.

The more modern ones have ceramic washers or O rings instead. The first type shouldn't need replacing unless you have a faulty product (in which case the manufacturer should replace it). The second is better left to the manufacturer's service staff, since you'll probably have to order the exact parts to fit your fixtures anyway.

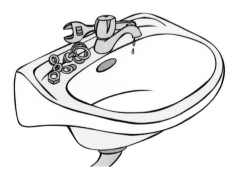

785. Painted wood, clean glass

Getting a little paint on the window panes while doing the frame or sill may seem inevitable.

• Mask the sill with tape before you start painting

Try this for splatters already there:

• Dip a sponge or rag in warm vinegar and hold over the stain to soften it.
• Now scrape the paint away with a sharp-bladed razor or craft knife.
• Rinse and wipe the window.

786. Smooth locks and silent hinges

Got a lock that sticks or a hinge that keeps creaking? Try this for a no-mess solution.

- Rub the offending hinge or the 'sticky' key with a graphite pencil.
- Now open and close the door (or wiggle the key in the lock) several times to distribute the graphite.

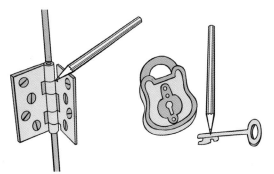

787. Vase with a 'vent'!

Your favourite vase sprung a leak?

Use a little food colouring to help seal the weak spot, then rinse clean.

- Let dry and dribble a little wax from a melting candle to seal – preferably from the inside.
- Alternatively, paint the crack on the wrong side with thickened nail enamel or acrylic paint.

788. Tangled jewellery?

Untangling the bling collection is always a problem for teenage girls; and every mother's nightmare. Reduce the confusion with a Hollywood greenroom-style mirror.

Make it big, possibly floor-length, and they won't keep popping into your walk-in wardrobe!

- Now chuck the strip lights and screw in an odd collection of assorted knobs – mix it up for extra funkiness.

Hang all the bits and bobs on those knobs for instant access. Tangle sorted!

789. Curb your herbs

Unless your kitchen garden sits in pots on the window sill, the more invasive herbs – such as mint – can quickly overrun their allotted beds.

Push sections of plastic builder's pipes into the soil to a depth of 7–10 cm/3–4 inches, and use them as 'planters'.

The open-ended cylinders give your herbs the benefits of being bedded rather than potted, yet keep them in their places!

790. Chalk marked

With some blackboard paint, almost anything becomes easier to label.

- Recycle ice lolly sticks as plant tags.
- Turn the skirting boards in the nursery into one long toddler-high drawing easel.
- On folding garden chairs, paint neat rectangles in which to scrawl guests' names to indicate the seating plan!
- Paint on paper or metal for rewriteable labels for boxes and jars (slip the label behind clear film so it won't rub off with regular handling).
- Scrawl a 'Busy' message on your home office or workshop door!

791. Fairy glow

Make your own magical string of fairy lights!

- Cut out circles 15–18 cm/6–7 inches in diameter from white and pastel card.
- Remove a 'quarter wedge' from each and make the wings – fold over, draw on a feathery edge (*see illustration*) and cut out.
- Roll the three-quarter circles into cones and snip off the pointed end.
- Sew on wings with small running stitches or use glue.
- Remove bulbs from your string of lights, push holders through each cone, screw the bulb back!

Warning: Don't try this with incandescent bulbs which might get hot and start a fire!

792. Ribbon-pleated light

Use a spool of satin ribbon to give a plain paper or fabric lampshade a pleated silk look.

- Using fabric glue, tack one end of the ribbon to an inside rim of the lampshade.
- When dry, wind the ribbon taut around and through the frame, overlapping the bands to look like pleats.
- When you've finished, fix the end in place the same way.
- For extra security, attach two lines of fabric tape along the inner top and bottom rims with glue to hold the ribbon in place.

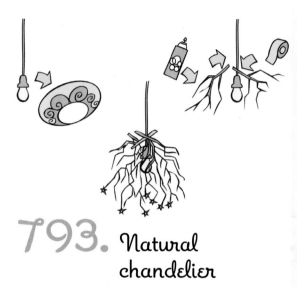

793. Natural chandelier

Make your own chandelier with dried twigs from the garden or local park.

- Remove the shade of your pendant lamp, making sure the socket can still hold the light bulb securely.
- Spray-paint the twigs silver.
- When dry, cluster around the light bulb and tie onto the pendant cord with metallic parcel tape.
- If you like, you can even dangle paper or tinsel stars or frost with fake snow.

Warning: Don't try this with incandescent bulbs which might get hot and start a fire!

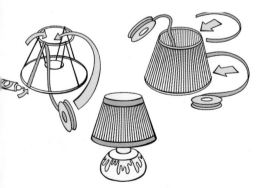

794. Light up, do!

Metal cigar tubes are perfect for making outdoor candles.

- Run in a wick (available at craft shops) to the bottom.
- Keeping the wick centred, fill the tube with wax granules (also from the craft shop).
- You can add a few drops of essential oil.
- Don't fill right to the top. Leave a 2.5 cm/1 inch gap and add scrunched-up paper to fill the space so that the wax and wick don't shift.
- Before lighting, remove the paper and anchor the tube a couple of inches deep into sand or soil.
- Never leave unattended!

795. Framed by the pane

An old window shutter or cabinet door with multiple panes can be easily converted into a picture frame for those happy family photos!

- Cut out a piece of glossy cardboard the same size as the door or shutter.
- Measure and mark the positions of the window panes on the cardboard.
- Centre a photograph in each pane and stick to the board base – use non-permanent adhesive or photo corners to remove easily.
- Carefully nail the cardboard to the back of the door/shutter frame and hang.
- Leave the doorknob on for a quirky touch!

796. Busy daisies

Brighten up a plain surface or piece of fabric by stamping with a row of flowers. You'll need fresh flowers for this – a daisy type, such as gerbera, will work best.

- Mix fabric or acrylic paint to a spreadable consistency with thinner (not water) in a saucer and press the flower into it face down.
- Blot the flower on a sheet of brown paper to remove excess paint, then begin stamping, holding the flower by the stalk.
- You should get 2 to 3 impressions per dip.

As a bonus, the brown paper will look good enough to save as handmade wrapping paper!

797. Candle in a tin

It's easy to make a perforated 'shade' for outdoor candles if you have some old tin cans to hand.

- Get a sturdy hole punch for metals.
- Remove any label on the tin, clean well, and use a can opener to remove the top and bottom, giving you an open cylinder.
- Carefully punch through the can wall at random to perforate.
- Add a light coat of clear varnish or car wax to prevent rust.
- Slip over your candle to use!

798. Paper for your drawers

This is a pep-up plan for that tired-looking but serviceable chest of drawers.

- Get some wallpaper to match your décor.
- Unscrew the drawer handles.
- Using double-sided sticky tape, position some wallpaper to fit the drawer fronts, not including the frame. Mark the size for each drawer on the wallpaper in light pencil.
- Remove the drawers, sand all the surfaces and paint the frame in a coordinating colour.
- When dry, paste the sections of wallpaper onto the drawer fronts.
- Seal the drawers and frame with a coat of clear varnish.

Pest Control

You don't want to be annoyed by buzzing insects, but you don't want to poison your own environment either! Here are safe, swift and effective ways to stall the creepy-crawlies' takeover agenda – and vanquish the weeds too. Banish them all from your garden, as well as from the pantry and cupboards and library...

■ Weapons and armour

799. Open with caution!

Fill a tight-shutting aluminium box with:

- Mousetraps
- A non-toxic insecticide safe to use in food preparation and dining areas
- A botanical garden insecticide
- A small bottle of lemongrass essential oil (keep two bottles – diluted in alcohol and vegetable oil – ready for use) and some citronella candles or incense
- A spray bottle filled with a weak solution of one part detergent or glycerine in two or three parts water

- A big box of borax
- Antiseptic wipes and disinfectant; kitchen paper
- Rubber gloves – disinfect with bleach solution after use

■ Flying menaces

801. Spritz and swat!

The simplest anti-insect measures can be the best.

• Spray insects with detergent/glycerine spray (*also see Tip 802*).
• Have a fly swat handy (or even a rolled up newspaper or magazine).

The mildly sticky solution hangs on to insect wings and weighs down creepy-crawly legs, making them less of a fast-moving target. Now swat them!

Warning: Never attack hornets, bees and wasps in this way – they may turn on you!

800. Flies stop here!

A strong-smelling set of herbs in your window box can deter all but the most persistent housefly – provided your kitchen is hygienic (therefore not too attractive!).

• Growing pots of mint or basil (especially the more intensely aromatic Thai basil) is especially effective.
• A small bay tree near the door will look pleasingly Mediterranean and provide an aroma unattractive to most insects but lovely in cooking.
• Trim the herbs regularly, or rub a few leaves between your fingers as you open the windows or door to release the aromatic oils.

802. Lacquer the mosquitoes!

You may be bothered with mosquitoes during a hot summer or when on holiday in warmer climes.

- When you see mosquitoes, spray the air with hair spray – it stiffens their wings and drops them.
- Swing the can around to cover a wide area quickly.
- Now swat!

803. Lemon grass mosquito wash

Lemon grass keeps mosquitoes at bay – most of these annoying buzzers seem to hate the lovely aroma!

- Add a few drops to your mopping water.
- Dab some on your cleaning cloths and sponges.
- Use the oil to wipe down wooden benches, window and door frames.

804. Swipe away bee stings

Swiping a bee provokes it to defend itself with a stinging attack! (Should you spot an entire swarm or hive, run!) If you have been stung:

- Don't squeeze; you'll drive the venom deeper (see that sac pulsing on the end of the sting?).
- Fish out your credit card and scrape at an angle to drive the sting out without squeezing.
- Dab on a solution of baking soda to ease the sting.

805. Wasp sting soother

Wasps and hornets, unlike bees, won't leave the stinger behind.

- Soothe with a dribble of lemon juice or vinegar to neutralize the venom – or get hold of an anaesthetic spray.

806. Maddened by midges?

Eucalyptus oil can keep most insects at bay. (It also takes care of lingering cooking smells, as most of us humans find it refreshing rather than repelling!)

- After you've finished cooking a barbecue supper and are just about to sit down to eat, throw a few eucalyptus twigs on the barbie before you grab your plate.

807. Get rid of wasps

As soon as you spot a wasps' nest:

- Place uncovered jars of sugar-water (half honey or sugar and half water) near the nest.
- The wasps love the sweet syrup so much, they'll die to get at it!

808. The bug-free barbecue

Ah, glorious summer, with its alfresco dinners and barbies! Beautiful – if only the buzzing cloud of insects would steer clear...

Make citronella your signature scent for the outdoors, on camping trips and even the back garden.

- The scented candles add elegance to your table.
- Garden torches and tealight holders 'planted' in pots help keep the swarms away from the vegetation they love to hide in.
- If you can stand the stronger smell, burn citronella-scented incense (coils or cones, or whatever's convenient) – the smoke acts as double deterrent.
- Burn a few coils or cones under the table to protect ankles from nips!

■ Creepy-crawlies

809. Infested with silverfish?

These insects love starch, endangering your library especially. They also attack photographs, cardboard packaging, textiles, papier mâché and toiletries with starchy fillers.

- In a pet- and child-free home, bait 'traps' with flour and borax. This should do the trick!
- Add packets of silica gel, as silverfish thrive on humidity.
- Decant packaged foods into tight-lidded containers.

810. Give those ants their marching orders

Borax to the rescue again.

• Follow them home. Now you can feed them to death.
• Mix sugar or coarse cereal (such as polenta or oatmeal) with borax.
• Leave spoonfuls of these near the entrance to ant homes. The insects will carry the grain back in with them, maximizing your chances of getting the whole colony – something spraying insecticides doesn't do.

Warning: Make sure children can't get at the borax-tainted bits.

811. Roach attack!

In the event that you come across pests on holiday, borax will be your best friend again.

• Make a stiffish paste of flour, sugar and borax.
• Leave near cracks, crannies, drains and under cabinets.
• Place a saucer of water nearby if there isn't a source of water close.

The cockroaches will eat the bait and get thirsty, then they'll drink water, swell up and explode!

■ Rodents (and other storecupboard thieves)

812. Your pantry is bugged!

Any evidence of mothlike insects, weevils or white maggots in cereal grains, dried pulses and flours? Unfortunately, there's no way back for infested foods.

- Throw out any jar with a hint of movement, 'floury' bits at the bottom or 'tunnels' pockmarking the surface of flours.
- Empty the cupboards.
- Wash *everything* in hot soapy water – containers and shelves.
- Dry everything in the sun if possible.
- Spray non-toxic insecticide into every crack and crevice.
- Dispense with all loose lids and paper packages.
- Decant foodstuff into sealed transparent jars.

813. Rats!

Rats are a real health hazard and you must keep them at bay at all costs.

Cleanliness and tidiness are the only answers.

- No stray crumbs and spills, no dirty dishes in the sink, no uncovered food or bins.
- Dispense with clutter – full wastepaper baskets, mattresses that leak stuffing, old rags, soiled dishcloths, smelly mops.
- Plaster any cracks and crevices in the walls.
- Wrap tape around pipes where they meet walls.
- Set traps near vents and ventilators.
- Use wire mesh screens on windows and doors.
- Seal gaps under doors with felt (saves on heating too).

814. *Mouse attack!*

Baiting the mousetrap?

- Wash your hands with vinegar to eliminate any odour and don rubber gloves – mice have a good sense of smell, and will avoid anything that smells odd, such as humans!
- A blob of peanut butter or a stiff ball of porridge is a better bet than the traditional cheese – mice are carb-loving rodents, which is why they like the farmer's fields!

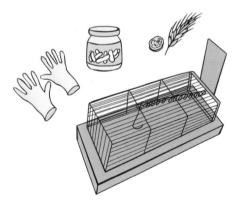

815. *Save your silks (and cashmere)*

Dry cleaning's kind to delicate fabrics and should kill any moth eggs hiding in there. Clean everything before putting away for a season. Even woollies marked safe for a cold machine wash are better off being dry cleaned.

- Moths are attracted to food smells and perspiration, so long gaps between deep cleans means trouble.
- Upholstery and carpets need a seasonal steam-clean.
- All garments that can take a hot wash should get one before being put in storage – with plenty of mothballs.
- Freezing works well, too – seal clean garments in a re-sealable bag and place in the freezer for at least four hours.

816. Clothes safe in the chest

Storing winter clothes in a cedar or camphor chest provides great protection from munching insects.

- Use fine sandpaper lightly on the inside to refresh the aroma.
- If using other woods, dab camphor or cedar essential oil (diluted with vegetable oil) down the sides. Repeat as the scent wears off.
- Leave the used cotton balls in your drawers to protect smaller garments.
- Small muslin sachets with chips of cedar or camphor wood help, as does dried lavender.
- Once the chips (or lavender buds) seem to be losing their smell, burn them on your log fire.

817. Feed the birds to save your garden

Not only might you save your precious buds and blooms, inviting a feathered flock means natural insect control!

- Many birds like to supplement their seed snack with a protein-rich caterpillar or a juicy gnat.
- Others will make straight for the insect course if you give them a shady playground and some water.
- The birdfeeder and birdbath needn't be fancy – strings of popcorn and a sturdy shallow basin or an old trough will work well. Change the water daily though, to avoid it turning into an insect-breeding ground.

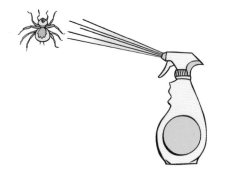

818. Shower away spiders

They may give you the heebie-jeebies, but most garden spiders are your allies against insect pests.

- If they do bother you, spritz water from a spray bottle to send them scurrying.
- If they're building cobwebs in the kitchen and it's hygiene you're worried about, persistent removal usually persuades them to choose another location.

819. Shell the snails!

Mount a shell attack on garden slugs and snails.

- Strew crushed seashells, fine gravel or coarse sand over the soil in flowerpots, window boxes and small beds to deter soft-bellied snails and slugs, which love to feast on your tomato leaves.

820. Plant-type pests

Don't use a chemical cocktail of weed killers if you can possibly help it.

- For weeds coming up between paving stones or through cracks and crevices, just scald with some boiling salted water.
- For weeds in flower pots and beds, mulching is your best bet – it saves you water (and watering time) too.

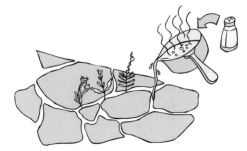

■ In bed with the bugs!

821. Pet peeves

Fleas and ticks, like many other insects, are repelled to some extent by strong smells. The trick is choosing products that are safe for your pet as well.

- Consider adding brewer's yeast and garlic to your pet's food.
- Strew your pet's basket, bed or sleeping area with rosemary, eucalyptus or rue leaves, or fennel seeds.

822. Give those mites the brush-off!

- To kill the mites and remove residual allergens, wash bedlinen at temperatures above 60°C/140°F.
- Cold or warm water will swill out the allergy-causing bits, but won't kill mites that cling on.
- Dry cleaning can kill mites, but the dead bodies will stay – and continue to irritate every time you breathe them in.
- If your bedding can't stand a really hot wash, dry cleaning and then washing may help.
- Hypoallergenic covers and synthetic fillers will help.
- Keep your pet out of the bedroom.

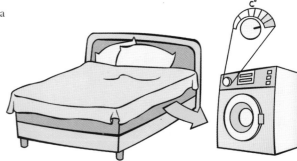

Pet Care

Because your pets are as entitled to a safe, comfy home as you are, we have tips that help you settle in a new addition, treat every species (canine, feline, avian and rodent) right, and pet-proof your home to boot!

■ New among us

823. One at a time

If you've got a pet, try to plan any pregnancies for when the pet is grown-up and secure.

- During your pregnancy, playing with a baby doll and going through cuddling motions will help you spot any signs of jealousy.
- Mark the bedroom and nursery off-limits.

- Be loving and attentive to your pet.
- Have a child over often so it gets used to small people.

Preferably wait until your child settles in school before getting a pet. Start small – a fish, a bird or a rabbit make good first pets.

824. Home, new home

Playing with a new young pet immediately upon arrival can be rather unsettling for it.

- Set up bedding, litter (for a kitten), food and water bowls in a quiet, warm corner.
- Put your pet there first – offer company, talking in a low, soothing voice.
- Let it explore in its own time but keep an eye out.
- A ticking clock tucked in the blanket and a warm water bottle at bedtime will help.
- Try to bring a familiar piece of comfort from the kitten's or pup's first home.

825. Your pet and your pre-school

Learning the rules early means growing up together is safe and fun.

- Teach the children – by example and advice – to wash their hands after playing with their pets or handling the pet's food dishes or toys.
- Supervise playtime together and ban the pet from the nursery until your child is at least five.
- Teach children that it hurts to have tails, ears and whiskers tugged. (Compare it to their hair being tugged.)
- Let them help with brushing coats, putting out food and filling water bowls.

■ Young animals

826. Cardboard comfort

Don't invest in a fancy wicker basket just yet!

- Wait until your cat or puppy is fully house-trained and past the teething stage.
- Until then, a warm bed of old clean throws and clothing in a cardboard box is easiest to replace in case of accidents, or when it gets soiled or worn.
- When you do choose a permanent bed, washability should be your main consideration.

827. Well groomed!

Establish a grooming schedule.

- Start early.
- Designate a quiet spot, where your pet can stand up on a wide bench or table.
- Get it used to standing still. Praise and pet continuously.
- Help it get used to examination. Pick up the paws, look in the ears, open its mouth and touch its teeth.
- Brush its back in short sessions, speaking soothingly throughout.
- Go on to its legs, neck, head, belly and chest.
- Never punish during grooming.
- Never threaten a pet with a grooming tool.

828. Learning through play

Cats and dogs learn through play. So let your pet learn its place in the family from playing!

- Young cats love to play predator.
- Young dogs interpret 'winning' as a move up in the pecking order. Never lose a game of tug of war.
- Teach it to 'drop it' or 'let go' before it gets too big for you to beat at the game!
- Never encourage wrestling matches with your pup.
- With dogs, make sure all toys are 'handed' back to you at the end of play to establish dominance.

829. All together now

Pets get bored if left on their own and love it if you play with them.

- Cats love hunting – favourite prey includes fabric or paper butterflies tied to (non-fraying) ribbons, or catnip mice.
- Dogs and cats love balls – roll a small ball on the carpet for kitty or puppy to chase!
- Adult cats and dogs enjoy retrieving – even scrunched up paper (avoid newsprint). However, it should be too big for your pet to swallow!
- Puppies can get quickly bored with an 'old toy'.

830. Home alone

Emergencies can occur which mean you have to leave your pet.

- Have someone trusted look in on a young pup a couple of hours after you leave and perhaps take it out for a quick walk.
- Secure it in a large barred crate with safe toys and perhaps a rawhide chew.
- Play the radio softly in the next room – the sound of voices helps young dogs feel secure.
- Pet and praise when locking and letting it out.
- But avoid melodramatic drawn-out goodbyes and excited arrivals.

831. Net over cot

Babies and young animals can transfer germs and parasites to each other, overloading their delicate immune systems.

- If you have a young pup or kitten, fit a net over your baby's pram and cot. After all, the warm, soft spaces are very tempting for pets to curl up in!

■ Pet safety

832. Keep safe

A pet has the same safety needs as a toddler.

- Use a sturdy child gate at doors, windows and stairways you don't want it to have access to.
- Restrain it repeatedly to cure attempts to climb or jump out.
- Wire fencing isn't really the best bet; it has 'give', which can allow a dog or cat to burrow or slip under it.
- If you take your pet out in the car and it is too big to crate, invest in a harness that clips on to seatbelts.

833. Clamp up the cables

Teething pups will chew anything rubbery and curious kittens love trailing ropes, which is dangerous if they choose electrical wiring.

- Make sure all cables are either enclosed or clamped well above reach of a pet.
- Any that you can't enclose or move higher, you need to enclose in rigid plastic casing.
- If you can find nothing else, use rigid corrugated pipes – fang-resistant metal or sturdy plastic.
- Train your pets to avoid adopting these for chews and toys – this may save your garden hose and tyres later!

834. Play it safe with solids and substances

Your sewing basket or craft kit could turn lethal.

- Plastic or metal bits can kill if swallowed. So can larger objects that splinter under attack.
- Glue, varnish and paint stripper fumes are dangerous. Whenever you use these, shut your pet out of the room! Allow them back in only after the room has been well ventilated and supplies put away.
- Beware cigarette butts.
- Concentrated detergents or washing up liquids are unsafe.
- Beware small batteries, which can choke and poison.
- Tinsel and sewing thread can cut a cat's intestines!

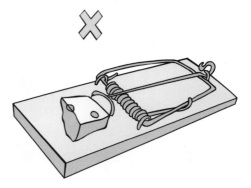

835. Save the trap

Avoid putting down rodent traps and baits while your pets are at home.

- If you've got a cat or terrier-type dog (one of the ratter breeds), don't even think about using poison in mousetraps! If they catch a poisoned rodent, your pets could get poisoned.
- Do not use spring-loaded mousetraps in which a paw, tail tip or whisker could get caught!
- If you have an infestation, either leave your pet in a temporary home or take a family holiday while the pest control people do their job.

836. Lick alert!

Cats and dogs lick themselves clean. If they've got toxic chemicals on their coat, this is dangerous.

- Avoid using chemicals in the garden. Even after using 'natural' solutions, keep your pet indoors.
- Certain plant oils are toxic to pets. Avoid using these on surfaces they inhabit.
- Keep your workshop and workroom off-limits.
- Never use solvents to clean a spill off a pet's fur! Take them to the vet immediately.
- If your pet accidentally gets a splash of a chemical, wrap them in a towel and take them to the vet immediately.

837. Poisonous plants

Some common houseplants are poisonous:

- Lilies and other plants that grow from bulbs – daffodils, crocus, hyacinth, iris and narcissus
- Ivy, holly, mistletoe and poinsettia
- Rhododendron
- Cyclamen
- Foxglove
- Hydrangea
- Laburnum
- Lantana
- Rhubarb
- Taro (elephant's ear)
- Wisteria
- Yew
- Certain types of sage, verbena
- Fruiting trees and stones or seeds of apples, pears, cherries, aubergines, tomatoes, apricot, peaches and plums.

Just part of a leaf of some plants can be dangerous! Check with your local garden centre and your vet. Don't grow or use them in floral arrangements.

838. Quick! Make it sick!

If you spot your pooch swallowing something poisonous or toxic, try to get it to throw up.

- Give your dog some salt – one teaspoon for smaller breeds, two for larger ones should do it.
- However, if you didn't catch it in the act, don't waste time. Get to a vet immediately with a sample of the substance or its packaging.
- Even if it did throw up at once, you should still see the vet. Call immediately after making the dog sick.

839. (B)right on the road

Accidents happen, but you can take precautions. Make your pet visible by dotting its collar with reflective stickers or patches.

- If unavailable at your pet shop, check a sports shop. Bands or reflective tape can be cut into spots and used.
- Dot the collar with patches at 2.5 cm/1 inch intervals or, if using tape or cutting from a reflective fabric jacket, wrap fabric all round.
- Use fabric glue and let dry for a day.
- Watch out for adhesive allergies when you put the collar back on. If there are any, repeat the process with a needle and thread.

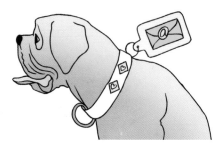

840. Fence in close

Fences and railings keep your pets home and safe.

- Check regularly for loose boards and bent rails; also banister rails and those bordering balconies and terraces.
- With a new pet, especially diminutive breeds, your fencing and railings should be higher than their shoulders.
- Ensure that the gap won't be a very tight fit for their heads or paws – you don't want them to get stuck.

841. Dog@mail.net

Putting your contact information on the back of your pet's tag or collar is the standard safeguard for a pup or tomcat prone to playful straying. However, you may feel that including your telephone number may compromise your privacy.

- Get your pet his own email address or a profile on a social networking site! Put that on the reverse of its dog tag. It helps more than an address if you're moving house or travel often.

■ General care

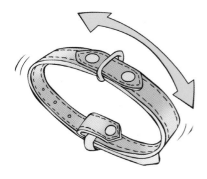

842. Soft collar

Pet collars can irritate and may damage fur around the throat.

- Minimize damage and discomfort by choosing a soft material – the softest leather; or a fabric one padded or lined on the inside.
- For greater safety, choose one with a little stretch or add an elastic insert. Should your pet get caught in a hedge, it can still pull free.
- Adjust the collar so that your pet can pull free of the collar in an emergency.

843. Cuddly beds

A household pet's bed calls for even more care than your own – especially since it can't clean it.

- Hot-wash and disinfect bedding every week for dogs and cats.
- For small caged pets, such as hamsters, clean out the cage and change the bedding material daily or every other day (this depends on how many occupants there are).
- Make sure bedding is dry – if there seem to be water spills, change the bedding at once.

844. Pristine pet food

Serve your pet hygienic rations.

- Fix times, place and dish for meals.
- Remove the food bowl after an hour (earlier if they're finished) and wash – separately.
- Disinfect their eating area.
- Bin leftovers separately.
- If possible, fit a separate sink in the utility room for your pet's things; if not, use the sink in the garden shed.
- Clean water bowls twice a day and refill several times.
- For caged birds, change the water daily.
- Ensure seeds, cereals or nuts for rodents and birds aren't rancid.

845. Keep the weight down

Obesity can precipitate a whole host of diseases – from hip problems in a dog to fatality in smaller mammals such as gerbils.

- Make sure active species get enough exercise.
- Never skip the dog's walk.
- Hamsters need their treadmills for exercise.
- Smaller rodents such as gerbils should be fed a varied diet, with not too many of the oily seeds they love. Give them plenty of green stuff and vegetables, as well as hay for fibre.

846. Flea attack!

Whenever you groom your pet:

- Lay down some newspaper and have your pet stand on it.
- Before disposing of the paper in the outside bin, dab at the debris with dampened tissue – any reddish specks indicate flea droppings!
- If you see either fleas or their droppings, it's time for treatment – for your pet (keep proprietary products out of children's reach) and upholstery. Carpets can harbour flea eggs for years before they hatch!
- Hot-wash pet bedding regularly through the treatment, and replace when you've run the course.

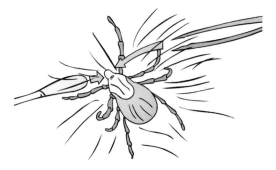

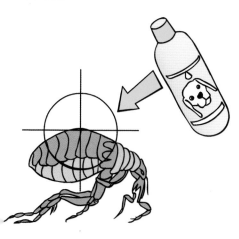

847. Tweeze those ticks!

Turn surgeon for your pet.

- Get a pair of long-nosed pointed tweezers and a bottle of rubbing alcohol.
- Keep your tweezers in your right hand; if your pet's jumpy, get someone to hold it.
- Use a cotton bud, in your left hand, to dab a good drop of the alcohol on the tick's head.
- Quickly grip the tick by its head and pull off.
- With a magnifying glass, check that the jaws are out. Should you suspect you've left one behind, visit the vet as soon as possible.

848. Popping pills

- Put the pill inside a pellet of a favourite food.
- Open its mouth and drop the pill on to the back of the tongue.
- Stroke its throat to encourage swallowing.
- If it licks its nose, the medicine went down!
- Offer water immediately afterwards.
- Deliver liquid medication in a dropper or bottle – open its mouth, press the dropper's mouth against its cheek (outside the teeth) and hold the muzzle closed before squeezing.

849. Pet hair problems?

To enjoy canine or feline companionship, be prepared to deal with pet hair.

- Brush furry coats regularly.
- Comb carefully – if it hurts, they'll avoid it. Cut away snarls rather than tug.
- If your dog lounges on the sofa, get a throw that can be washed in hot water.
- To get hair off upholstery in a hurry, use a piece of synthetic carpeting – brush to generate static in the pile, then pull over the surface, moistening lightly with water and run over again gently.
- Don't have carpets or rugs in pet-accessible areas – hard flooring is the best option.

■ Canine companions

851. House happy

Dogs need house training.

- Puppies squat slightly even to urinate. Pick it up (hands behind forelegs from the back) and put it where it should do its business.
- Cover its entire play area with newspaper – except its bed. It will avoid soiling the bed.
- Put it on the covered area when it is outside its crate.
- Gradually reduce that area.
- Once it is comfortable with a single square of paper, move it slowly to where you want it – even the garden.
- Gradually use less paper till you dispense with it entirely.

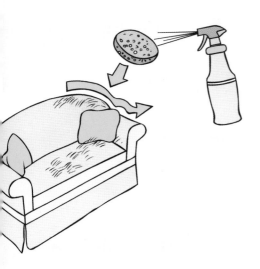

850. Quick fix for fluff

Two quick wipe-ups for pet hair:

Wrap masking tape around your fingers sticky side out, then 'wipe' over furniture. Change as soon as it gets furry.

Wring out a damp facial sponge and wipe over the upholstery. The hair will stick to it. Wash the sponge frequently and repeat.

852. Learning curve

Train your pup early.

- If you don't want the adult dog on your bed, don't put the pup there!
- A pup may cry at night but don't sit up with it! Keep its bed somewhere it can see or hear the family.
- Don't let your pup teethe on your fingers. It tells it that biting is acceptable!
- Take away unsuitable objects at the teething stage with a firm 'no'.
- Don't let it jump to greet you. Hold its paws and apply gentle pressure on the rump, saying 'Sit' firmly. Then praise it.

853. Lead on!

Teach your pup its name and to wear a collar and lead. Reward it initially.

- Choose an easy name. Use it whenever it comes to you.
- Start calling from further away.
- Put on a soft collar. Offer a treat to distract it. Let it go free, then try the collar again. Do this several times a day in short sessions. Increase collar time gradually.
- Attach a light lead and let it trail. Don't restrain it at first.
- Get it used to you picking up the lead.
- Gradually wind it in.

854. Car barkers!

One easy way to get your dog to stop barking out of car windows is to restrain it with a firm 'No'.

- Put it on a short leash.
- If it continues barking, don't raise your voice. Repeat a firm 'No'; pull it below window level. Hold it there and ignore it until it stops.
- Praise and pet lightly when it stops; wait a few minutes before giving a second chance. Be prepared to repeat.
- If it hasn't stopped by journey's end, be prepared to start over on the next leg!

855. Who is top dog?

These things can establish obedience from a dog.

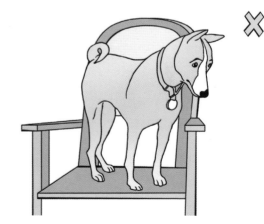

- If your children play on the carpet while the pup sits in your chair, its position teaches it that it's dominant! Don't let it sit on sofas and chairs.
- Don't bring your dog food or treats; let it come and get them.
- If it's come to its accustomed place for food, make it wait to be served.
- When it comes to play, you start the game and you stop it.

If all this sounds cruel, it isn't. Dogs are pack animals!

856. Doggie bowl

For your dog, the whole family is its 'pack'.
Establish the pecking order kindly and
carefully.

- It's best to feed your dog only after the
  family has eaten.
- Let your child put out its food – the dog will see
  this small human as its master or mistress.
- Train a pup to sit quietly while the family eats
  or at least while you serve it.
- Teach it early to wait for your command to
  begin eating – this prevents impulsive gobbling
  of anything seemingly edible.
- Never offer table scraps – it encourages begging.

857. Hot under the collar

On a blistering day spare a special thought
for your furry friend.

- Walk your dog on grass rather than tarred or
  paved streets. Avoid standing still for long.
- Never leave your pet in a parked car on a hot day.
- Leave some time between a walk and a feed.
- Snub-nosed and short-muzzled breeds
  suffer more, especially if they are elderly
  or overweight.
- You could clip back the fur of long-haired breeds
  in summer. Don't go so close that the skin shows,
  or your pet risks sunburn!

858. Dog day at the beach

A day at the beach means taking a few extra precautions.

- Dogs can get overheated quickly. Make sure your pet has a cool, shady place to lie down in.
- Fill its bowl with fresh water first thing. Sea water is not a healthy drink.
- Sea salt isn't kind to your pet's fur. Hose it down or give it a bath in fresh water if it's been in the sea.
- Don't give the dog ice cream! Rather, put a couple of ice cubes in the water bowl.

859. Dog with a bone

A juicy bone isn't necessarily the safest chew.

- Bones can splinter and stick in the mouth or injure the gut. Never give your pet chicken bones (brittle) or slender ones (sharp and prone to splintering).
- Rawhide chews are a good compromise.
- If you must give a bone, choose a really large, sturdy one – preferably hard-baked (available at pet stores).
- If it's teething time or your dog usually eats soft food, a good chew will help strengthen its jaw and clean its teeth. Carrots work as well!

860. The vegetarian dog?

Dogs aren't exclusively carnivorous.

- Your pet needs carbohydrates besides meat. Add rice or bread and vegetables (including starchy ones) to home-mixed food.
- Minus the spices and salt, most vegetables, beans and carbohydrates you eat are fine by your canine!
- Avoid excess sugar and fat.
- Add 'fresh' food to feeds.
- For a primarily vegetarian pet, provide enough whole grains, pulses and seeds along with powdered milk products.
- The occasional egg is a nutritional boost whatever his diet.

■ Felines in the family

861. Kitty litter

If you have a cat but no access to a garden, you'll need to have a litter tray.

- Place the tray in a low-traffic spot that is also easy for the cat to access.
- Put the litter box on a large washable rubber mat; change daily (get two).
- Alternatively, stand the box on an opened out and flattened cereal box. Discard daily.
- Wearing gloves, empty the litter at least every other day. Scoop up faeces when you notice any.
- Clean up any 'accidents' at once.
- If you're pregnant, let someone else clean the litter.
- Always wash hands with soap and hot water afterwards, and disinfect the gloves as well.

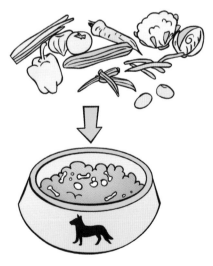

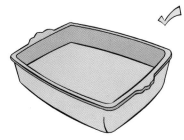

862. Not litter!

Buy a proper, purpose-made product for your cat's litter tray.

- Do not use shredded newspaper, sawdust or wood shavings for litter – first, they aren't easy to collect together for changing and can easily be trekked all over the house; second, the shreds and splints can lodge in paws or in muzzles.

863. Scratching cats

Cats need scratching posts to keep healthy.

- To ensure kitty uses your preferred post, dangle a toy from it when he's a kitten.
- The post should be sturdy and tall.
- An alternative to the post wrapped in sisal rope or textile is a section of sisal carpeting (or similar upholstery) stapled to the skirting board.
- Keep the post near the cat's bed or curl-up spot.
- If the cat has used your furniture for scratching, get it cleaned to remove the scent marking.

864. Knit-free kitty

We all love the traditional image of a kitten playing with a ball of wool or a knitted throw. However:

- Little claws can easily get snagged in knits and be damaged.
- It's also possible for a cat to develop a habit of chewing wool if you keep giving it woollies to play with.
- The fibres, especially now that so many 'wools' are really blends, can collect in and plug up the digestive or respiratory system.

865. Couch kitty

Unlike dogs, cats are better off indoors.

- Typically, cats don't wander except for territorial display or mating. Neutering or spaying helps avoid this and a host of other health problems.
- A cat who isn't used to the outdoors will be happier indoors. Make kitty feel 'at home' from day one.
- Let home be stimulating and secure so the allure of the outdoors is reduced – offer toys and a warm quiet spot.

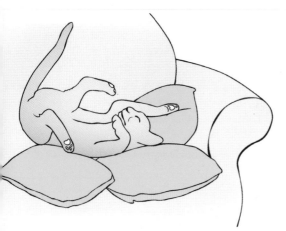

866. Not on my chair!

Rescue your favourite reading corner from your feline friend!

- Place the basket near the radiator or build a window seat over it – the warmth will lure it.
- A cushion filled with catnip should win it over to the sleeping spot of your choice.
- Use a stronger, pungent fragrance in your own spot – mist with a linen spray filled with a spicy or intense floral aroma.
- Push a bag of cloves down the side of the chair.

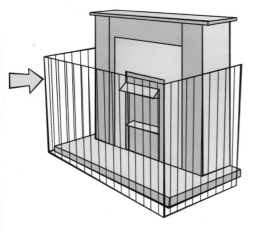

867. Hot spots for cats

Cats' attraction to warmth often draws them towards vibrating machinery!

- Always keep the washing machine and dryer closed when not in use. Do check for errant felines before filling!
- Do not encourage cats in the kitchen.
- In the hearth, always use a sturdy fireguard and keep any small unstable objects well clear.
- The boiler or heater is tempting, but if it's in a basement (for instance) a build-up of carbon monoxide is possible. Keep the door shut at all times to keep your cat out and have the heater serviced regularly to keep emissions down.

868. Tumbles hurt!

Yes, we know the old saying, but a startled cat may not always land on its feet. And anything could scare kitty off balance.

- Keep windows and doors leading to terraces and balconies shut.
- If your home has narrow ledges near the roof, add railings (to guard against falls) or roofing tiles (so they can't walk there to begin with).
- Make sure you have cat flaps in both the front and back doors.

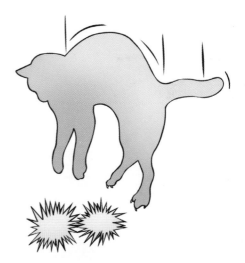

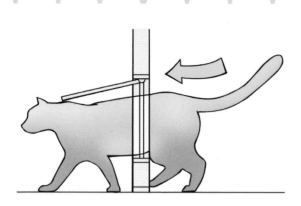

869. Cat in a flap

Teach your kitten to use the cat flap.

- Try when it is in a playful, calm mood, just before a meal.
- Place its favourite food on the other side; hold the flap open to let it see it.
- Encourage it to go through with a gentle push.
- Let the flap drop. Wait a bit before opening it and calling it back in.
- Repeat by pushing it through without actually holding up the flap.
- Holding the flap slightly open, let it return on its own.
- Now try it without food.

870. Home for tea

For cats, the pack mentality doesn't apply. However, food can still be used as an excellent behaviour modifier.

- With cats that are prone to wandering, set a schedule of feeding later at night to encourage it to come home.
- A delicious 'free meal' at the end of the day is often all the incentive a cat needs to regard a house as 'home'.

■ Rabbits and other rodents

871. Bunny litter?

Like a cat, a rabbit can be trained to use a litter tray. However, it doesn't come naturally (like it does to kittens).

- Choose a low-sided tray for easy access.
- Early on, put the litter tray inside a pen with the bunny. Confine it to the pen until it is quite used to using the tray.
- By way of introduction, scoop some of its droppings onto the litter (as a hint!) and put bunny in the tray to do its business.

872. Gnawing rodents

Rodents' front teeth keep growing – in natural circumstances they would get filed by gnawing constantly. This may not happen with a pet given prepared foods.

- Provide something in the cage for them to gnaw.
- Crusts of bread toasted in the oven or a sturdy twig from a fruit tree are good ideas.
- When picking up your rodent, allow it to sniff your fingers first. Never make a sudden grab, as rodents have poor sight.
- Get rats, mice and gerbils used to your scent by hand-feeding them a treat occasionally.

873. Hay for bunny

Bunnies need more than carrots.

- Make sure they always have ready access to grass and/or hay – for essential fibre.
- The tougher texture of hay makes it a good chew too – encouraging your rabbit to choose it over, say, a chair leg or the carpet for a nibble!
- If the hutch is outdoors, make it a moveable one you can shift around the lawn – that way bunny can nibble while using the rabbit run, and the grass can grow back when he is moved.

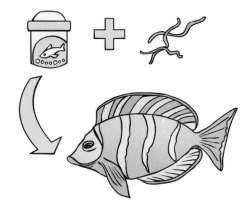

874. Less fresh!

While fresh food is good, watch out.

- Introduce fresh foods to rodents gradually. A sharp change in diet can affect their health.
- Rabbits and guinea pigs consuming their droppings for nutrients is normal.
- Ask what your new pet has been used to and replicate that diet for the first two weeks. Introduce new foods gradually.
- For larger mammals, mix the new food in small amounts with the old initially.

With some fish too, little fresh food and excessive pellets result in constipation. A few juicy worms will help.

■ Piscean pals

875. Fresher for fish

Whiffy water is a common problem with fish tanks.

- You'll need to clean the aquarium a little less often if you add a few charcoal pellets along with the gravel at the bottom.

- From time to time, recharge the charcoal by removing, washing well in a little vinegar-water, rinsing thoroughly and drying in the oven. (That will get those trapped whiffs out and ready the porous surface to absorb them again.)
- Of course, make sure the pellets are too large for your largest-mouthed fish to swallow!

■ Feathered friends

876. Mirror half

Caged birds will get very lonely – restless, even depressed – if single.

- Until you find a friend, attach a large enough mirror (securely!) to the cage's side.
- Some birds' mating rituals include offering food to a prospective mate (budgerigars and lovebirds). A solitary male may offer food to its reflection! This will pass and does no harm.
- However, most smaller species, which tend to be social creatures – finches, canaries – will need friends if they are to be well adjusted.
- A companion encourages songbirds to be vocal.

Bringing Up Baby

You need special safeguards to make your home child-friendly: precautions to take when you learn of the new arrival; playground rules for indoors and outdoors; travel tips and teething troubles sorted; shopping advice and daily routines to make sure your little one's secure.

■ Safety locked

877. Three, four, lock the door...

Some doors should always stay locked with children at home, keeping locks and keys out of their reach as far as possible:

- Cabinets and cupboards, all drawers and filing units.
- Storage for cleaning supplies, medicines, pet supplies, gardening equipment, matches, lighters, knives, razors and other sharp or heavy tools.

- The garage, basement and loft.
- Doors to the garden or terrace, especially if you have a pond or pool.
- Heavy-lidded trunks and chests.
- Sewing kits, toolboxes, craft supplies.
- The toilet lid – yes, such a product does exist!

878. Special equipment

You're right to be suspicious of 'must-have' gimmicks. However, there are a few bits of safety equipment you should invest in:

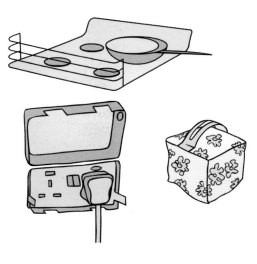

- A hob guard for the kitchen.
- Socket covers.
- Childproof catches for low cabinet doors.
- Sturdy doorstops that don't have removable parts (to avoid finger-in-hinge accidents).
- Fireguards for fireplaces and wood-burning stoves.
- A sturdy, well-padded playpen that's not likely to topple if a toddler throws his or her weight at one side.

879. Gate those steps

Fit safety gates at all danger spots:

- At the top and the bottom of stairs until you're confident the child can climb up and down sturdily.
- In the doorways of dangerous rooms – the kitchen, bathroom and home office.
- At the bottom of low or French windows, especially in upstairs rooms.

880. Danger – water!

Any container that's large enough for a small child to fall into presents a danger. If a small child falls into a large barrel with even a few centimetres/inches of water, he or she could drown.

- Any barrels, buckets or drums that can hold more than about 10 litres/2½ gallons of water should be stowed out of reach or banished entirely.
- Keep all large containers empty, and turn them over for good measure.
- Use a chain and lock on any larger containers in use – water butts, water storage tanks, etc.

881. No-lock loos

With young children at home, you don't want bathroom lock-ins.

- Install locks that can be opened with a key from the outside.
- If you have very young children (under six years of age), instead of locking the door, use hotel-style doorknob tags.
- Help children cut out and colour cardboard door tags announcing: 'Occupied!' or 'I'm inside!' Let the whole family get into the habit of using these – even if adults are using the locks, they should still use the tags so that children see it as a non-discriminatory family rule and adopt it readily.

882. Ring that bell

Children love chimes. Make this your excuse to:

- Place a loud wind chime near every door so it clangs every time the door is opened even a crack.
- Add strings of bells to windows as well – large sleigh-bell type Christmas ornaments are perfect, or a noisy rattle will do.
- This way, you can hear curious fingers opening up exit routes and avert danger.
- Of course, these are additional measures. Your first stop is fitting bolts on every door and window – and using them.

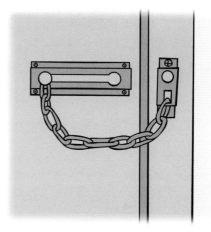

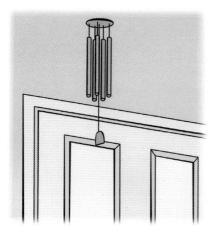

883. Safely shut

Not everything can be locked. For all those other doors and drawers, there are safer shutting options.

- A magnetic clasp on drawers and cabinet doors won't keep out a determined toddler; but if sturdy enough it will prevent younger infants from crawling right in.
- Use rubber stops at the tops of cabinet and cupboard doors to prevent doors shutting on tender fingers.
- Alternatively, for doors you don't want the baby going through in the first place, a short chain near the top is best.

884. Low locks

Sometimes door handles are too low to keep out your toddler.

- Install door knob safety covers, designed to allow an adult to open the door but keep it shut against children trying to turn the knob.
- Fit internal safety catches, which have to be lifted and released to open the door, in cabinets that can't be locked.
- For double-door cabinets, the half with the inner lip (as opposed to the door with the overlap, which you must open first to free the second 'inner' door) should have a bolt at the top.

885. Childproof? Think child resistant!

Believe it – there is no device so ingenious as to be completely childproof!

- You must double- and triple-layer the protections.
- You cannot relax your vigilance just because you have installed safety devices.
- Keep even childproof medicine bottles locked up – a child can learn to open them, or even manage to crack them accidentally!
- Even if the cabinets are locked, put sharp objects, matches and lighters, and cleaning supplies on higher shelves.
- Don't just close the stair gate, shut the door to the nursery as well.

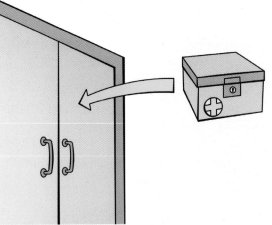

■ Electrical safeguards

886. Flexes away

A child can strangle itself with a trailing flex or pull down dangerous electrical appliances with dangling cords.

- Lock away the iron when not in use.
- Never leave a hot iron unattended – if you are interrupted while ironing, unplug and place the iron on a high shelf with its soleplate to the wall. The ironing board is not a safe place to keep an unattended iron!
- Get short spiral flexes (like the ones on telephones) for all your appliances so they can't dangle or trail.
- Use a wiring tube to hide computers and home entertainment system flexes – looks neater, too.

887. Light of your lives

Keep lighting baby-friendly.

- Recessed lighting is best: avoid lamps that can topple, flexes that can cause havoc, or jutting parts to tug on.
- With a small child, brighter ambient light allows you to spot spills and hazardous objects early!
- If the living room or nursery doesn't have enough daylight, consider adding a skylight, if possible.
- Choose nightlights that are cool to the touch and place them beyond the child's reach.

888. Light the way

Consider using photo cells or occupancy sensors for light fittings in children's rooms.

- It teaches them about conserving energy.
- It also means that entering a room 'in the dark' holds fewer frightening possibilities.
- Plus, it means the light will turn off even if they forget to switch it off, saving electricity.

■ Fire alert! (& other alarms)

889. Firewatch!

Keeping open flames to a minimum (even outside the kitchen) is common sense with an inquisitive infant around.

- Avoid lighting candles for ambience.
- If at all possible, avoid having an open fire.
- If you have an open fire or a wood-burning stove, use a sturdy fireguard.
- This is your best excuse for not smoking – a lighted cigarette tip entrances your baby, who is very likely to make a grab for it just when you are distracted. Big ouch!

891. *Hot water!*

With a young child in the house, you need to watch out for overheated water from the pipes as well.

- Turn the heater thermostat low enough that water is never hotter than 50°C/120°F. If your heater doesn't come with this feature, you can usually get a plumber to install a device to make this possible.
- Don't allow toddlers to turn on hot taps unsupervised – remind them red is for 'danger'!

890. *Alarm call*

Install alarms for safety.

- Install alarms on doors to dangerous areas – back garden, basement, loft, utility room, cleaning cupboard, toolshed, garage, roof/terrace and pool.
- Use a chime that rings by your headboard with the switch near the child's bed, which he or she can use if they feel frightened or unwell at night.
- Install smoke alarms everywhere, including cellars, lofts and sheds.
- Put a sticker on the most accessible window in your child's room so that in case of a fire, rescuers know where the child sleeps.

892. All about baby

Update the list of emergency numbers by your phone (*also see Tips 524 and 525*) once you have a baby.

- Add your baby's weight to the list – it is an important factor in determining safe dosages for small children; update regularly.
- Give a copy to your babysitter and point out the location of the medicine cabinet and its keys.
- If your baby has any known allergies or drug sensitivities, jot those down on the emergency list as well.

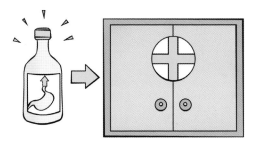

893. Bitter brew

With a young child at home, an emetic is an essential addition to your medicine cabinet. Ask your pharmacist to recommend one suitable for young children.

- If your child has ingested something harmful, this will make him or her throw up.
- However, check with the hospital first to ascertain a safe dosage.
- If you know what has been ingested, let the hospital know – you shouldn't make a child throw up if a corrosive substance has been swallowed for instance, and it is useless in case of fast-acting toxins, so let the nurse guide you.
- Even after the child has thrown up, take them for a check-up.

■ More 'home remedies'

894. Soft landings

The surest way to spot danger at baby height is to 'be a baby'. Do this before baby comes home! After the arrival you will not have time or energy for this.

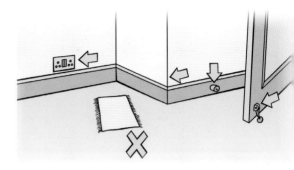

- Get down on all fours (or get Dad to do it) and crawl all over the house.
- Before your due date, deal with enticing nooks; delicious-looking non-edibles; sharp corners and edges; electrical fittings and so forth.
- Put covers in electrical sockets.
- Add rubber corners and bumpers to sharp edges.
- Remove loose mats wherever possible.

895. Free-fall flooring

Since your baby will spend most of his or her first years at floor level, you may as well start making it child-friendly.

- Fix loose tiles or flagstones, repair cracks and crevices.
- Cold, hard floors – tile or stone – need a soft covering. Wood is not as hard on hands and knees, nor as cold.
- Wall-to-wall carpets will need frequent vacuuming and shampoos.
- For carpeting, choose darker colours – brown and grey are best, or dark blue, red or green – and make sure it's washable.
- Lots of floor cushions are a good idea.

896. Trusty tables

Once you have a young child at home, it's time to clear the tabletops.

- Tabletops will inevitably get tugged and bring everything on the table crashing down. Put away your ornaments for now.
- Don't put the tablecloth or mats on the table until immediately before the meal; remove as soon as the plates are cleared.
- Get rid of the paperweights and stationery items (from pens to staplers and clips). Give them new homes in boxes placed out of reach.

897. Low life

Now that the pretty knick-knacks have moved up high, what can you keep on those lower shelves and surfaces?

- Keep the low tables empty for the baby's changing mat and nappy bag.
- Put the toy baskets on the shelves.
- Near floor level is ideal for the throws, rugs and pillows that will help ensure a soft landing when your little one goes exploring.

898. Furniture fix

No furniture is entirely childproof.

• Keep furniture minimal in the early years. Apart from the hard knocks, it also obstructs your view so you won't know at once when your child gets up to mischief!

• Ideally, all furniture should be too heavy to pull over, and padded to avoid scrapes and bruises.

• Make sure lighter furniture is really light – too light to seriously injure or trap a child if it falls. Choose plastic, or light aluminium and cane.

• Check that lighter furniture isn't brittle – avoid glass insets or wood that is prone to splintering.

899. Storage safer

Baby can challenge your versatile storage!

• Make sure heavy-lidded baskets and solid chests are securely locked. Those that aren't must have a lightweight lid and perforations for ventilation should an infant manage to get trapped inside.

• Stacked furniture – tall modular bookcases or a stack of graduated trunks – should all be reorganized.

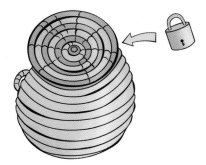

900. Screw it safe

For children's rooms, stand-alone furniture that you can adapt is the most versatile solution. However, all but the sturdiest can be pulled over by a determined tot.

- Keep all standing furniture safe by drilling through the back wall and screwing it to the wall behind.
- Holes in the walls can be filled up with putty when you remove the furniture – a small price to pay for your child's safety.

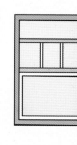
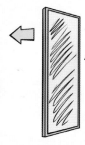

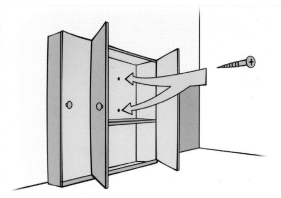

901. Window on their world

For the children's room, traditional window hangings are fraught with unpleasant possibilities.

- Curtains and blinds get stained and soiled, and can be brought crashing down – pelmet, rods and all – by a persistent toddler. So keep them short and washable.
- Avoid curtain ties and blinds with cords that dangle or can be pulled free.
- Use a fixed screen for privacy, which also lets in diffused morning light, rather than curtains or blinds, until your children are older.
- Also consider fixing an 'etched' pane on the window to provide adequate privacy for now.

902. Period pitfalls

Certain features of period homes enhance their value, but can be hazardous. Some things you can't change. For others, there are solutions.

- Many older homes used lead paint. Paint over with latex; watch for children teething on banisters, railings and window sills.
- Fix netting behind any railings with hooked shapes or wide gaps.
- Make sure the wiring is earthed!
- Replace brittle glass with tempered glass – in doors, windows and shower enclosures.
- Block up unused fireplaces and laundry chutes; lock up the dumb-waiter.
- Be vigilant about collapsible grilles in lifts and dumb-waiters.

903. Glow in the dark

For those living with chronic conditions such as asthma or epilepsy, sudden attacks that call for quick relief are nothing new. When the patient is a child, though, finding their medication or an alert alarm that rings in your room can be difficult in the dark.

- Use a fluorescent sticker on the child's inhaler bottle or outline the alarm switch with fluorescent paint.
- Make sure it gets enough light during the day to recharge.
- Check that it's glowing bright before turning the lights off at night.
- Use fluorescent stickers on the nursery ceiling, to outline doorways (nursery, bathroom, your bedroom) and skirting boards along corridors.

904. Canny kitchen craft

Yes, we know it's impractical to completely ban the baby from the kitchen.

- Select a 'safe cabinet' near ground level for toys or empty plastic storage containers with no small parts. That's for baby, and the rest belong to Mum and Dad.
- Put a label on it so the baby knows it's his or hers, and the others are not.
- As your child gets a little older, you might want to let the little one stack his or her 'junior chef' toys in there.

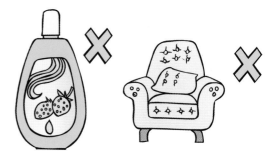

905. Hidden hazards

With a small child, even seemingly safe substances and objects can present dangers.

- Keep all medicines and toiletries out of a child's reach, especially if jumbo-sized. Certain herbs and spices, mouthwash, deodorant, shampoo and meat tenderizers can cause serious harm if ingested in large enough quantities.
- Avoid buying toiletries that are food-flavoured until the child is old enough to know the difference between edible-smelling and edible! Yes, we mean that chocolate-scented body wash and the strawberry-'flavour' baby shampoo.
- Avoid beaded or sequinned furnishings and buttons (on cushions or pillowcases).

906. Good gardening

Some extra safety tips for the garden when you have a small child in the family:

- Make sure you don't have any poisonous plants here or inside the house – your local hospital and garden centre can both advise.
- Consider removing plants that attract bees.
- Otherwise move them and make that part of the garden off-limits – put them near the water butt, compost heap and tool shed, all clustered together to contain the danger.
- Don't allow under-fives to play in the garden unsupervised.
- Avoid having laddered fencing or garden gates, as they can encourage a child to climb – vertical boards or railings are best.

907. Perilous plants

Not all houseplants are safe if baby decides to have a chew!

- Many common indoor plants – such as philodendron and other members of the arum family – contain oxalates in the leaves, which can result in a painful mouthful!
- It's always best to check with your doctor whether any of your plants are especially unsafe.
- In any event, it's best to keep plants out of reach – not just the leaves, the soil too.
- However, make certain too that houseplants aren't on a shelf of such a height that a persistent toddler will pull the planter down on himself or herself!

■ Play it safe

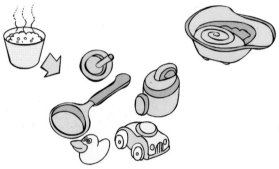

909. Soft-toy spruce-up

These are the worst culprits for dust and dirt, and they harbour germs and grime.

- Choose soft toys that can be machine-washed, preferably in hot water. Slip into a mesh laundry bag and use the delicates cycle.
- Non-washable ones can be freshened up with baking soda too – sprinkle through their 'fur' like powder, rub in lightly, leave for half an hour, then brush out.
- Vacuum soft toys gently after cleaning.
- Wipe sticky and slimy non-washable soft toys with a damp cloth dipped in a gentle soap solution.

908. Play clean

Toys always find their way into a toddler's mouth. Even non-toxic toys are bound to have a host of bacteria and dust. You need to wash toys regularly as well as disinfect surfaces daily.

- Carpets aren't particularly hygienic – a washable rug with non-slip backing that can stand a hot wash is better.
- Wash plastic toys in warm soapy water.
- Wipe wooden toys with a damp cloth moistened with a mild baking soda solution.
- For easier bath times and cleaner toys, give rubber, plastic and washable cuddlies a bath with your child.

910. Playground rules

Choose safe play equipment for the garden.

- Don't hang swings using S-hooks – the sharp points can be dangerous if they become detached. Use ring fasteners and check weekly.
- Make sure ropes or chains are strong enough to support an adult.
- Use soft or lightweight swing seats that won't cause injury on impact.
- Anchor play equipment in a sand bed to minimize injury from falls, or make sure the grass is soft and clean. It should extend at least 4 feet from the equipment and be at least a hand-span deep.

911. Best baby food

Bottled foods are convenient, but they contain additives, so are nutritionally diluted.

- Consider feeding your baby a milder version of your traditional cuisine, provided your diet is nutrient-dense.
- It's a good idea to go beyond the popular bottled flavours to more esoteric ones. Babies taste very keenly!
- If you decide to make your own baby foods (*see Tips 334–346*), greater control over your baby's diet and lower costs can offset the time and thought.

912. Not so sweet

Avoid adding sweeteners to your baby's food. Sugar will help your child develop a sweet tooth. And there are health implications too.

- Fruit and vegetable purées and cooked grains are naturally tasty. The sugar habit only makes these naturally yummy foods taste 'pale'.
- Never give honey or golden syrup to a baby under 12 months. They may contain bacterial spores that cause botulism, and your baby's immune system isn't strong enough yet.

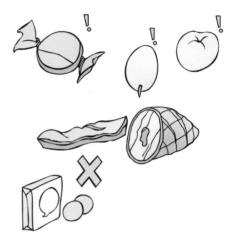

913. Choke alert!

Many foods are a potential choking hazard for infants under two to three years of age. Even for the two-plus brigade:

- Look out for small foodstuffs that can lodge in the throat – seeds and nuts, raisins, small hard sweets, whole grapes or cherry tomatoes.
- Other foods require proper tooth-tongue coordination to chew before they go down – tough meat chunks (including bacon or ham), popcorn, and sticky peanut butter.
- Encourage your child to take time to chew.

914. Avoid cured meats

Cured meats are high in nitrates, which can cause anaemia in young infants and so are best avoided early on. Nitrates are also naturally found in some vegetables.

- Wait till your baby is nine months old before you start giving nitrate-rich foods.
- Meat products to avoid include cured ham, bacon, sausages and salami.
- Common vegetables to watch out for are beetroot, carrots, green beans and spinach.
- Check with your baby's doctor for a comprehensive guide.

915. Hay fever hints

If your young children seem prone to hay fever, you might want to watch out when serving them certain foods.

- Oats, rye, kiwi fruit, tomatoes, celery, carrots, apples, pears and some spices contain compounds similar to the ones that make pollen so painful for them.
- Watch for any aggravation of symptoms when you wean them on to these foods. It'll save many a sniffle if a reaction is spotted early.

916. Greens are good

It's a misconception that children 'naturally' hate vegetables, especially greens.

- Rethink shopping and cooking strategies. Buy fresh and seasonal. Stir-fry or grill rather than boil.
- Ensure that even adults can't say 'no' to anything you serve. Doubters can take a smaller serving – two spoonfuls for adults and a single spoonful for children under ten.
- Never allow anyone to say 'I hate that stuff!' when it comes to food. Strong words engender strong feelings. Tell children it is impolite. They (and adults as well) can say 'I'm not too fond of it' instead.

917. Tot-friendly temperatures

Babies and toddlers have no idea what piping hot food will do to their tender mouth! It's up to you to prevent pain.

- Always check the temperature of food before feeding your child.
- For children under five, the temptation to reach for what is set before them is overwhelming – so don't even plate the food until it's cool enough for them to eat.
- For babies up to 18 months, it's best to serve foods lukewarm or at room temperature.

918. Hiccup helpline

Can't stop those hiccups? Not all home remedies are old wives' tales, but some will suit your child better than others!

• Hold your breath!
• Eat a piece of dry bread.
• Swallow a spoonful of dry sugar.
• Drink a glass of water.

Try the remedies in the given order, with about 20 minutes between. Once you know what works best, you can go straight for that next time!

919. Ring, ring!

There's a lot of scary stuff a child can get up to while you're answering the door or phone.

• Install cordless phones. With a baby in the house, the fewer cords the better!

A cordless phone also means you can walk with it – which means not sacrificing business or social calls because you have a small child. It also means you can supervise bath time, cook or keep an eye on them as they play in the garden without having to turn your back or go to another room.

920. Blissful bath times

For safe, pleasant bath times:

- Have a store of bath toys to rotate for novelty.
- Put a rubber mat or spare towel in the bottom of the tub for a non-slip surface.
- Then run the water, making sure it's not too hot.
- Never, for even a minute, leave an under-five alone with a filling or filled bath.
- Even with older children, the door should stay unlocked during bath time, and you should stay within easy earshot. Any sudden silences should be viewed with suspicion!

921. Safely penned

Start baby's day by setting up the play pen.

- You don't have to use it all the time – just while you're busy in the kitchen, in the loo, answering the door or on the phone in the next room.
- Have a separate set of playpen toys.
- When you're called to the door or the phone, put your child in the playpen with a favourite toy (if it's handy) before you attend to callers.

923. Motion sickness cures

You don't have to shop for (or cart around) expensive concoctions and concentrates to ward off motion sickness.

- Have some stem ginger, peppermint sweets, gingernut biscuits or peppermint tea handy when you travel. All safe for kids as well!

922. Overnight easy

Spending a night away from home – whether on holiday or with extended family – can be unsettling for young children.

- Bring along their favourite toy and night-time read.
- Pack a portable nightlight.
- For infants, take along a brand of baby food they know and like.
- If possible, avoid combining a host of strange faces with a strange place in the baby's first couple of nights away from home. Positive early experiences mean less anxiety later. So let the first visit be to grandparents, or a family friend.
- If the child is past toddler stage, explain that the time away from home is just temporary and that you will all be going home again.

925. Safe away from home

Here's a list that applies to children of all ages while they are away from home.

- They must know their full home address and telephone number – and your work address and telephone number.
- Younger children should carry cards with all these details, but not their own names.
- Tell them not to accept lifts or gifts from people they don't know very well – not even from casual acquaintances. Ask them to say they cannot do so without your permission.
- Teach them to walk confidently and stay alert on the road.
- Tell them to avoid loitering, especially when they are alone.

924. Avoid traveller's tummy

You know not to give tender tummies any water other than bottled in places of questionable sanitation when you go globetrotting en famille. But if they brush their teeth with tap water, it's that same contaminated fluid you're risking!

- Get them to use bottled water to rinse their mouths and toothbrushes too, as well as to wash hands when you don't have access to soap or disinfectant.

■ Good little habits

926. Easy riders

Make a set of rules for using bikes, roller skates or skateboards. Make sure these rules are followed by all members of the household, young adults no exception.

- Always wear a helmet, and preferably elbow and knee pads as well (especially with skates).
- Don't ride or skate while wearing headphones or while talking on the mobile phone.
- Avoid riding bikes at night, and definitely don't use skates or skateboards unless the pavements are well lit.
- If they must ride after dark, make sure they wear reflective gear and that the equipment itself has reflective stickers.

927. Tidy tots!

If your toddler is old enough to drag Teddy downstairs, he or she is old enough to bring it back to the nursery. Discipline is a habit – like brushing your teeth.

- Start children on the clear-up-before-bed game as soon as they are old enough to cart their clutter around – and it'll become second nature as long as you do it too. (If it's yet another bedtime battle you're afraid of, ask yourself: would you rather do the battles with a knee-high now, or wait for the teenage nagging wars?)

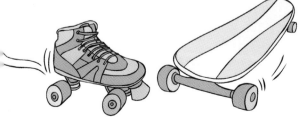

928. Tuck in the quilts

It looks luxurious, a bed with a big quilt overflowing its sides.

- Make sure you tuck it in at the bottom of the bed, though, to prevent it sliding off the bed and onto the floor as the sleeper shifts (or throws it off, especially if your child is a restless sleeper).
- It's good safety practice to keep babies and even toddlers tucked in tight. Indeed, with babies, aim to have all three sides well anchored to prevent any possibility of smothering.

929. Safely stored

Your bedroom, and your child's, may have several little gremlins in them!

- Put away perfume bottles.
- Lock up jewellery – even costume jewellery – lest it pricks or presents a choking hazard.
- Don't leave sequins and beads lying around. These are a choking hazard and are often found up children's noses.

930. Clothes for kids

Think before you buy!

- Buy clothes in stretchy (with 2 per cent Lycra) rather than woven fabrics – it'll mean less ironing and they won't grow out of them all that quickly.
- Avoid ties, buttons and hooks on clothes and footwear. Velcro, zips and large press fasteners are much safer.
- Make sure all sashes and ties are sewn on firmly.
- Avoid clothing decorated with sequins and beads.

931. Mesh is best for bags

For children's toy and laundry bags, avoid suffocation hazards:

- Choose breathable mesh or netting rather than tight weaves and plastic.
- Rather than plain drawstrings, have elastic cords for closure – this will reduce the likelihood of children putting their heads in and pulling the fastening too tight across the throat.
- Check buttons regularly to make sure none are coming loose.
- Velcro closures or open rigid rims are probably the safest choice.

Home Aesthetics

The thoughtful extras that make your house a *beautiful* home: from lights, flowers, aromas to action in the back yard, with art and aesthetics factored into every single step.

■ Flowers & other fragrances

932. Flower foods

Add any of these to the water in your vase to help flowers last longer:

- A small aspirin tablet
- A pinch of baking soda
- A few grains of sugar and a single shake of salt

933. Fitting in the flowers

Too few for your big vase?

- Gently lift them out and ask someone to help you tie them.
- Pop the posy back in the vase.
- Fill the gaps with scrunched up cellophane paper – in toning colours or transparent.
- Some pretty pebbles or marbles help with stability.
- Add water.

For a dressier look, large leaves or feathery ferns can fill the gaps. This arrangement won't last as long because the leaves will start to rot underwater. But it's stunning!

934. Bedhead blooms

You wouldn't wear a heavy spicy perfume in summer, would you?

- Similarly, flowers with a very heady fragrance can become oppressive on a hot night.
- Worse, they start to decay faster in the heat too – definitely not a welcome fragrance!
- If you have any in the house, move them out of your bedroom to another (well-ventilated) room.
- In other rooms, too, try to place them near an open window.

935. Scents or aromas?

At a meal, it's the aroma of your food that should take centre stage.

- Avoid scented candles in strong floral fragrances.
- Avoid using very heady flowers as table decorations – no gardenias to compete with the curry.
- Better options are fruity fragrances – spices or citrus, or herbs such as lemongrass.
- Some flowers are nice for meals if mild – roses, violets, fruit blossoms, and fragrances suggestive of edible ingredients.
- Foliage such as lemon balm or chocolate geranium adds a novel note.

936. Perked-up potpourri

You've run out of the fragrance refill and your potpourri is smelling like, well, nothing!

- Zap in the microwave for 10 seconds on low heat to revive before guests arrive

It doesn't last forever, but it's a good temporary fix.

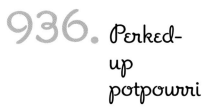

■ Livelier lights

938. Skirted lights

This is an easy way to keep changing your lampshades without actually changing them.

- Make a skirt – a cylinder really – of your chosen fabric to exceed the maximum circumference of the lampshade by an inch.
- Gather the top of the cylinder and sew on a band of elastic, as if sewing the waistband of a skirt.
- Now all you have to do is slip the shade on.
- If you use a washable material, so much the better – just wash whenever it's a bit grubby and replace on the shade.

937. As fragrant as a lightbulb?

It's the simplest diffuser you could have.

- Dab your lightbulbs with a little essential oil, or tuck a cotton wool ball impregnated with a few drops in the light fixture.
- When you switch on the light, the heat will help the fragrance diffuse into the air!

Warning: Don't apply on a still-warm bulb – especially if you're using an alcohol-based fragrance product.

■ Arts & crafts

939. Ring a ring of stars

- Get a wire wreath frame and starburst bows (homemade or those sold at a stationer's) to cover it, plus some smaller starbursts for extra dimension.
- Staple a point of each smaller starburst to a bigger starburst.
- Glue the starbursts to the frame to cover it.
- Staple together the touching points of adjacent stars.
- Make a starry garland in the same way to wind down the centre of your dining table or swag along the banisters.
- If you're making the bows yourself, why not use paper reserved for recycling – cut into inch-wide strips for 'ribbon'?

940. Not your usual pricey print

Customize 'art' to match your room's décor.

- Frame wallpaper and carpet samples identically.
- Line up a trio of toning patterns or similar prints in two or three same-family colours (blue, navy, violet or green, blue, yellow).
- Frame parts of a larger pattern from the same wallpaper.
- One long rectangular frame can add depth to stairwells and narrow corridors.
- Substitute a filled frame for a headboard.
- Try the same with leftover fabrics and a set of embroidery hoops.

941. Winter wonderland

Whatever climate you live in, this arrangement will deck your home for winter.

- Slip a sprig of sturdy evergreen – a conifer twig or an ivy leaf or some holly – into half a dozen clear baubles.
- Stack in a deep clear vase with pine cones.
- For greater height and drama, add an interesting dried branch with pine cones dangled off it like ornaments – secure ribbon or garden twine to the 'stem' of each cone with a loop of wire.

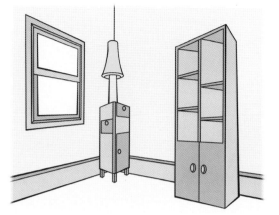

942. Nowhere to go, but up

Small rooms can easily be overpowered by large-scale furniture, unless it's high rather than wide or chunky.

- Height draws the eye up, making you aware of vertical space above eye level.
- It also distracts from the lack of floor space.
- It can mean a great deal of extra storage, which in turn can free up lower surfaces in the room, making it seem more expansive.
- Keep the lines clean and light for best results.

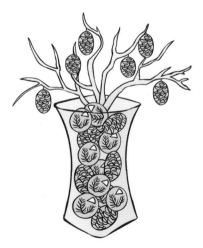

■ Window dressing!

943. String up some trinkets

Neutral, the easiest colour scheme, and white, the most adaptable, can be rather bland, especially in cold or cloudy weather.

- Take out your old boxes of trinkets, key chains, Christmas ornaments, seashells, toys, napkin rings and biscuit cutters.
- Tie different lengths of colourful ribbon to curtain rods and knot a pretty bauble to the end of each.
- Add a ribbon to the back of each chair at your dining table.
- String some baubles from the banisters.

944. Hangings straight

Help curtains close without that annoying crack of light where they come together!

- Attach 1-inch lengths of Velcro tape along the reverse seam of the curtains, at intervals of about 45 cm/18 inches.
- Make sure they are at the same level on all curtains. No need to keep track of which pair goes together!
- Of course, you need Velcro hooks on one side and Velcro loops on the other to fasten!
- Put the 'loop tape' on the right-hand edge of every curtain and 'hook' tape on the left-hand seam of each.

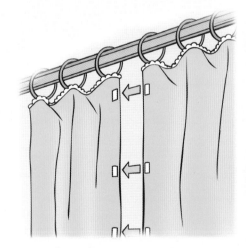

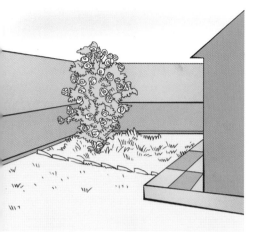

945. White for garden light

How would you brighten up a north-facing room? Let nature come to your rescue.

Grow some bright white flowers there – choose big massy blooms, whether lilies, lobelias or hydrangeas. The reflection of light works just as well – and is even prettier – if you can trail them up a pale trellis. How about a trailing rose, in *Sleeping Beauty* style?

946. Multi-purpose mulch

Mulching the surface of the soil can prevent loss of water through evaporation. It can also be a decorative accent if you choose some interesting materials. Try:

- Coloured gravel, the kind used in the bottom of aquariums
- Decorative ceramic pebbles
- A cache of old-fashioned glass marbles
- Even a sea of shells (particularly effective with pots painted cornflower blue!)

947. Windowbox winners

To make it easy to update your windowbox selection of greenery, plant them with pots!

- Choose containers in similar material to fit your window box.
- Vary heights and shapes a little for interest, as well as to suit different kinds of plants.
- Fill gaps with garden pebbles, stone chips or gravel for neatness, or hide the evidence with a few trailing vines.

This way, you can put together plants with quite different soil needs, and readily switch plants with every season and on a whim!

948. Indian summer colours

The end of summer and beginning of autumn is when gardens look drab.

- Make the inorganic bits of your garden stand out from the greens and browns.
- White, blue and bluish-purple or pink garden furniture liven up foliage.
- Many flowers and seedheads dry to a lovely sculptural shape. Spray-paint these. Sandwich the stem to be sprayed between the can and a sheet of cardboard or metal to protect the foliage behind. Work in short, light sprays to prevent drips.
- Garden fixtures can add colour too.

949. Amusingly utilitarian

Even a kitchen garden can look bright.

- You can use the foliage and flowers of vegetables if you mix up the planting. Courgettes and pumpkins, runner beans and onions all produce stunning blooms.
- Not all greens are the same; mix hues ranging from bluish to red.
- If the light and soil conditions don't allow you to mix crops in one bed, add a container plant needing similar light but different soil.
- Add a quirky touch with the props and containers. A wind chime of forks and spoons; bread bins for potting; a teapot for herbs.

950. Blooming lawns

Live where the skies open up often?

- Sow a few rain lilies in the lawn. These crocus-like plants react to rain by perking up with pink blossoms overnight – and they flower as long as fresh rainwater falls on them!
- Otherwise, they're no thirstier than lawn grass.
- You don't have to completely supplant the existing ground cover either – just a few clumps will spread rapidly with the seasons, until you have a waving pink carpet to rid you of those rainy-day blues.

Welcome to Our Home

For a home that's not just aesthetic but inviting, we have ideas to spoil your guests silly, whether they're new friends, old pals or little visitors. These easy-to-execute extras cost you hardly any time or effort, but will gild your reputation as a gracious host or hostess with all comers. Statutory warning: put all these tips into play at once, and your guests will feel entirely at home!

■ House-proud hosting

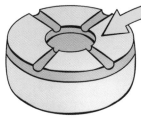 

951. Scented smokes, please

Whether you're inviting smokers into your non-smoking home or anti-nicotine neighbours to your cigar-redolent den, the lingering tobacco trail makes for neither good manners nor a good impression.

- To stop the stench at source, put lots of little ashtrays around – but first pour in some scented potpourri! The smouldering butts will tease out more aroma from it.
- Make sure there's a layer of sand or water below so you don't end up with flaming ashtrays!
- Before and after you have guests, leave a couple of saucers of vinegar around to deodorize the living room thoroughly.

952. Fragrant rooms

Greet guests with air that is aromatic and environmentally friendly to boot.

• Pour a few drops of lemongrass oil on balls of cotton and tuck them in corners where they will be out of sight but will still be in contact with the air... elbows of CFL bulbs for instance. This will also help keep out unwanted pests.

Warning: do not place near incandescent light to avoid fire hazard.

953. Floor protectors

A hardwood floor you'd rather not see scuffed, or a white sheepskin rug whose pristine fleece you fear for? Offer your guests some slippers.

• Keep a stack, in drawstring bags, in the hallway.
• Stock children's sizes, plus standard adults sizes for women and men – 12 pairs in four sizes is plenty.
• Avoid cutesy motifs and 'gendered' colours. Stick with a basic carpet slipper pattern, in perhaps bold red, chocolate brown, or nautical navy stripe.
• No pastels – they look grubby quickly.
• Sand the soles to prevent slippery accidents!

954. Raincoats for loan

Live in a shower-prone area?

- Keep a basket of thin roll-up macs by the door for guests and visitors caught out by a minor deluge – the disposable or short-use type made of transparent plastic are fine.

955. Child distractions

It pays to have a quiet distraction on hand when a friend or relation drops in with a fractious toddler in tow.

- Have some favourite children's reads and crayon colouring kits in the cupboard at all times – even in a child-free household.

While the child reads or doodles, it gives you and your guest time to actually catch up!

■ Stocking the guestroom

956. Just for guests

Keep these supplies in stock for those unexpected overnight guests.

- Soft disposable foam earplugs
- Adaptor plug – in the dressing-table drawer
- Bottled water
- Pocket-size pack of tissues as well as the regular box in the bathroom
- Selection of guest soaps
- A pocket-sized torch, plus spare batteries
- Small card or board game – for jetlagged insomniacs
- Disposable laundry bags or re-sealable bags for packing soiled garments or carrying wet swimwear or leaky cosmetics

957. Book supply

A stack of books catering to your house guest's tastes and interests is a thoughtful addition to the guest room.

- A swap shop or secondhand bookshop should offer something for most readers, and should be able to offer advice on subjects you know nothing about. The well-thumbed look is charming too.

958. Entertain at (arm's) length

Constantly keeping the guest company might not be restful for either of you, and disrupts a household with children or pets. There are books by the bed, but if your guest doesn't read much, here are some options:

- You could offer them free use of your den (if it's a usually quiet place)
- In-room entertainment – a portable radio or music system
- If there's a TV, you can hook up a DVD player with a choice of films
- For children, a new handheld video game can be pretty enthralling

959. Sleep like a baby

Don't feel that you have to create a 'grown-up' environment for guests – away from home, even the sophisticated city slicker may find a touch of nostalgia relaxing. Use your own childhood mementos or your children's.

- Pin an old patchwork quilt over the headboard or throw it over the armchair.
- Display vintage toys.
- Framed children's drawings or black-and-white prints will give the room a family atmosphere.

■ Ultra-friendly treats

960. Beyond basics

Your guests will find your home especially welcoming if you have these in a basket on the dressing table or in the bathroom:

- Hand cream in a gender-neutral fragrance
- New hairbrush of good quality, or a vintage one scrupulously cleaned after every departure
- Scented candles
- Miniature bottle of cologne
- Deodorant wipes, discreetly placed in the bathroom cabinet, perhaps next to the extra loo rolls
- Lip balm
- Sunscreen
- Pair of new socks for wearing to bed or around the house – even airline socks will do
- Spare bathrobe or dressing gown – again, stay gender-neutral

961. Fresh from the oven

Make your guest feel special with a batch of nibbles.

- Bake biscuits with personal appeal – cricket bats for an enthusiast; musical notes for a trombone player or dancer; cat shapes for a feline-friendly grandma; fruit and leaf shapes for a gardener; pound signs for a banker; trees for a happy camper. Write the guest's name on each biscuit in edible ink.

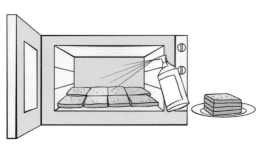

962. Flavoured waters

It costs little or nothing, but can dress up a simple repast and make a guest at your table feel honoured.

- Add a few fresh lemon or cucumber slices to every jug of water in the house.
- For narrow-necked bottles, a few sprigs of mint would be lovely.

963. Elegantly eclectic bookmark

A sprig of fresh rosemary or thyme, a sprig of lavender or a fresh bay leaf can make fragrant bookmarks.

- Offer one with the books you leave in your guest bedroom. The aromas from the crushed foliage will also keep many insects away (*see Tip 800*).

964. Sweet-scented dreams

Finding sleep in unfamiliar surroundings can be difficult. Encourage sweet dreams with a pillow pouch.

- Put a spoonful of dried lavender buds on a square of muslin or organdie.
- Gather the corners together and tie with mauve ribbon, threading through a 'Sweet Dreams' note.
- Sneak into guests' rooms after dinner to leave one on each pillow before they go to bed.

965. Foot refresher

Hold out the promise of a sensory treat for those travel-weary toes, with a home-made 'foot spa' at the bottom of the bed.

- Place a scoop of smooth pebbles in the bottom of a sturdy ceramic basin.
- Nestle in a small vial of essential oil – such as refreshing peppermint or tea tree.
- Slip in a note to 'Add hot water' in the folds of a towel laid on top.
- Lay out fleecy slippers next to it.

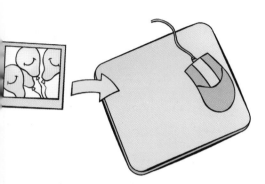

966. Thank-you snaps!

Here's an innovative way to say 'Thanks! I loved it!' or 'Great having you! Come again soon!'

- If it's a gift or dinner you're saying thank you for, send a Polaroid or digital print of you with your present or of the party. Add an appreciative note on the back.
- For a guest, slip into their overnight bag a print of special moments during their stay (maybe on a mouse mat or some coasters?) or the recipe for that jam they loved (use a fancy script on your word processor).

967. Triumph over jet-lag

Keeping up with the clock when travelling far to the east or west of your own time zone can be difficult. Gently lead jet-lagged guests into a new routine:

- If they travelled from the east, organize a few outdoor activities (not too hectic) – maybe tea in the garden – to help them stay awake until dusk.
- If they flew from the west, wake them up with a cuppa by a window – they need sunshine, ideally half an hour of it.
- Synchronize activities with daylight to reset their body clock.

968. Guest goodies

Maybe your guest is an early riser, or has a body clock that's still in a different time zone.

- Put a small electric kettle, a mug, a selection of teas and coffee, sugar, pods of UHT milk, and a teaspoon on the dresser.
- Offer an assortment of zingy waker-uppers as well as soothing bedtime teas – mint, chamomile and Earl Grey are a good basic team.
- Replenish regularly.
- But don't forget to offer your guest tea with the rest of the family as well, and make them a fresh cup if you find they have risen late.

969. Travel guide

Send first-time guests a route map and your address.

- You can post them a hand-drawn one with all the landmarks marked in.
- Or send a clear local map (the same one likely to be found at the airport) with the route and address marked in.
- Scan a copy and send it to them by email as well.
- Include your phone number, in case they get lost!

It's a Wrap

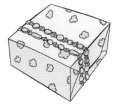

For special seasons and momentous occasions, as well as for everyday perker-uppers, a thoughtful gift given with extra care will make someone's day – and elevate you to the super-Santa club! Which means you'll never be out of ideas for the perfect present again...

■ Quick, clever present-ing

970. Gift-wrapped

Don't bother tying bows!

- Wrap your gift.
- Add a piece of double-sided sticky tape underneath.
- Secure one end of the ribbon to it.
- Wrap the ribbon around the gift like a sash – go round at least three times with each new band slightly overlapping the previous one.
- Tuck in the free end, securing to the piece of sticky tape.
- Add a small accent – a chopstick stuck into the ribbon 'obi'; a bauble threaded or hooked through; a feather or flower (silk or fresh); a bold leaf or sprig of a hardy herb (such as rosemary).

971. Petit parcel

These clever wrappings are for ribbon-phobes:

- Lay your gift diagonally on a square of wrapping paper or fabric. Gather the corners to the centre; seal with a sticker.
- Twist one or both ends of the paper closed (pop it into the cardboard core of a loo roll first if it's an awkward shape).
- Put it in a box and secure with an elastic ponytail ring with an appropriate accent.
- Got a pretty jam jar? Shred coloured paper or foil to fill the jar and hide the gift. Stick on a clever label.

972. Plain made posh

No wrapping paper or ribbon?

- Use computer stationery, baking parchment, greaseproof paper, or newspaper. Add a simple rubber stamp – monogram the recipient's initials or choose a paisley design.
- To a well-washed foil container, add an ice-cream stick 'tag'; write on plain paper, fold into a fan and stick on.
- Secure the top of a small flowerpot with foil, paper or clingfilm. Put a sticker label on top.
- For a small gift, try a well-rinsed yoghurt carton with an upside-down muffin case for a lid, secured with tape or a rubber band.

973. No-wrap presents

A pretty present may not need wrapping. Just tie a big bow around:

- A special stuffed toy
- Elegantly bound books, a tin of chocolate or soap, or some exquisite bed linen

However, don't do this if you're bringing the present to a big party, or if the recipient may set it aside and not open it immediately.

974. Pretty knots all in a row

Make knots rather than bows for an interesting package.

- Use stiff, slim (¼-inch) cord and tie the bow all the way through, pulling the loops through into a knot.
- Now repeat several times (4–5 at least) so you have several knots in a row.
- Shift the ribbons close together so that the knots are lined up against each other.
- Trim the ribbon ends to equal lengths and straighten so that they look like pleats.

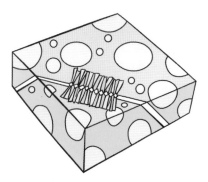

975. Trendy ties

Left loop too long, right loop too droopy…
Forget ribbons!

- Wrap cigars or special tobacco in a bright paper bag tied with a pipe cleaner in a contrasting colour!
- Wrap a book in plain paper. Use a leather thong as the tie. Slip on letter beads to spell the recipient's name, knotting at either end to hold the word together.
- Wrap a box of truffles or miniature art with plain white paper, securing with a decorative buckle.
- Hold a soft fabric parcel together with an elasticated bead bracelet or looped necklace.

976. Sweet grip

Make your own garland of sweets to dress up your gifts.

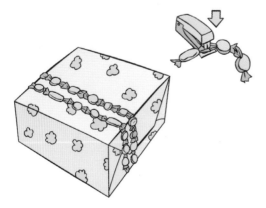

- You'll need a bag of wrapped sweets and a stapler.
- Staple the wings of the wrappers of each sweet to another. Continue until you have the necessary length.
- This string can replace the handle of a gift bag.
- You can wrap a long chain three times around a boxed gift. Staple the last 'link' to the one below.
- You can even use these as party decoration – up the stairs, along pelmets or window sills, and down the centre of the dining table.

977. Wine wrappers

Everyone likes a good wine. Here are some ways to wrap it:

- Use a length of no-sew felt to make a drawstring bag. Edge with a quick, bold blanket stitch in contrasting wool. Use a length of ribbon, braid or tassel to tie.
- Or wrap the bottle in crushed colourful tissue and slip it into a net bag.
- Or sit it in a large square of net fabric, gather up the edges at the top and tie with ribbon at the neck.
- Add a gift tag cut in the shape of a chalice.

978. The label's the thing...

Giving a great vintage? Don't hide the label.

- Girdle the neck with a small wreath of herbs or evergreens.
- Tie a plain ribbon knot in a festive colour – red, gold or silver. Add a couple of bells or baubles to the ends of the ribbon.
- For a spicy red to pep up a curry, make a 'skirt' of bay leaves and dried chillies strung on string.
- For a New Year bubbly, tie on a noisemaker and a bag of confetti stars!

■ Smarter solutions

979. Treasure stasher

Disguise jewellery in an unexpected holder:

- Nestle in tissue or satin inside an egg cup.
- Put in an antique bottle filled with potpourri.
- Bubblewrap and hide in a spice jar or tea canister.
- Put in a coffee mug and top with wrapped sweets.
- Place in the bowl of a soup ladle. Wrap it!
- Slip it inside sporting gloves.
- Hide a girl's first jewellery in a toy! Place inside a set of nesting dolls, a CD case or pencil case.
- Use the folds of an umbrella or a favourite shoe!

980. Novelty nuts!

If you buy unshelled walnuts or chestnuts, save those that break open neatly.

- Place a tiny gift – a charm, a luxurious truffle or a single perfect seashell – in the shell case.
- Seal the halves with removable poster glue or old-fashioned paste glue. (Don't use strong synthetic adhesives – the halves should pull apart fairly easily, yet not fall apart while they are closed.)
- Hide them in a bowl of florists' moss or a bucket of popcorn for recipients to dip in.
- You can spray the shells with metallic paint for extra glamour.

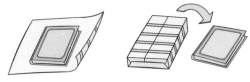

981. Birthday treasure hunt

Got the birthday boy or girl a big gift? Think beyond handing over the key or instruction manual with a bow on it.

- Arrange a treasure hunt.
- Hand them the first clue in a small wrapped box.
- This should lead them to further clues parked in apt places – for a car, it might be near a poster of a racing car or a favourite childhood toy truck.
- Finally, it should get them to the gift – draped in ribbons, tied with a huge bow or with a cake inside!

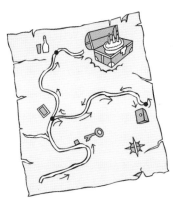

982. Wrap-a-book bag

For a quick gift bag:

- Select sturdy wrapping paper – even greaseproof (for biscuits) or brown paper.
- Wrap a hard-backed book, leaving the parcel a little 'roomy'.
- Secure the paper around the book and at the base, but leave the top flap open.
- Gently shake the book out, slip your gifts in, fold over the top and there's your gift bag!
- Close the flap with a stick-on label or tie a ribbon from base to top, securing the bow just in front of the flap.

983. All sewn up

For dainty presents, sew felt sacks!

- Cut out two identical squares of felt.
- Using a carpet needle and wool or sturdy yarn, stitch the squares together, leaving the top open.
- Turn the pocket inside out and knot the thread; turn right side out to hide the end.
- Add a line of large running stitches about 2.5 cm/1 inch from the top; leave the ends long enough to tie into a bow.
- Slip in the gift, draw the 'cord' in for a drawstring, and tie.
- Embellish with felt appliqués or sequins.

984. Stocking stashers

Knit simple socks to wrap awkward shapes.

- Knit long, narrow rectangles, sewing up one long edge and one short edge to give you a simple sock without heel or toe!
- This will camouflage awkward-shaped objects or hold an assortment of small stuff snugly – bottles and vases, a peculiar paperweight, an assortment of tree ornaments or small toys.
- Add a drawstring near the open end – weave some ribbon through or just tie with some crocheted braid.

985. Well-travelled treat

Giving someone a gift from an exotic point of origin?

- Bag it in a packet made out of a map of the area.
- This is a nifty way to present superlative tea, coffee or chocolate.
- To do this with a wine bottle, you'll need a taller and tougher bag. Laminating the map should do it, if you secure joins with strong double staples rather than adhesive.
- This is also a good way to present a souvenir from your own travels.
- You can seal the gift with a pretty stamp from that country!

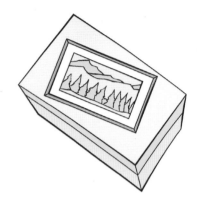

986. The present picture

For a gift meant for a special occasion, use a photographic clue in the wrapping.

- Make a photocopy of the photograph.
- Adjust the size of the image to the area you need to cover.
- Quite a plain container – old coffee tin, tennis ball tube, shoebox – can become wonderfully evocative when this image is pasted on.
- Make it a fabulous reminder – a wedding portrait for an anniversary, a landmark from the part of the world you wish to evoke or a vignette of the occasion or object you are saying 'thank you' for.

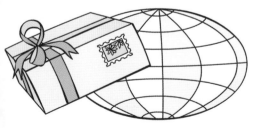

987. Gift matching

Consider matching the packaging to the gift – at a slight tangent…

- Put DVDs or videos inside a popcorn bucket.
- Artists' supplies could come in an old paint can.
- Give fireworks in a red fire bucket.
- Put seeds inside a terracotta flowerpot, place an upturned saucer over it, and tie shut with gardeners' twine.
- Got your friend a pedometer? Put inside a pair of sporty socks!
- Present exotic spices wrapped in muslin and bundled inside tea balls.
- Pile liqueur-filled chocolates into a brandy snifter.

988. No boring envelopes!

New covers for coupons, etc.

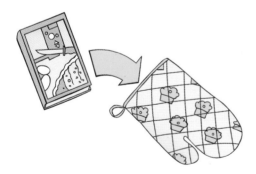

- Giving a cookery course? Slip the brochure inside an oven glove.
- A course in art appreciation? Put in a basic frame.
- Tuck tickets for a holiday in an accessory to match – beach hat or spa slippers.
- Hide an invite to the opera inside a roll of sheet music.
- Secure that gym membership with a terrycloth wristband.
- A pottery weekend? Pop the papers inside a small moulding dough tub.
- Tickets to a movie? Clip to a carton of popcorn!

■ Gifts accessorized!

989. (Heart) warming gift

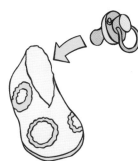

In winter, let the gift bag bring extra warmth!

- For infants, shape the bag into felt booties.
- For children, make mittens!
- For 'little ladies', a party purse.
- For teenagers, cut out a felt scarf, double over and sew up the sides. The recipient picks out the stitches before wearing!
- Adults might like a felt hat tied closed for a bag.
- Line a rectangle of felt with fleece, sew into a cylinder and close the 'bottom' with a separate yarn (unpicking this gives you a muff).

990. Batteries included

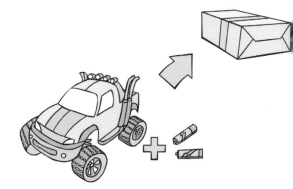

Don't leave the recipient short. Include any must-have item with your gift.

- If you're giving an electronic gadget, especially a child's toy, do include batteries in the right size.
- A non-digital camera? Add a few rolls of film.

991. Give generously...

... and add some useful extras.

- Buying a book? No one can have too many bookmarks!
- The cheeseboard and knife could do with a wedge of cheese for company.
- Add a colouring book (for children) or a sketch pad to a set of pastels or paints.
- Give a nice notebook with that fancy pen.
- Include a CD with headphones.
- Keys to a new car? Put them on a key ring.
- Gardening tools? Add a tube of hand cream.
- Teapot or mug? Add some good tea.
- Espresso machine or coffee mug? A bag of coffee beans, please!
- A fancy corkscrew? Where's the wine?
- Pop some biscuits in that nice ceramic jar.

992. By the basket

Beautiful wicker or cane craft is a worthy gift in its own right. But it's nice to top up the gift basket! Here are some traditional and some surprising basket fillers:

- Fresh produce – don't stuff the basket or it will seem like it's a gift of groceries; instead, choose a few extraordinary vegetables (perhaps an heirloom variety, or else an unusual exotic, or a surprising shape or colour such as purple cauliflower).
- Some farm-fresh eggs.
- Cut wild flowers *au naturel* – no tying into posies.
- Fresh herb posies tied with ribbon.

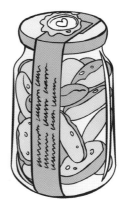

993. Sweetie pile

Smarten up a simple bag of boiled sweets for an easy, yet thoughtful, present.

- Instead of the typical gift boxes, cellophane bags or paper cones, get a small preserving jar to put the sweets in – most supermarkets stock them.
- For smaller sweets, such as jelly beans, you can even use a spice jar or jam jar.
- Add a little scoop or metal measuring spoon – 1 tablespoon or 1 teaspoon, depending on the scale of the sweets – when tying a bow round the neck.

994. Sealed with love

Giving homemade jam or biscuits? Add your own freshness seal and label.

- Wrap a sturdy strip of paper around the jar or box to go across the lid.
- Use an old-fashioned wax seal to secure the edges together on top.
- The paper strip can double up as a label – identify the contents up one side and write a 'use by' date down the other side.
- If your container is more futuristic stainless steel than traditional jars, use label tape for your message and stick on to seal!

■ Notes and cards

996. ID-it!

Take a break from the scrawled names on gift tags.

- Stick on a polaroid of the recipient, and punch a hole at the top or in a corner to hang off ribbon.

997. Okra greetings!

A quaint vegetable stamp, this!

- Lop the top off a large-ish okra and dip it in paint to stamp.
- Stamp first on a piece of sponge to get excess paint off.
- If it starts to get sticky, slice off another 1 cm/½ inch and continue.
- Do pinks and purples on white for summery flowers.
- In winter, stamp with white or silver paint on a midnight blue background for snowflakes.
- Gold on red or red on black always looks festive.

995. Season's greetings from us all

Make your own picture postcard!

- Photocopy favourite snaps of your family. Or use strips from the photo booth.
- Select stiff-ish paper in a bright colour.
- Snip and paste these on your card forms; leave at least half the area empty for writing.
- Cut larger prints into strips an inch wide and reassemble at random.
- For smaller photos, put them together like window panes or line up along the card's bottom.
- Scrawl your messages on the plain background.

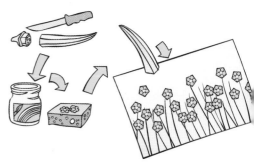

■ Exceptional ideas

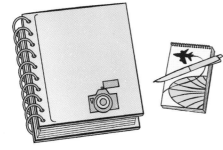

998. Traveller's tales

For a globetrotter who likes recording memories, a notebook is the perfect gift!

- Buy a basic book, spending on good, sturdy cream or white paper rather than paying for a fancy binding.
- Or get a photo album for the snap-happy tourist.
- Photocopy a picture of a favourite destination, laminate and fold over to make a dust jacket.
- Make a sentimental fabric cover that carries memories of home – a parent's signature suit material, a fleece that matches a partner's favourite pullover or a baby blanket, etc.

999. Glasses very full!

Giving glasses? Fill them up!

- For a hostess gift, present glasses in an open box, part filled with water and a single flower floated in each. Instant table décor.
- For a birthday or anniversary, fill with popcorn that hides a liqueur chocolate at the centre of each glass.
- Tall tumblers for a nifty cook? Add a test tube of exotic spice to each.
- For the cocktail addict, consider a double-decker gift of bar tools slipped into each highball glass!

1000. House warmers

Some great ideas for a first bachelor pad or a new couple's first home.

- A tray of potted seedlings.
- A temporary tabletop garden – in a plastic-lined trug, place a container of wheatgrass bordered with pebbles and flowers held in florists' foam. Stick in a 'signpost' with their new address.
- A batch of moth-chasing sachets – stuffed with sage, cedar chips, bay leaves or lavender – rolled up in a fleece throw.

1001. Crafty cupcakes

A sweet birthday treat for children, confectionery chefs or crafty types.

- Bake half a dozen cupcakes – with plain white vanilla icing.
- Line up an equal number of sturdy foil muffin cases.
- Fill the foil cases with cake decorations – sugar flowers, shredded coconut coloured blue and green as well as some plain white chocolate curls or chocolate vermicelli, some hundreds and thousands or sprinkles.
- Place in a box and toss in some small ready-to-use icing tubes in the gaps.

Index*